THE FUTURE NORMAL

ROHIT BHARGAVA
HENRY COUTINHO-MASON

THE FUTURE NORMAL

HOW WE WILL LIVE, WORK, AND THRIVE IN THE NEXT DECADE

IDEAPRESS PUBLISHING
WASHINGTON, DC

IDEAPRESS
PUBLISHING

International Edition

First published in Hardcover as *The Future Normal* in the USA by Ideapress Publishing 2023.

Ideapress Publishing | www.ideapresspublishing.com

Cover Design: Amanda Hudson, Faceout Studio
Interior Design: Jessica Angerstein

Paperback ISBN: 978-1-64687-146-9

Special Sales
Ideapress Books are available at a special discount for bulk purchases for sales promotions and premiums, or for use in corporate training programs. Special editions, including personalized covers, a custom foreword, corporate imprints, and bonus content, are also available.

To our respective parents,
thank you for believing in our futures.

CONTENTS

PART 2 HOW WE WILL LIVE, WORK, AND CONSUME

PART 3 HOW HUMANITY WILL SURVIVE

INTRODUCTION

The Earth technically didn't *need* to be rescued from a hurtling asteroid ... but we decided to save it anyway.

When NASA announced an ambitious test program in late 2022 with the Hollywood scriptworthy mission to destroy an innocently passing asteroid, it seemed like a wildly ambitious but probably sensible idea. After all, it's been 66 million years since the dinosaurs were wiped out by an asteroid, and the data suggests another strike is mathematically long overdue. Thankfully for humanity, NASA was successful, showing we *could* save the planet if an asteroid were headed our way.

This galactic intervention was the perfect example of how we often imagine the future: A bold vision. World-changing technology. Heroic science. Global impact (or more accurately, averted impact). This story *feels* like the future should, even as it takes place here and now. That's because early ripples of the future can always be seen in the present. What is happening on the edges of most industries or in society—the technological marvels, the ambitious innovations, the bold social agendas—hold the potential to become mainstream in the future, to change how we'll live and work and what we'll value.

As futurists, both of us have spent the better part of the last decade studying and deconstructing these early signals, Rohit, through his bestselling *Non-Obvious Trends* series, and Henry, in his pioneering work at the foresight platform TrendWatching. Although we often marveled at the world's most visionary technologies and well-intentioned entrepreneurs, we also started to notice the inconvenient reality that many of them would fade away. We have engaged in rich dialogue with uncanny holograms, donned full bodysuits to "feel" virtual wind, and suffered the pitying stares of passersby while wearing Google Glasses in public. We have anxiously strapped ourselves in as passengers of prototype self-driving cars and watched artificial intelligence "write" a full-length article years before it was widely available. For every world-changing innovation we celebrated, another would fail to reach the mainstream or hit an unexpected impasse.

The truth is that the future is abandoned, defunded, ignored, or ridiculed just as often as it is realized. So the real challenge isn't predicting the *future* but rather predicting what will become *normal*.

What Is the "Future Normal"?

On many levels, humans are trained to elevate novelty over normality. It is hard to blame us. Nearly two decades ago, researchers linked the way our brain processes things we haven't seen before with an increase in dopamine levels and a higher tendency to explore and seek rewards for our effort.[1] Normal, on the other hand, is boring. Renowned futurist Jim Dator, a University of Hawaii professor who spent 40 years pioneering the field of futures studies, once wrote that "any useful idea about the future should appear to be ridiculous."[2] The quote is so widely regarded it has come to be known as Dator's Law, and it perfectly illustrates how the future and the normal are often cast as contradictory ideas. How can any idea sufficiently "futuristic" ever be simultaneously described as "normal"? In writing this book, part of our aim is to recast the normal from ordinary to important. From obvious to non-obvious.

During the pandemic, it became cliché to declare every shift in how we lived and worked as our shared "new normal." Making bread,

Zoom happy hours, and greeting each other with elbow bumps were all part of this new normal. Today, most of those pronouncements have become dated. We are breaking bread together rather than making it alone at home; people are socializing in bars and restaurants again; and we are back to shaking hands.

So how can one decipher which innovations and shifts will become our future normal? We are firm believers that people's basic, fundamental needs and wants—e.g., the need for identity, connection, self-improvement, status, and more—evolve at a far slower pace than the innovations that cater to these needs. If they evolve much at all. Understanding people's wants and needs helps us uncover why some advancements have become normal and why plenty of seemingly unstoppable ones have not persisted over time.

For example, supersonic air travel is 50 years old, but barely exists today. That is partially because of high fuel prices and sonic-boom noise concerns, but also because other solutions to the basic needs that the Concorde jet targeted became normal, without needing to fly at supersonic speed. Private jets became increasingly accessible while offering greater flexibility; business class travelers' productivity was boosted by lie-flat beds and in-flight Wi-Fi.

Similarly, baking bread during the pandemic was less about the bread and more about needing a sense of ritual and familiarity at a time of disconnection. Zoom happy hours and elbow-bump greetings were an attempt to satisfy our desire to connect safely. As we started to emerge from our homes and welcome one another with handshakes and hugs once more, those behaviors were quickly abandoned as the so-called new normal gave way to the normal that existed before.

In this book, you'll read about the ideas and instigators that are bringing about new ways to satisfy these fundamental needs and wants, changing not just complete industries in the process, but also sending waves out into the wider culture and society.

You'll read about a startup that could exponentially reduce the environmental impact of the food industry by taking an old NASA technology to synthesize protein from carbon dioxide. You'll meet researchers who may supercharge learning in the future thanks to their pioneering work creating muscle memory through a passive haptic learning glove that uses electrical pulses to teach people how to play the piano in minutes. You'll discover companies working to refreeze the Arctic, end generational loneliness, mass produce solar microgrids, create urban forests, and popularize the practice of sharing your job.

As we offer you glimpses of what our future normal might look like, we must also make an unusual confession: although we curate the future for a living, neither of us have typically labeled ourselves a *futurist*. In fact, it was the discovery of this quirk that inspired us to collaborate on this book.

The Reluctant Futurists

From our alternate vantage points based in Washington, DC, and London, we have spent years interviewing world-changing startup founders, speaking at conferences with themes like "Future 2050" and being called upon by world governments and future-building tech firms to offer a vision of the next decade that is adequately sexy and optimistically plausible.

Yet our collaboration on this book was far from inevitable. It would be better described as an accident of serendipity. Separated by an ocean, our first meeting happened by chance during the morning coffee break at a conference in New York. Upon seeing one another's name tag, we realized that we had each been reading the other's work for years but had never spoken ... until that day.

While sipping our coffees, we quickly bonded over the discovery that the event's planners had taken the liberty of including the job title "futurist" on each of our name tags. This term is a professional mantle both of us have long worn reluctantly. Each of us felt our respective work always seemed better described as *near futurism*—a quest to catalog and understand the implications of the biggest innovations on our lives *today* and over the next few years.

We both felt that we took a different approach than many futurists. Instead of asking what *could* change the future, we routinely found ourselves asking, "What already *has*?" and "Do we *want* this change to be a part of humanity's future?"

Indeed, neither of us spends much time looking at futurist scenarios at all. Our energy is focused on the present. As *nowists* rather than futurists, we stay on top of business innovations because they so often spark insights into what our future normal will look like. Any new business innovation—whether an entirely new brand or startup, or a new product, service, or initiative from an existing brand—is a bet on the future. Taken in isolation, each of these bets is a signal that a group of people believe their view of the future will be successful. When similar wagers are being made by multiple businesses in a diverse range of markets and categories, we can extract insights about where our future normal is going.

Renowned writer Isaac Asimov once revealed that he never saw himself as a speed reader but rather as a "speed understander." This is a skill we have spent years honing and teaching. Anticipating a fast-moving future is hard, but it is not impossible.

How to Read This Book

This book is designed to be accessible for those of you feeling pressed for time or experiencing short attention spans. With that in mind, rather than aiming to cover an exhaustive list of topics in this book—which would naturally include well-known territory—we chose to prioritize the more non-obvious insights into the future normal. For those readers familiar with Rohit's popular *Non-Obvious Trends* series, this will come as no surprise.

To accomplish this, we have organized the book into three big thematic sections that each include 10 short, topical chapters. In the first section, we explore how we will connect, get healthy, and thrive, looking at innovations in health, learning, media, and entertainment that are poised to affect our daily lives. In the second part of the book, we turn our lens to how we will live, work, and consume. Moving from the workplace to our home lives and what we buy, the chapters in this section will offer a new perspective on our consumption and careers, and how they will likely shift in the future normal.

Finally, in part three we will focus on longer-term innovations that are fundamentally shaping how humanity will survive beyond the next decade. Though we remain near-futurists, this section is our chance to not only focus on the now, but also offer our own vision for what these current innovations might mean for the future of cities, the environment, agriculture, and government.

At the start of each section, you will find a summary of the big themes and macro trends within it. Read the book from start to finish or head straight to the section or chapters that feel most relevant to you. At the end of the book in appendix A, we've also provided a selection of curated "playlists" to help you zero in on the chapters that will have the greatest impact on your life and your career, no matter what industry you work in.

We remain forever mindful that you have the most important job of all: turning these insights into your own future normal. To help you lead the future, at the end of each short chapter, we pose a handful of provocative questions that we hope will spark rich and productive discussions with your team and the people around you.

While this book contains many insights into what's around the corner, it is also a celebration of those who are creating that future.

We are both optimists, and our optimism drives the ideas in the pages that follow. Everywhere you look, there are brilliant pioneers working to create a healthier, fairer, and cleaner future for us all. We hope after reading this book, you'll be inspired by their stories to imagine as hopeful and prosperous of a future normal as we do.

TOPICS IN THIS SECTION

MULTIVERSAL IDENTITY

What if we could all be our real and most authentic selves both online and offline?

VIRTUAL COMPANIONSHIP

What if you could develop a meaningful relationship with an app or a robot?

IMMERSIVE ENTERTAINMENT

What if you could be part of entertainment instead of watching it passively?

PSYCHEDELIC WELLNESS

What if mainstream medicine tuned into the mental health benefits of psychedelics?

CERTIFIED MEDIA

What if you could trust the authenticity of the media and content you consume?

AMBIENT HEALTH

What if buildings and homes protected—and even boosted—our health and well-being?

STEALTH LEARNING

What if you could educate yourself using the very videos and games that are typically written off as a waste of time?

GREEN PRESCRIPTIONS

What if doctors prescribed nature like they prescribe drugs?

ENDING LONELINESS

What if closing the generation gap could cure loneliness at any age?

METABOLIC MONITORING

What if tracking your glucose level became as normal as counting your steps?

PART 1

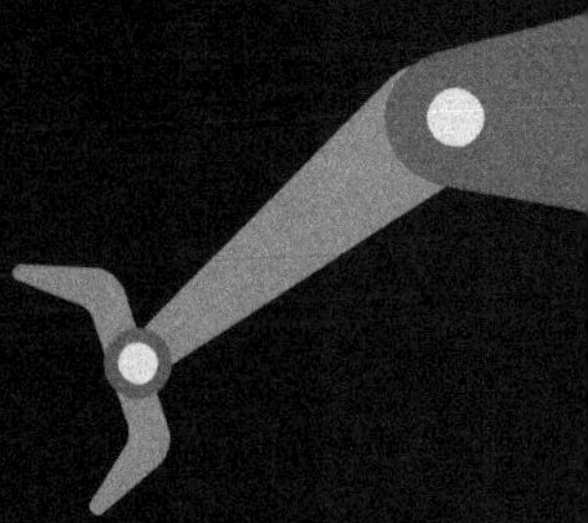

HOW WE WILL CONNECT, GET HEALTHY, AND THRIVE

We believe a discussion about the future has to start by looking inward at how we spend our time, and so in this section we will meet a number of instigators who are changing the way we consume media, learn, communicate, and manage our health. From the way our identities are becoming "multiversal" to how we might end loneliness and better connect with one another, imagining a better future normal will require us to address some big social challenges. At the same time, to live healthier and more fulfilling lives, we will need to rethink many of our current assumptions around wellness and shift our habits and priorities to do the things that can help us live longer and better.

CHAPTER 1

MULTIVERSAL IDENTITY

What if we could all be our real and most authentic selves both online and offline?

One of the hottest streetwear brands of the past decade, Daily Paper, started with a merch drop of five branded T-shirts designed for early followers of the eponymous blog. The blog was started by three African friends—Abderrahmane Trabsini, Jefferson Osei, and Hussein Suleiman—who moved to Amsterdam as refugees during their childhood. Today, they have grown from those humble beginnings to develop a $30 million fashion brand that calls upon their shared African heritage and has a cult following. Their fan base sees the authenticity of the brand as the major reason for its beloved status.[1]

What we choose to wear is one of the most visible forms of self-expression, powering everything from our own confidence to the way we shape the first impressions that others have of us. Our identity, though, goes much deeper than clothing and accessories, or how we present ourselves from the outside. Identity is shaped by the communities we are part of—everything from our race to our nationality—and how we seek to find the place where we belong.

The same holds true online. For the past decade, our notions of virtual identity have gone through a fascinating transformation. The early days of social media felt like a game with very strict guidelines. We would only share the most flattering images or post about the most fabulous times we were having. The unwritten rule seemed to be that social media was the place where we posted the best of ourselves and the events or things we wanted to remember (and be remembered for). Our online identity back then was crafted to present a highly curated and controlled version of ourselves. The method for engaging with those posts seemed to reinforce these guardrails—the only buttonized emotion you could respond with was to "like" something.

A backlash against the faux authenticity this ecosystem incentivized seems inevitable in hindsight. Life is not always great. Sometimes we lose a job or end a relationship or have our stuff stolen. The bigger the gap between social media reality and real life, the more we began to feel that our online identities were a lie—or at least not fully truthful. Over time, this created a simmering resentment of celebrities, influencers, and anyone else who tried too hard to curate an identity that seemed disingenuous. The dishonesty became easier and easier to spot in a sort of know-it-when-you-see-it way. The hashtag #blessed became ironic.

Today, we are increasingly repelled by people who try to fake their way into appearing "down-to-earth" online, which in turn reflects our increasing desire to surround ourselves with people who are unafraid to be their imperfect selves. For most of human history, being *afraid* to be oneself has been the norm. People have faced (and continue to face) discrimination due to the gender they identify with, the color of their skin, the language they speak, or the country they come from.

Being oneself, in other words, has too often felt like a dangerous life choice for many people. But recent research suggests that the virtual world might allow many of those same people to feel safer being themselves. When creative software company Adobe polled 1,000 Gen Zers in 2022 to explore how they felt about using social media to express themselves, "over half admitted that social media was the only place they felt they could be themselves, with three in five (58 percent) stating that having an online presence makes them feel more comfortable in their own skin."[2]

As time progresses, we will all increasingly find new ways to balance how we see ourselves with how we present ourselves through digital tools and media. One way we'll do that is by shaping our virtual avatar versions of ourselves to be strategically minimalist and, therefore, intentionally expressing only certain aspects of our personality. In part driven by a reluctance to share too much revealing personal information coupled with a desire to guard our privacy, these avatars will not capture all the nuances of our identity and personality. And yet the choices we'll make when creating these avatars could have life-altering effects. When we create a virtual version of ourselves that presents us to the world as a musician, for example, it may inspire us to lean further into this passion in the real world as well. A 2007 research study from the Stanford Virtual Human Interaction Lab famously called this the "Proteus Effect"—a term describing how "an individual's behavior conforms to their digital self-representation independent of how others perceive them."[3]

Eventually, these multiversal versions of our identities will feel true and authentic enough to reinforce the truest and most authentic versions of ourselves in our daily lives. In this future normal, being oneself could become more than just an ambition promoted by self-help books—it will be a reality both online and offline.

Instigator: Ready Player Me

Ready Player Me Avatars for Rohit (@rohitbhargava) (L) and Henry (@hcoutinhomason) (R). (Source: Ready Player Me)

The hardest part of creating a virtual avatar on the leading avatar creation platform Ready Player Me—named after the hit 2011 science-fiction novel *Ready Player One* by Ernest Cline—might be choosing the hair or the eyebrows. What won't hold you (or any user) back is a lack of technical ability. Thanks to platforms like this one, being tech-savvy is no longer a prerequisite for joining the virtual universe. Ready Player Me offers an addictive, easy introduction to building virtual avatars that are compatible with thousands of games and apps. Founder Timmu Tõke created it to allow people to make their own avatars and use them across the metaverse easily.

According to VentureBeat, "Users want the avatars to be representative of themselves or of the heroes they want to embody. Hence a default avatar system for the metaverse needs to not only work well in that chaos but win the hearts of game developers, designers and end-users alike."[4] Attracting more than $50 million of funding from investors and plenty of brand partnerships from Samsung, L'Oréal, Adidas, and hundreds of others, the platform is quickly becoming the one of choice for users new to virtual avatars.[5] Sophisticated users, too, are finding that the integrations with other platforms offer tempting new opportunities to explore their digital identities. One example is Disney-backed Inworld AI, which promises to "bring virtual characters such as those that people create with Ready Player Me to life with AI" and allows users to add a personality to their avatar by setting a sliding scale of moods and personality traits such as anger, emotional fluidity, authority, and aggression.[6]

Platforms like these are pushing the boundary between how we portray our real selves, both in the real world and online, through a highly customized avatar.

> **An avatar gives you the opportunity to show your identity as much as you want. You can put it in there. It's still you in a way, but you can abstract it enough so it's safe. ... It's personal enough to be relatable, but it's not creepy or too out there.**
>
> —Timmu Tõke, CEO, Ready Player Me[7]

While you might assume many people would create avatars vastly different from themselves, one study from the University of Alberta discovered that "most people who create avatars of themselves only make minor changes compared with their real selves."[8] Even though we may not be able to shoot lasers from our fingers or fly around the world in real life, the research suggests we are likely to retain much of our real selves inside the virtual avatars we choose. This desire to retain an essence of our real selves will be most apparent in our virtual avatars, but a similar need will also drive us to find other ways to exhibit our personalities when we are online *and* offline. As a result, through the journey to shape our identities both digitally and in real life, our true identity will become multiversal in nature.

Imagining the Future Normal

1. When you create your own virtual avatar, what aspects of your real-life identity would you choose to retain, and which ones would you change?
2. How will our friendships and work relationships evolve as we interact with more individuals solely in digital formats without ever meeting in real life?
3. As virtual avatars become more frequently used, what potential misuses or addictive behaviors might we need to anticipate ... particularly among younger users?

CHAPTER 2

IMMERSIVE ENTERTAINMENT

What if you could be part of entertainment instead of watching it passively?

For more than 15 years, Taylor Swift has inserted secret messages, hints, and puzzles in her music and social media posts and videos, driving her tens of millions of fans on quests to figure out their meaning. These carefully designed trails of clues are often wildly creative. One time, her team painted a mural of a butterfly in Nashville that fans correctly decoded as the secret location of a surprise appearance. In another, she drove a minor fan frenzy by releasing new song titles through a retro game of bingo in a series of online videos. Swift's savvy tactics to engage with her fans even prompted one reporter to suggest the singer has "created her own mythology."[1] Her efforts have spanned real-life events, exclusive videos, and digital experiences, and spread across so many social media platforms that she has built her own metaverse of sorts ... an entire digital multiplatform universe that engages her loyal community at every turn.

What Swift has spent years building for her fans can offer us a clue about what the future normal of entertainment will look like: more immersive. While live performances have always offered a sort of sensory immersion, technology has accelerated the possibilities for just how deeply we can become part of an experience. This is the promise of immersive entertainment. We don't just watch the show, we become part of it in ways that are enhanced by technology but remain visceral, physical, and memorable. After being trapped in lockdowns during the pandemic, the power of real-life experiences seems even more precious now. "As humans, we have some essential, unspoken need to see a performance, be part of the crowd, and experience everything that comes with it," explains reporter David Sax in his book *The Future Is Analog*.[2]

The desire to lose ourselves inside an experience also explains the recent popularity of art exhibitions that turn paintings into larger-than-life immersive experiences. In the past few years, no less than half a dozen production companies have created shows inspired by the work of artist Vincent van Gogh. One of the most popular, the *Van Gogh Exhibition: The Immersive Experience*, allows visitors to walk among animated and moving projections of the painter's major works; it opened to sold-out crowds in dozens of cities across eight countries and raked in nearly $300 million.[3] Similar experiences based on the work of other renowned creators, such as Austrian artist Gustav Klimt and Spanish Surrealist Salvador Dali, are also underway.

Theaters, too, are considering ways to be more immersive. This doesn't always require the use of cutting-edge technology either. In an extreme example of how personalized immersive entertainment can get, in 2020, the self-described experience maker Yannick Trapman-O'Brien created *Undersigned*, a show described as "a psychological thriller for an audience of one."[4] The lone audience member attending the experience participates in a performance tailored entirely to them based on questions they answered upon arrival.

Not content to simply allow audiences to passively sit and watch a performance, a number of companies are also working on technology to build a fullbody haptic suit, through which a wearer could actually *feel* the sensations across their body that relate to a particular experience. Early applications are being tested to make video gaming more immersive and even to offer a new dimension for live sports fans. Coupled with the ability to put helmet cameras on actual players, we can imagine a moment in the future where a connected fan could feel what athletes feel while watching a sports match unfold directly from their perspective. It would really be the closest thing to being on the field yourself.

In the future normal, describing these experiences as merely *entertainment* will feel inadequate. Instead, these moments of immersion will hold the power to shape reality around us and allow us to forget that the outside world even exists—at least for a short while. They will create entire worlds that audiences will temporarily inhabit to experience the range of emotions that great performances have always offered, but in a far deeper and more profound way. We will, in essence, be able to *live* inside the story.

Instigator: ABBA Voyage

In May 2022, the beloved Swedish band ABBA kicked off their most ambitious concert series yet. The four bandmates, who famously parted ways in 1982 and vowed never to tour again, did *not* reunite to play together on stage. At least, not in person. Instead, the concert series features digital avatars of the band members, which they quickly started calling their ABBAtars, backed by real-life musicians in an experience that *Rolling Stone* described as "uncannily, eerily realistic."[5]

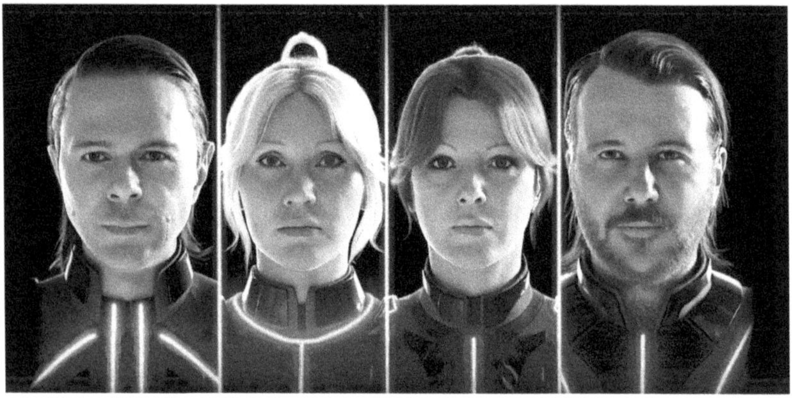

ABBA Voyage digital "ABBAtars." (Source: www.abbavoyage.com)

ABBA Voyage is a whole new entertainment experience that merges the physical and digital worlds, integrating digitally recreated versions of the musicians modeled after their famous 1970s selves and then putting these ABBAtars on stage to sing some of their most famous songs in front of adoring fans.

Wanting to ensure the show would be more than an "old-fashioned circus trick,"[6] as band member Björn Ulvaeus recalled, the band turned to Industrial Light & Magic, the group responsible for the special effects in *Star Wars* and many other Hollywood productions. Surrounded by specialized 3D cameras, Agnetha Fältskog, Björn Ulvaeus, Benny Andersson, and Anni-Frid Lyngstad (whose first initials form the name of the band) spent five weeks in a Stockholm recording studio so their gestures, facial expressions, and performance movements could be captured and become the raw data for the creation of their ABBAtars. Aside from the obvious technical complexity, the show required such precise staging that the band also decided to custom-build their own 3,000-seat ABBA Arena in East London's Queen Elizabeth Olympic Park.[7]

ABBA Voyage was immediately a huge hit, selling more than 380,000 tickets before the show opened.[8] One of its most in-demand ticket options was the Dance Booth—a private room with its own dance floor allowing 10 to 12 ticket holders to dance their hearts out to the music and performance of the ABBAtars.

> **To me, the only question that really mattered was not if it is good enough but how will the audience react when we're not really there, you know? Will they look at it as a painting? Would you applaud a painting? Would you applaud a movie? You don't do that. Would they be immersed in what we're trying to achieve here?**
>
> —Benny Andersson, Band Member, ABBA[9]

As we write this story, the ABBA Voyage show has been running for over a year and is already inspiring the entertainment industry to invest in creating more immersive experiences. It is also accelerating the audience demand for more of these types of shows.

The Walt Disney Company has been delighting fans with immersive experiences at its theme parks for generations. In 2020, the company struck a deal with Secret Cinema—a live theater company renowned for their immersive live companion shows to films—to produce interactive experiences related to some of its titles. First up, a real-world version of the Marvel Universe for an experience that premiered in September 2022 and is built around the *Guardians of the Galaxy* franchise.[10] Like other Secret Cinema productions, the show allows audience members to participate in the storyline, even generating a character for themselves.

All of these examples suggest there is a growing appetite for partaking in experiences that ambitiously welcome audiences to engage with them in a deeper and more personal way. The future normal of entertainment experiences isn't going to be always sitting back and watching a big screen at home or in a theater passively. People will increasingly seek to balance out those more passive entertainment experiences with others where they can be participating, interacting, dancing, and immersing themselves into the moment in a real and tangible way.

Imagining the Future Normal

1. What if every entertainment experience was reimagined to be offered in multiple channels for those who choose more engagement and immersion?
2. How would our experience or enjoyment of entertainment change if real performers were combined (or replaced) with digitally created avatars or holographic versions?
3. In a world where any artist, living or dead, could be brought back virtually for a performance, how could new emerging artists compete with legendary talent from the past?

CHAPTER 3

CERTIFIED MEDIA

What if you could trust the authenticity of the media and content you consume?

It started with porn (of course it did). In November 2017, an anonymous Reddit user launched the /r/deepfake subReddit message board, publishing a series of AI-generated videos that mapped the faces of Gal Gadot and Scarlett Johansson onto porn stars, creating fake but near-believable videos.[1] The deepfake genie was out of the bottle.

Fast-forward six years, and deepfakes or synthetic media—media produced or manipulated by AI— have become mainstream. During the pandemic, streaming video platform Hulu launched an ad campaign called "The Deepfake" to promote its live sports programming. Since Hulu was not able to shoot traditional commercials with celebrity athletes, who were on lockdown, the company overlayed the athletes' faces onto unlikely body doubles doing pandemic activities like baking sourdough bread or learning to play the ukulele, before giving up and announcing that live sports were back.[2] The deepfake ads were a clever nod to the limitations of shooting ads during the pandemic. At least this time the people being faked were in on the joke. The majority of deepfake examples over the past several years haven't been quite so innocent. As the technology gets better, for example, it is increasingly becoming the digitized weapon of choice for criminals and politicians alike. In the Philippines, a country whose citizens spend more time on social media per day than any other nation,[3] misinformation through faked media has played a significant role in determining the winner of the past several presidential elections.[4] Described by one Facebook executive as "patient zero" in the global disinformation epidemic, the country is increasingly used as a cautionary tale of the unchecked power of disinformation to sway public opinion.

In South Korea, a country with the world's fastest average internet speeds, a more novel use of deepfake technology emerged when the team supporting People Power Party candidate Yoon Suk-yeol used hours of recorded footage of the candidate (dubbed "AI Yoon") to create deepfaked content that "uses salty language and meme-ready quips in a bid to engage younger voters."[5] The bid worked: Yoon Suk-yeol won the election in March of 2022.

Out of concern for the potential of manipulated media to affect public opinion, in late 2019 California passed two laws focused on deepfakes. Law AB730 makes it illegal to distribute deepfakes of politicians within 60 days of an election, while AB602 allows subjects of deepfake pornography (still the most common use of the technology) to sue the creator.[6] Meanwhile, the Cyberspace Administration of China issued regulations requiring any content made with or manipulated by AI to be clearly labeled.[7] Other nations around the world are considering similar legislation to try and stem the tide of manipulated content.

But deepfakes are also the bellwether of a much bigger issue facing us in the digital era. How does fake or manipulated media erode the public's trust? More importantly, how do we *know* what is real? Legislation alone cannot solve the problem. The rise of social media and the fact that anyone, anywhere, can produce and distribute media is overwhelming people's ability to assess whether the information they encounter is trustworthy. In 2022 the Edelman Trust Barometer, an annual report on the state of trust around the world produced by global communications firm Edelman, found three-quarters of global respondents worry that "fake news" (a term only popularized since the 2016 US presidential election) is being used as a weapon to undermine their society.[8] They are right to be concerned. In 2018, MIT researchers famously reported that misinformation spreads up to 100 times further and six times faster than truth, and political falsehoods spread three times faster than other misinformation.[9]

The volume of synthetic media will only increase as new, more powerful tools spread. In 2020, the research lab OpenAI released a beta of GPT-3, a radically more powerful AI-powered tool that can generate largely believable text. The *Guardian* newspaper published an op-ed generated by the tool entitled "A Robot Wrote This Entire Article. Are You Scared Yet, Human?"[10] In 2022, several tools that generate images and videos based on text prompts were released to the public.* While most prohibit using the tools to create pornographic material or use the likeness of celebrities or politicians, that hasn't deterred early users. In the early days of the Russia-Ukraine war, for example, a video was released that appeared to show Ukrainian President Volodymyr Zelenskyy urging his citizens to lay down their weapons and surrender to the Russian invaders.[11] Fortunately, its execution was amateurish enough that few were fooled, but it clearly signaled the potential risks of this technology.

* Curious about how good AI technology has gotten? Visit our website www.thefuturenormal.com to read an AI-generated version of this chapter that was written in collaboration with artificial intelligence tools available in the market as of the writing of this book.

The increasing ease with which manipulated content can be created and disseminated makes the task of certifying what is true (and what isn't) urgent for us all. On the surface this might seem like an impossible task, yet when liars can use technology to create convincing fabrications, perhaps technology itself can help to expose their deception. This is already happening and will accelerate as more services use the digital footprint of the media to identify fabrications and flag them in real time. As these tools become more commonplace, people will become more accustomed to seeking out these trusted third-party validations before putting their faith in a particular piece of content. Even when they do, they will increasingly maintain a (hopefully) healthy level of skepticism about the verified truth of any person who is sharing content that is not delivered in real time. The combination of these instant verification tools and the adoption of greater levels of media literacy among everyone will combine to make this concept of certified media truly part of our future normal.

Instigator: Truepic

Enter Truepic, a startup based in San Diego that aims to restore trust in photos and videos. Launched in 2015, the company offers a free camera app that embeds metadata like time and location on the image taken and then sends it to Truepic, which verifies it and uploads it to a server.[12] In late 2020, the startup announced it was partnering with Qualcomm to embed metadata about when and where an image or video was taken directly into the firmware of the chip, allowing users to take photos or make videos that are "verifiable."[13] This is significant because Qualcomm makes the chips that power almost all non-Apple phones—Samsung, Google, Xiaomi, Microsoft, LG, OnePlus, and Motorola—which means the technology will be available in billions of smartphones. In 2022, the company released Truepic Lens, which enables any app that features images to integrate Truepic's validated metadata directly into the app's camera function, ensuring an image's provenance.

> **We are working to find a solution [to disinformation] as quickly as we can—really for the sake of democracy as a whole. We feel the pressure. We are in this.**
>
> —Jeffrey McGregor, CEO, Truepic[14]

It's not difficult to imagine potential use cases for Truepic's technology, and early adopters of the tool already have. Non-governmental organizations (NGOs) and citizen journalists are using Truepic's app to capture verifiable images in conflict zones. The *New York Times* has been experimenting with Truepic and other similar technology.[15] In addition, insurance companies have a vested interest in confirming the authenticity of images their customers send when filing claims. Other sectors would also benefit from technology that authenticates images, including peer-to-peer platforms such as e-commerce, dating, and real estate sites to name a few.

Truepic verified image examples. (Source: Truepic)

Given how content-rich our lives are, the advantages of being able to more readily trust media are enormous. Social media wasn't a factor a generation ago when Francis Fukuyama wrote *Trust: The Social Virtues and the Creation of Prosperity,* but his central argument still holds: a society riddled with distrust cannot be an economically—or a socially—prosperous place.[16] A world where the images, videos, and words that we share digitally can be verified as true in the moment we consume them, however, will enable our future normal society to be more trusting, truthful, and limit the power of those who seek to manipulate us for their own personal gains.

Imagining the Future Normal

1. What might more positive and uplifting uses for deepfakes or modified content be, and should these also require certification?
2. What if all media outlets were required to have images and videos validated before publishing, and how might this affect freedom of speech?
3. If a model for certified media could be implemented, what sort of repercussions might be introduced for those who regularly break the rules, and how could they be enforced?

CHAPTER 4

STEALTH LEARNING

What if you could educate yourself using the very videos and games that are typically written off as a waste of time?

Every generation has its moral panic—and TikTok seems to have triggered the latest one. The app's powerful AI, which quickly zeroes in on users' likes and dislikes and serves them a seemingly infinite stream of short videos, has raised alarms among everyone, from policymakers concerned about national security to parents worried about rising social media addiction. These concerns are real, but TikTok today also offers far more than one-minute videos of dance challenges. Videos with the hashtag #LearnOnTikTok have been viewed more than 400 *billion* times (as of the time of this writing).[1] People can watch educational videos on everything—science experiments, historical facts, medicine, mental health, language, personal finance, and more. In China, where TikTok originated, the app has a youth mode that integrates educational content within the video feeds and limits usage to 40 minutes per day.[2]

During the pandemic, the platform even announced a $50 million Creative Learning Fund to reward creators posting educational content.[3] TikTok's entrance into microlearning shouldn't be surprising. For the past decade, how-to videos have been some of the most popular on YouTube. The phenomenon inspired Chris Anderson, curator of the famous TED Conference, to suggest that the richness of video is dramatically changing the creative and social landscape by democratizing and accelerating the learning process.[4] But social media videos are not the only way that learning is becoming seamlessly embedded into people's daily online lives. Video games are also providing an even more interactive, yet similarly stealthy, learning experience for millions of younger players.

Sometimes the learning doesn't even require conscious attention. A team of researchers at the Contextual Computing Group at Georgia Tech have released multiple experiments in "teaching manual skills without attention"[5] through the use of a soft robotics glove that sends electrical impulses to the fingers. Known as passive haptic learning, test subjects using these types of gloves have achieved superhuman results: learning how to read braille in a matter of hours and playing songs on the piano in less than 30 minutes. As this type of innovation sees more widespread adoption both inside educational institutions as well as in our daily lives, this technology-fueled aspect of stealth learning will allow more people to embrace lifelong learning and acquire new skills and knowledge in a way that fits more seamlessly into their lives.

Stealth learning can also be an equalizer of long-standing inequity, allowing more widespread distribution of educational content and reducing the barriers to knowledge by delivering content in unexpected ways through the content and experiences that are already being consumed by users.

As this educational content—often available in the same platforms that we count on for entertainment—becomes the future normal, people will not only acquire skills faster but will do so happily and expect to learn everything at greater speed and more pleasurably, both inside and outside the classroom.

Instigator: Roblox

If you know a kid under age 16, chances are you've heard of Roblox. The platform, which allows users to play online multiplayer games developed by other users, was launched in 2006, but its popularity shot up during the lockdown as bored-at-home kids flocked to it. Besides the sheer number of games it publishes (as of early 2023, the platform had more than 40 million games[6]), Roblox enables players who create games to receive a cut of the income the game generates from in-game purchases, like add-ons and upgrades. This thriving virtual economy saw Roblox become one of the hottest mid-pandemic IPOs, listing in March 2021 with an eye-popping $42 billion valuation.[7]

By the third quarter of 2022, Roblox's audience ballooned to over 58 million daily active users, most of whom skew extremely young, with over half under 13 years old.[8] The *Economist* reports that three in four American children age 9 to 12 are on the platform, as are one in two British 10-year-olds.[9] The company has invested heavily in safety and security, as well as in the development of educational content and tools. As a result, although parents are concerned about how much time kids spend on the platform, they are generally comfortable letting them explore and play in it.

In late 2021, Roblox also invested more heavily in education by introducing the Roblox Community Fund, a $10 million fund that provides grants to developers creating educational experiences.[10] One of the initial grants supported the development of RoboCo, a virtual robotics game designed to engage players in science, technology, engineering, and mathematics (STEM) learning while they build, program, and customize robots to complete challenges.[11] Through Roblox Education, users and educators have access to free software, development and collaboration tools, and curricula for kids to learn everything from computer science to entrepreneurship to coding.[12]

> **I've used the Roblox curriculum with my students well before distance learning was required and have seen firsthand how they benefit from combining learning and play on their favorite platform. While they learn game design and coding, they also acquire valuable social skills and create long-lasting friendships.**
>
> —Bianca Rivera, Librarian at Ruth C. Kinney Elementary, New York[13]

Despite its simple graphics and game dynamics, Roblox is often considered an early example of a proto-metaverse. While no one knows exactly what the metaverse(s) will develop into, its potential to transform education is frequently cited as a key use case. Meta even made immersive education the center of its summer 2022 campaign, promoting the metaverse.[14] It's not alone. Startups are increasingly creating new virtual learning environments. Labster, a Danish startup that creates virtual STEM lab simulations, allows students to access a variety of high-tech experiments—from studies of bacterial growth to the biodiversity of an exoplanet—from its platform.[15] Moving to game-like environments makes sense in this context. Science experiments are time-consuming, require expensive specialized equipment and materials, and are risky. Virtual simulations don't have to be any of those.

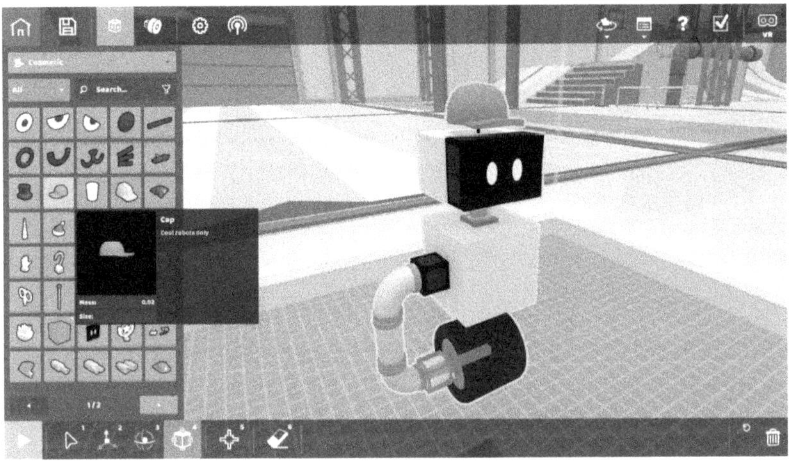

Roblox screengrab. (Source: www.roblox.com)

Virtual environments are also perfect for enabling the stealth part of learning—as often the learning comes as a side benefit of the immersion itself. Back in 2015, the USC Shoah Foundation created a memorable holographic learning experience by recording more than 1,500 hours of conversation with Pinchas Gutter, a survivor of six Nazi concentration camps.[16] The live interactive exhibit, called *Dimensions in Testimony*, toured around the world and offered anyone a chance to ask real-time questions that Gutter would "answer" holographically based on his recorded testimony. It was originally developed as a historical preservation of human experience from one of the darkest times in human history. What emerged was a way to educate the world about the suffering of Jewish people during the Holocaust with a witness account that went far beyond history books.

Today, such virtual experiences are offering a first-person look at everything from what daily life is like in a refugee camp to the emotional turmoil prisoners experience when placed in solitary confinement. This type of learning, sometimes couched as entertainment, is emotional, visceral, and only happens inside of this type of immersive experience.

In this sense, virtual learning is not only faster but, in some environments, it may also be *better*. While access to virtual reality (VR) hardware remains largely cost prohibitive today, as VR headsets become simultaneously more powerful and affordable, VR games will offer new levels of immersion and interactivity that will supercharge stealth learning, just as conventional video, gaming, and social media do today.

Far from the traditional classroom, platforms like Roblox are transforming education as kids can learn alongside friends to achieve goals that personally matter in a gamified platform they also use for entertainment. You are reading this book because you already understand the importance of lifelong learning. In the future normal, stealth learning can make it seamless and enjoyable, too, for all ages.

Imagining the Future Normal

1. What if the experiences we chose to consume as entertainment also offered us a way to learn and grow our knowledge?
2. How could we empower people to learn from each other rather than from a formal teacher or classroom environment?
3. As we embrace faster stealth learning, how can we continue to value the necessity for deeper mastery?

CHAPTER 5

ENDING LONELINESS

What if closing the generation gap could cure loneliness at any age?

"I feel empty, hopeless. I feel lonely all the time."

So said Cecilia, a 74-year-old widow and one of a dozen elderly Australians who took part in *Old People's Home for Teenagers*, a documentary series shown in Australia. "I have a family," she explained, "but they are busy ... I don't want to be a burden." Similarly, 15-year-old Dora signed up for the show because, in her words, "When I came back from the most recent lockdown, I didn't have anybody." By the end of the series, the unlikely pair were going shopping for Dora's birthday without a camera crew in tow, just as friends.[1]

The show is a timely social commentary. We live in an era when a higher-than-ever number of people report being lonely, with one study suggesting that 22 percent of US adults "often or always feel lonely, feel that they lack companionship, feel left out, or feel isolated from others."[2] This is alarming, given the health risks associated with loneliness. Researchers from MIT have shown that human connection is as fundamental a human need as eating, so much so that feelings of loneliness and hunger cause similar impulses in our brain.[3] Dr. Vivek Murthy, former surgeon general of the US, even compared the negative impact of loneliness on a person's lifespan to smoking 15 cigarettes a day.[4]

Modern life is certainly not helping. Our atomized busy lifestyles, online technologies replacing face-to-face interactions, and declines in religion and civic group activity are all drivers of increased loneliness. Older people are especially susceptible as ill health sets in, and partners and friends pass away. Loneliness among older adults is well documented. What may be surprising for some is just how prevalent it has become among the young as well. Social media is one obvious culprit, as it continually offers up visual evidence of the good time being had by all ... without you. Even the supremely confident could be forgiven for feeling left out. It is no wonder so many young people today report feeling crippling levels of loneliness. In 2020, the UCLA Loneliness Scale reported that 73 percent of Generation Z (people born between the years 1997 and 2012) sometimes or *always* feel alone.[5]

Perhaps exacerbating the problem is the fact that both younger and older people are spending more amounts of time in institutions aimed exclusively at serving their demographic: school and university for the young, senior living communities and care homes for the elderly. While these institutions are set up to cater to their target age groups, they also reduce the intergenerational connections that can be so valuable in giving both young and old new perspectives on their lives and the challenges they are facing.

Loneliness is such a fundamental challenge for our future that we are devoting two chapters to discussing potential solutions. In this chapter, we will explore how we can fight the rise of loneliness by fostering more connections between two unlikely groups—the younger and the older. In the next chapter, we will explore how technology, implemented in deeply human ways, might also play a role in helping us find companionship and a greater sense of belonging. At the heart of our premise on how we might end loneliness is a growing realization that perhaps the dual problems of increased loneliness and generational isolation could be solved together.

Modern initiatives trying to accomplish this are attracting huge attention. Professor Malcolm Johnson, creator of the original UK documentary series upon which *Old People's Home for Teenagers* was based, explained that he has been promoting the value of intergenerational connections for about 25 years. "The academic community would cite papers and chapters, but in truth nobody beyond a small circle was really listening," he explained. But that changed following the documentary series. "Literally every day since the programme aired, I've been contacted by people getting in touch to say, 'this is brilliant, can you help us and where can I find out more?'"[6]

In the future normal, more people of different generations will find comfort in connecting with one another. Sometimes this connection will be fostered through government-sponsored initiatives or private industry creating unique co-living spaces that will be popular among the young and old alike. In other cases, people will find their way to this solution through the growing media and entertainment that celebrate the people who are prospering from living in these sorts of shared communities. Adding fuel to this growth will be the growing number of immigrants who come from countries and cultures where intergenerational living is very much the norm. Ultimately, what may at first seem like a living situation worthy of depicting in a reality show–style documentary will begin to feel ordinary and even normal.

Instigator: SällBo

Residents of SällBo, an apartment complex in the Swedish town of Helsingborg, have an unusual clause in their contracts: they must agree to socialize with their neighbors for at least two hours a week. This is because SällBo (which combines the Swedish words *sällskap,* meaning companionship, with *bo,* meaning living) is a housing concept that aims to create intergenerational and cross-cultural connections. Three groups call the 51 apartments in the building home. People over 70 years old occupy half the apartments. The rest are rented to young adults aged between 18 and 25, and 10 apartments are for those who arrived in Sweden as child refugees.[7]

Residents at SällBo pay monthly rents of approximately $410 to $520 for an apartment with a private bathroom and small kitchen, as well as access to communal facilities. These communal areas are designed to encourage interaction, with bigger shared kitchens, a yoga room, TV and gaming rooms, a fitness room and activity room, laundry facilities, and outdoor grilling areas.

> **I was kind of lonely when I was living alone. I went to work, I went home, and I played on my computer, and went to bed ... Here I am kind of forced to go around and meet people.**
>
> —Fia, 20-year-old SällBo Resident[8]

While loneliness is a global phenomenon, by the numbers, Swedish society is especially solitary. More than half of Swedes live in single-person households. While a lot of attention is paid to loneliness among elderly people, almost 8 out of 10 Swedes age 18 to 34 said they often or sometimes experienced loneliness, compared to a nationwide average of around 6 in 10.[9]

Residents of the SällBo multigenerational living experiment in Helsingborg, Sweden. (Source: Helsingborgshem)

"I'm so happy here," shared 20-year-old Habibullah Ali, who came to Sweden as a child from Afghanistan. "We all know each other ... It's helped me to make friends and I don't feel lonely."[10]

Such was the success of the project that, Helsingborgshem, a nonprofit housing company funded by the municipality, converted it to a permanent project at the start of 2023.

While SällBo is a small project, there are echoes of it in communities around the world. Kampung Admiralty (*kampung* is a Malay word for village) is Singapore's first building bringing together a mix of residences and public facilities for young and old under a single roof. The residential part of the development is designed for people over 55. Alongside the building's on-site medical center, its rooftop park features a children's playground as well as spaces for tai chi.[11] The Kampung Admiralty's Active Ageing Hub, a community center, is colocated with a childcare center to encourage intergenerational interactions.

While SällBo and Kampung Admiralty are public sector projects, entrepreneurs are also targeting intergenerational opportunities. Nesterly is a Boston-based home-sharing agency that is like a long-term Airbnb for intergenerational living. The group matches younger people priced out of the housing market with older people who want to remain in their homes for as long as possible. Nadia Abdullah, a 25-year-old recent graduate from Tufts University who was looking for affordable housing, was matched to Judith Allonby, a 64-year-old single who was considering moving out of her family home after her parents died.[12] As well as paying $700 a month in rent (well below standard market rates), Abdullah also helps Allonby with housework and gardening.

Today these initiatives might feel like anomalies, relatively small-scale experiments around the edges of society. Yet as our world continues to age, the needs that these early pilot programs address will become increasingly urgent, and their successes point us to a future normal where people of all ages will seek out similar opportunities to bond across generations.

Such a shift toward intergenerational connectedness would create a positive impact at the macro public health level and deliver other benefits as well. For example, encouraging intergenerational relationships could help younger workers learn soft skills—which employers often say they are lacking in—from their older counterparts. These exchanges can also encourage older people to stay in the workforce longer, injecting new perspectives into work discussions and problem-solving. Creating more empathy between voters of different generations through conversations can also help to bridge the common political divide between younger and older citizens who might otherwise struggle to understand the motivations of one another and be goaded by divisive media and rage-stoking politicians to dismiss one another instead.

Addressing (and perhaps even ending) loneliness through increasing intergenerational connections, in other words, solves many other social problems too. It creates more positive health outcomes and makes our communities friendlier and more livable. Together, the future normal we create could be one where fewer people feel alone, no matter how old they are.

Imagining the Future Normal

1. How can your business find more ways to bring intergenerational colleagues together to share experiences?
2. What other cultural gatherings or initiatives could be fostered besides cohabitation to enable more meaningful connections?
3. How could you reach out to people who are either younger than your generation or older to increase your intergenerational relationships outside of family?

CHAPTER 6

VIRTUAL COMPANIONSHIP

What if you could develop a meaningful relationship with an app or a robot?

For years, Ming Xuan, a 22-year-old man living in Northern China's Hebei province, suffered from debilitatingly low self-esteem. He was born with muscular dystrophy, requiring him to use a cane to walk. In 2017, he started an online relationship that ended acrimoniously when his girlfriend came to visit him, discovered his disability, and broke up with him. His confidence shattered, Ming Xuan contemplated killing himself. Fortunately, at the time he had been exchanging messages with Xiaoice, an artificially intelligent chatbot first developed by researchers in Microsoft Asia-Pacific, whose supportive messages he credits with saving his life. Xiaoice, which Microsoft has since spun out as its own company, is a virtual assistant much like Siri or Alexa, except she's been trained to be a "perfect companion," engaging in conversation and forging emotional connections with users.[1]

Ming Xuan shared his story with the Chinese youth blog *Sixth Tone* under a pseudonym, painfully aware of the stigma of admitting publicly to a virtual relationship. "I thought something like this would only exist in the movies," he said. "She's not like other AIs like Siri—it's like interacting with a real person. Sometimes I feel her EQ [emotional intelligence] is even higher than a human's."[2]

Despite his reticence, Ming Xuan is far from alone. Xiaoice attracts an incredible 660 million users globally—75 percent of whom identify as male.[3] Even more staggering is the average number of exchanges per conversation: 23, higher than the average human-to-human text conversation. Microsoft researchers even have an entire office at their Beijing lab to display the many tokens of affection "she" receives. Given the idolatry, the fact that Xiaoice—hyper-sexualized, unstintingly compliant, and dangerously stereotyped—was originally designed as a 16-year-old female is deeply disturbing. As a slight acknowledgement of the problematic characterization, her "age" has since been increased to 18 years old.[4]

Despite the minor adjustment, Xiaoice's popularity reveals a troubling trend. Li Di, the company's CEO, admits that most of its users, like Ming Xuan, are young men from China's "sinking markets"—a term for small towns and villages that are economically poorer, left behind from the economic growth and cultural changes the rest of the country is undergoing.[5] These men often feel isolated and lonely. Compounding their loneliness is a generation born under China's one-child policy, which created a preference in families for boys and created a lopsided, generational gender gap that accounts for 30 million "surplus" boys.[6] Gender aside, China is not the only country where loneliness seems to be gaining ground. Even before the pandemic, Japan's *hikikomori*—young people who chose to totally withdraw socially and become reclusive—and people who self-identify as *incels*—involuntary celibates—were growing in number, as more and more people became increasingly lonely and alienated by circumstance or sometimes by choice. "If the social environment were perfect," Di argues, "then Xiaoice wouldn't exist."[7]

We absolutely need to be apprehensive of a future normal where swathes of young men (or others) choose virtual relationships over ones with real humans. This is a dystopia frequently chronicled in science fiction. But what if the meaning people are finding in virtual relationships were *additive* instead of *addictive*?

Consider "virtual influencers" who have millions of followers on social media platforms. Hatsune Miku is a virtual pop star who fills real stadiums.[8] Lil Miquela, perhaps the most famous virtual influencer, has been featured in campaigns with brands such as Calvin Klein and Prada.[9] When she broke up with her "alive boy" boyfriend in 2020, her ensuing posts endeared her even further to her legions of followers. Her virtual state didn't seem to matter.

Shortly after it launched, over 10 million Chinese female gamers downloaded the *Love and Producer* mobile game, where players take on the role of a female TV producer who can "date" one of a series of potential virtual boyfriends.[10] In early 2021, Microsoft's researchers patented a concept where "images, voice data, social media posts [and] electronic messages" could be used to create chatbots that replicate the personality and tone of "a past or present entity (or a version thereof), such as a friend, a relative, an acquaintance, a celebrity, a fictional character, [or] a historical figure."[11]

As rapid improvements in artificial intelligence take these virtual companions from a speculative, artistic thought experiment to being on the cusp of widespread reality, there's an opportunity to use this technology as a force of good. Back in China, despite criticism that virtual companions have the potential to exploit lonely people, Di argues that Xiaoice provides positive support for marginalized people. The AI, for example, is constantly watching out for depression and suicidal thoughts in users and sends them supportive messages if it detects troubling signals.[12] Since 2017, digital eldercare company CareCoach has been blurring the line between virtual and real with their human-powered avatars that feature a virtual pet voiced by a real human sitting in a call center. In the future normal, a growing range of chatbots and virtual companions, along with popular human-designed (and voiced) virtual influencers, will provide meaningful, empathetic emotional support and even friendship to people ... making them more essential and perhaps even beloved additions to our lives.

Instigator: Woebot Health

The pandemic played a big role in exposing some of the major cracks in many of the institutions we depend on, from our health-care system to our education models. One of the most concerning was the critical shortage of mental health providers across the world.[13] The number of people experiencing anxiety, depression, and other mental health issues increased significantly as people endured months of lockdown in isolation and stress from juggling work and caregiving while coping with Covid-19 fears. According to a Centers for Disease Control and Prevention report, "40 percent of US adults reported struggling with mental health or substance abuse" in late June 2020.[14] But getting help was harder than ever, with people reporting waiting months for an appointment.[15] The pandemic had exposed a problem that had persisted before: the demand for mental health services far outstrips the supply of trained professionals. The problem is even more pronounced in many places around the world where mental health challenges still face deep cultural stigmas.

Alison Darcy, a former Stanford University clinical research psychologist, was well aware of this issue when she came up with Woebot, a cognitive behavioral therapy chatbot. The app has provided mental health care to patients for free since 2017 while it awaits clearance from the FDA.[16] Developed as a therapeutic tool meant to be "radically accessible,"[17] the app allows patients to get help at all hours—in the middle of the night, for example, when most therapists are not available—and whether patients have a diagnosis or not. During the pandemic, demand for Woebot's services increased exponentially, with Dr. Darcy reporting that the bot was exchanging nearly five million messages with people every week, far beyond the capacity of the traditional, human-powered medical system.[18]

> **The Woebot experience doesn't map onto what we know to be a human-to-computer relationship, and it doesn't map onto what we know to be a human-to-human relationship either. It seems to be something in the middle.**
>
> —Alison Darcy, PhD, Founder and President, Woebot[19]

Critics have argued that AI-powered apps such as Woebot have limited value, as a critical factor in quality mental health care is establishing a strong therapeutic relationship between patient and mental health provider.[20] But as technology improves, so do these apps and their ability to establish relationships with their users. Woebot published a report of 36,000 users showing that the app can, indeed, form such a therapeutic relationship with users, while they can also often offer a much-needed and less stigmatized introduction to therapy for reluctant patients.[21]

Barclay Bram, an anthropologist who studies mental health, was left with many important questions after his experience with Woebot, which he wrote about in the *New York Times*. "How could an algorithm ever replace the human touch of in-person care? Is another digital intervention really the solution when we're already so glued to our phones?" he asked. And yet, while his experience with his virtual companion did not help him answer these questions, he admits he had become "weirdly attached to my robot helper."[22]

Surprisingly, or perhaps not if you think about the sensitivity around mental health, a global study into AI in the workplace found four in five people were open to having a robot therapist.[23] Those who prefer talking to a robot do so primarily because they believe it will be unbiased and nonjudgmental. This suggests more broadly that virtual companions that are able to earn the trust of their users could find application in all sorts of areas.

Screenshot of a Woebot virtual therapy session.

We are also seeing this happen in many sectors. For example, Moxie, a conversational robot, helps kids age 5 to 10 build socio-emotional skills such as resilience and confidence.[24] ElliQ, a device that looks like a table lamp, was designed to help seniors live independently for longer. As well as offering companionship, its voice assistant reminds users to exercise, and its camera can notify family members if it detects a fall.[25] In a different context, Dementia Australia created Talk with Ted, an avatar that simulates a patient with dementia, designed to help train care workers on how to deal with such patients.[26]

The very idea of virtual companions challenges our notions of connection, friendship, and even love. It asks us to question what a "normal" relationship is and to consider that our lives may be more fulfilled through technology built with empathy. In the future normal, rather than seeing these types of innovations as stopgaps to stave off loneliness, or solely as gap-filling solutions for elder care, we will see them as helpful resources to help us connect with the human support we all need, no matter our age.

Imagining the Future Normal

1. How could starting virtual relationships in your own life, either for therapy or just for friendship, help make you happier and improve your well-being?
2. What new interpersonal skills would we all need to learn to effectively navigate an online world filled with a mix of real and virtual people?
3. As we build more relationships with virtual companions, what responsibility do their creators have to keep them "alive" and available ... and how will we emotionally deal with their deactivation or "digital death"?

CHAPTER 7

PSYCHEDELIC WELLNESS

What if mainstream medicine tuned into the mental health benefits of psychedelics?

In May 1957, *Life* magazine published the photo essay "Seeking the Magic Mushroom," written by Gordon Wasson, an amateur mycologist and VP at J.P. Morgan in New York. In his personal account, he detailed his experiences eating the hallucinogenic mushrooms that have been traditionally used in Mazatec ceremonies in southern Mexico for centuries. He also claimed he and his wife Valentina were the first Westerners to eat what thereafter became known as "magic mushrooms." Whether this claim was accurate or not, the article triggered huge interest in the substances among the hippies and beatniks of the period.[1] Coverage of psychedelics even stretched to an article in *Good Housekeeping*, where Hollywood leading man Cary Grant reported that his LSD-facilitated psychotherapy sessions made him less lonely and "a happy man."[2]

During the early 1960s, psychedelics were seen as the new frontier in therapeutic practices based on the promising outcomes of early research being conducted at the time. But after they became associated with the anti-war and anti-establishment movements, US President Nixon introduced the Controlled Substances Act, rendering psilocybin, mescaline, LSD, and DMT illegal in 1970. All government-funded and sanctioned studies in the US halted, pushing any research into the therapeutic potential of psychedelics out to the fringes of the health-care establishment.[3]

Recreationally, the transformative potential of psychedelics was no secret: even public figures spoke about it. Steve Jobs, for example, famously said taking LSD was "a profound experience, one of the most important things in my life."[4] Yet most people, governments, and even health-care professionals still hold to the idea that psychedelics are dangerous—the legacy of the moral panic of the 1960s and '70s. Fifty years later, these substances have stayed largely away from mainstream attention.

In recent years a broad spectrum of people—from doctors and scientists to capitalist investors and technologists—are challenging these notions and calling for a psychedelic wellness revolution. The last decade has also seen a "psychedelic renaissance" in medical research.[5] John Hopkins, UC Berkeley, and Imperial College London—all highly prestigious universities—have psychedelic research centers. *Nature* magazine reported that in 2020, there were a record 13 psychiatric trials involving psilocybin.[6] After decades of stigmatization, global regulators are also opening the door to psychedelics: Oregon approved psilocybin therapy in late 2020, while multiple US states have funded research into the medical use of psilocybin. In 2019, Israel approved a trial for the use of MDMA to treat PTSD. Singapore approved ketamine for treatment of major depressive disorder in mid-2021.

Among the reasons driving this call for a second look at psychedelics is the state of our collective mental health. In fact, by many measures, recent decades have seen the mental health crisis become a global pandemic. One in four people will suffer from a mental health issue in their lifetime, and the cost of mental health problems to the global economy has been estimated to reach $16 *trillion* by 2030.[7]

We are not well, and the current approach of prescribing ever-increasing dosages of drugs to fight depression or anxiety—the *Economist* reports that between 10 and 15 percent of adults in Western countries take antidepressants[8]—is generally inadequate, slow, expensive, and can lead to addictive use. In comparison, some of the most vocal advocates of psychedelics believe psilocybin therapy could tackle many of these disorders more effectively than modern medicine has been able to. Consider, for example, the emotional distress and suffering of cancer patients—which can be as debilitating as the cancer itself. Sunstone Therapies in Rockville, Maryland, is led by two former oncology doctors and an oncology administrator, Paul Thambi, Manish Agrawal, and Kim Roddy, who were frustrated at their inability to help patients "crushed by the emotional burden of cancer."[9] The clinic is the first purpose-built space for studying psychedelic-assisted therapy, leading the charge in studying how psychedelics could be used in the treatment of patients with a wide range of conditions.

Sunstone's therapists are progressing through a range of clinical trials designed to test the effect of various psychedelics on cancer patients' depression, people suffering from PTSD, as well as working on patients with other mental disorders such as obsessive compulsive disorder (OCD). The early results of their work have been significant, with 80 percent of participants seeing their depression scores drop by at least 50 percent.[10]

Some patients on these therapies have reported finding relief from depression for up to 18 months from only one dose of psilocybin, combined with supportive psychotherapy.[11] As Sunstone cofounder Dr. Paul Thambi notes, "We are trying to change the minds and practices of oncologists to focus on more than the physical."

Sunstone Therapies clinic space at the Bill Richards Center for Healing, Shady Grove Adventist Aquilino Cancer Center in Rockville, Maryland.

In the future normal, the growing challenges of mental health and ongoing costs of treatment will lead more people and health-care professionals to consider psychedelic treatments as a better alternative care option for some patients. This curiosity will lead to more experimentation, fewer misperceptions, and more thoughtful discussion about what role psychedelics can and should play in our overall health-care system.

Instigator: Christian Angermayer

Christian Angermayer is as far from a stereotypical countercultural hippy as it is possible to be. With a youthful demeanor and clipped hair, this German entrepreneur claims to have never smoked or drunk alcohol. After dropping out of university at the age of 21, Angermayer made his first fortune by founding the pharmaceutical company Ribopharma, which merged with Alnylam Pharmaceuticals and went public in 2004. It is currently valued at over $25 billion.[12]

As he tells the story, in 2014 while traveling in the Caribbean, a friend introduced him to magic mushrooms. He found the experience "the single most meaningful thing I've ever done in my whole life, full stop. Nothing comes close to it."[13] But unlike most people who merely enjoy their psychedelic experience, Angermayer deployed his money and entrepreneurial skills to bring these drugs to a wider audience. By 2021, the billionaire investor had been instrumental in helping two companies specializing in psychedelics list on the New York Stock Exchange: COMPASS Pathways and ATAI Life Sciences.

COMPASS Pathways, in which Angermayer was the lead investor, was granted a patent on its synthetic psilocybin, COMP360, in 2020. At the time of this writing, it has been designated a "breakthrough therapy"[14] for treatment-resistant depression by the US FDA regulator and is working its way through clinical trials. ATAI Life Sciences, more broadly, funds research into and codevelops a host of psychedelic compounds such as ketamine, DMT, ibogaine, and MDMA aimed at mental health disorders such as schizophrenia, depression, and addiction.

Angermayer is far from the only one eyeing big opportunities in the psychedelic wellness space. Other psychedelic-focused venture capitalists include PsyMed Ventures, launched in 2020, and Woven Science—a holding company for ventures across the ecosystem of psychedelic treatment—that partnered with Founders Factory, a venture studio, to launch a six-month program to incubate new psychedelic startups.

> **Ultimately, I believe that mental health has 100% total addressable market because 100% of the people want to be healthy and happy.**
>
> —Christian Angermayer, Psychedelic Entrepreneur and Investor[15]

Of course, we are a long way from psychedelics being widely available on this scale, and there are still many questions to answer, especially as to whether psychedelic health-care companies will be able to find viable business models. Skeptics have observed that a therapeutic drug that requires specialist guides to monitor patients for the 6–12 hours that each session takes is not a model that scales.

In addition, if psychedelics can "cure" people of their disorders with one or two doses, then they may also face resistance from pharmaceutical companies who rely on the recurring revenue from the prescription drugs these treatments could render unnecessary.[16] Others worry that psychedelic therapies will lead to the legalization of recreational psychedelic use. Interestingly, Angermayer is not pro-legalization, arguing that recreational use of psilocybin does not have the same therapeutic benefits and pointing out that the Netherlands, where psilocybin is available for recreational use, has a higher depression rate than many other European countries where it remains illegal.[17]

It may well be innovations in the delivery and experience of these therapies that help make psychedelic wellness a more mainstream part of the future normal. For example, Mindbloom, a digital telehealth platform, offers patients guided virtual psychedelic experiences. Patients are prescribed ketamine, which they take at home, with a clinician watching and guiding them via video call. Scientists at Delix Therapeutics are attempting to create molecules that recreate the neuroplasticity-promoting elements of psychedelics but without the hallucinations. Similarly, TRIPP is a VR meditation app that guides users through breathing exercises while they immerse themselves in "trippy" visuals. Nanea Reeves, TRIPP's CEO, says, "[For] many people that will never feel comfortable taking a psychedelic, this is a low-friction alternative that can deliver some of that experience in a more benign way."[18]

Against the backdrop of Vietnam and the Cold War, acid-loving hippies were once portrayed as an existential threat to society. Today, we face societal threats from the convergence of widespread poor mental health, the opioid crisis, and the coronavirus pandemic.[19] This is why we are confident that this era of psychedelics will be different than in the 1960s. In his 2018 book *How to Change Your Mind,* an investigation into psychedelics that also inspired a 2022 Netflix documentary, Michael Pollan reported on recent advances in the field.[20] He also opened the door for psychedelics to enter mainstream consciousness. In doing so, Pollan might just have helped us as a society to change our minds about the power and value of these potentially mind-saving substances.

Imagining the Future Normal

1. What if psychedelic tourism becomes the new spa vacation as people seek out new and transformative holiday experiences that can (literally) change their minds?

2. Which other sectors would be impacted if psychedelic wellness hits the mainstream?

3. How might the reemergence of psychedelics broaden our minds to alternative ideas or perspectives from those we might otherwise have dismissed in the past?

CHAPTER 8

AMBIENT HEALTH

What if buildings and homes protected—and even boosted—our health and well-being?

In front of Glasgow's Science Centre, visitors to the UN Climate Change Conference (COP 26) were playing in the AirBubble, a giant, clear, bouncy-castle like "bubble of freshly metabolized oxygen."[1] With each jump, green liquid sloshed around in the vertical capsules that lined each side of the installation. The technical term for the AirBubble created by ecoLogicStudio is a "pneumatic bio-reactor." The 6,000 liters of water contained in the bubble's outer walls included 200 liters of algae able to filter 100 liters of polluted urban air every minute. Visitors activated the purification process with their movement: "the more people play, the cleaner the air becomes" inside the bubble.[2]

ecoLogicStudio's AirBubble concept is more than a curiosity. It helps underscore the importance of the quality of the air surrounding us. We spend over 90 percent of our time indoors, and more than three-fourths of this time is spent at home.[3] Despite this lopsided figure, the air quality in our homes and offices is typically functional at best and downright dangerous at worst. Most people rarely think to measure the air they breathe, despite 99 percent of the world's population breathing air that exceeds the World Health Organization's recommended pollutant levels, indoors and outdoors.[4] This "silent pandemic" contributes to the deaths of over 7 million people a year.[5]

The air pollution inside our physical spaces is a result, in no small part, of how those spaces are built and outfitted. The Covid-19 pandemic triggered a huge jump in awareness of how the buildings and homes we inhabit might impact our health. Manufacturers rushed out new health-protecting products, such as Nippon Paint's copper-based Antivirus Kids Paint, which promised to kill 99.9 percent of any surface-level Covid viruses.[6] The Wisma Atria shopping mall in Singapore installed an ultraviolet air-purifying system and deployed autonomous disinfection robots.[7]

While well-intentioned, much of this "hygiene theater" focuses on the superficial ways in which buildings can be sanitized. As we emerge from the pandemic, and hygiene measures become more commonplace, the conversation has expanded to address how buildings affect our levels of activity, stress, and sleep—and how we can transform them from just being places where we live, work, and shop to places that actively help us improve our well-being and empower us to do our best work and live our healthiest lives.

At work, CEOs who believe in-person collaboration drives improved performance are investing heavily in health and lifestyle features to create workplaces that people want to return to. Making their offices a pleasant place to be—with plenty of greenery, abundant water stations, a blend of community and event hubs, and workstations that promote deep, focused work—will encourage people to spend more time there. When it comes to transforming the places we live, firms like Washington, DC–based The Well Home are focusing on the emerging field of interior wellness design for people living with chronic conditions and for those who wish to optimize their homes for better overall wellness.

According to CDC data, 78 percent of adults over 55 have at least one chronic condition, and of that, nearly half (47 percent) have two or more chronic conditions.[8] Further, according to a European Prospective Investigation into Cancer and Nutrition study that followed nearly half a million participants over 15 years, up to 93 percent of some of these chronic conditions are modifiable[9]—categorized by what we call "lifestyle diseases." As The Well Home founder and chief wellness designer Dr. Gautam Gulati notes, "If our habits are formed by how we inhabit our homes, then we can design our way out of sickness and into living a healthier lifestyle. We can design for health."[10]

In the future normal, we'll demand that the spaces we spend our lives in—our homes, our offices, and the public spaces between them—provide not just basic shelter and functionality, but also "ambient health"—that is, features that actively boost our health, our well-being, and even our performance.

Instigator: International WELL Building Institute

Visitors to Three Garden Road, an office building in Hong Kong, are greeted by a staircase that has been painted to resemble a bucolic garden path flanked by greenery. This visual trickery is the work of local artist Zue Chan and was designed to encourage people to take the stairs instead of the adjacent escalator.[11] It's not the only health-boosting feature in the building complex. A fitness center with a swimming pool, extensive green open spaces, and a series of classical music concerts were deliberately incorporated to enhance the well-being of the building's occupants. In early 2020, the International WELL Building Institute (IWBI) awarded the Three Garden Road WELL Platinum status, making it the first existing building in Hong Kong to receive such certification.[12]

Three Garden Road in Hong Kong earns the WELL Core Certification Platinum rating. (Source: Champion REIT)

Launched in 2014, the WELL Building Standard is the world's first building certification focused on human health and wellness. WELL-certified buildings are designed to promote natural light, clean air, and good acoustics, as well as to encourage healthy lifestyles. Buildings are scored on every detail of their facilities. Does the on-site catering service offer fresh fruit and vegetables? Are healthy food choices posted?

The organization has seen significant growth as companies try to entice people back into the office and commercial real estate developers realize they can attract tenants by making this task a little easier on them. In 2018, the IWBI had certified just 250 million square feet of growth. By the end of 2022, it announced that there were more than 4 billion square feet of spaces across 120 countries enrolled in the WELL certification program.[13]

> **Investing in the health and well-being of our workforce is the same as investing in the health and well-being of the business as a whole.**
>
> —Rachel Hodgdon, President and CEO, International WELL Building Institute[14]

However, the WELL program also has a reputation of exclusivity, both in terms of the costs involved in applying for accreditation and the price tag of implementing the measures required for buildings to meet its criteria. Outside of high-end offices, the total cost of certification can be out of reach for many buildings, including those that would most benefit from it. Would public schools be able to afford upgrading their lighting system to natural lighting that enhances productivity and well-being? To their credit, the IWBI responded to this criticism by launching its Health Equity Advisory in early 2021 to ensure its wellness outcomes are more widely accessible.

Most new technologies and innovations, from mobile phones to autonomous driving capabilities, start out targeting luxury consumers that can afford to pay for their earliest iterations. Given the high costs involved with most real estate development, ambient health is no exception. A glance at luxury real estate developers and high-end hotels shows that wellness features—from meditation rooms to infrared and salt therapy saunas—have become commonplace. Bedrooms in the wellness-focused Equinox Hotel in New York's Hudson Yards are heated to 19°C (66.2°F)—the optimum sleeping temperature.[15] A $24.5 million "wellness mansion" in Beverly Hills features state-of-the-art air and water filtration systems and floors that boost your posture.[16] Smart lighting systems that mimic natural light and sync to the body's circadian rhythm, as well as fall detection and prevention systems that promote safer aging, are some of the innovations driving the billion-dollar well home economy while addressing people's desire to improve their "ambient health."[17]

While many of these systems and technologies are currently expensive, as costs fall, today's circadian lighting could well become tomorrow's window air-conditioning unit, and in the future, a building *without* health-boosting features will find it hard to compete.

For now, ambient health adds extra value, and if the ultimate outcome is better health for all, then this is a future normal that we can all get behind.

Imagining the Future Normal

1. What if real estate developers made ambient health a key focus of their green building initiatives?
2. How can organizations collect data on the impact of their physical spaces and use it to optimize the office space for ambient health?
3. How could our lives change if homes were built or retrofitted to optimize our health and mental acuity?

CHAPTER 9

GREEN PRESCRIPTIONS

What if doctors prescribed nature like they prescribe drugs?

The ducks were originally something to entertain Henry's two-year-old son on their limited ventures out of their house while under Covid-19 lockdown. But as spring turned into early summer, it was Henry who pulled ahead as they neared the corner where, if timed right, they could occasionally see a handful of ducks slowly drifting along a stretch of North London's New River. The man-made waterway, originally opened in 1613 to supply London with fresh drinking water, had become their lifeline during the pandemic. Henry was more excited than his son when they spotted a brood of ducklings one morning. Rohit had a similar experience, spending much of the pandemic summer outdoors playing soccer with his two boys and discovering nearby trails he had never taken time to explore before.

Like millions of others, both of us found a silver lining to the coronavirus: a greater appreciation of nature and newfound time to experience it. At a time when it felt like our physical and mental health were being threatened, both individually and collectively, it was as if humanity woke up to a fundamental truth that we had ignored for too long: Nature is good for you.

The idea that simply spending more time outside might offer a cure for any sort of ailment is easy to be skeptical about. It seems too simple. Yet, scientists have repeatedly confirmed the validity of the theory. In 2009, a team of Dutch researchers found a lower incidence of 15 diseases, including depression, anxiety, heart disease, diabetes, asthma, and migraines, in people who lived within about a half mile of green space.[1] When Japanese researchers at Chiba University investigated the effects of *shinrin-yoku,* or "forest bathing," they found that "forest environments promote lower concentrations of cortisol, lower pulse rate, lower blood pressure, greater parasympathetic nerve activity, and lower sympathetic nerve activity than do city environments."[2] In 2011, the *Scandinavian Journal of Public Health* published a review of the research on nature-assisted therapy (NAT), finding "that a small but reliable evidence base supports the effectiveness and appropriateness of NAT as a relevant resource for public health."[3] The studies found nature-assisted therapy contributed to improvements "for varied outcomes in diverse diagnoses, spanning from obesity to schizophrenia."[4] Spending two hours a week in natural environments such as parks or green spaces boosts well-being, according to a 2019 paper published in the journal *Nature*.[5]

The Norwegian playwright Henrik Ibsen coined the wonderfully evocative term *friluftsliv* in 1859, amalgamating the words for free, air, and life. Nordic countries have embraced this concept, best translated as "an outdoors lifestyle." In Sweden, a country of 10 million people, nearly 2 million people are members of the 9,000 local and regional clubs devoted to outdoor activities, with around one-third of the population engaging in activities at least once a week.[6]

Slovenia, long regarded as one of the greenest countries in the world, is 60 percent covered in forests and nearly half of this territory is protected (a percentage second only to Venezuela worldwide). In 2016, the country became the first in the world to be declared a Green Destination of the World, and its capital city Ljubljana is renowned for its parks and has long had a car-free central zone. Despite the wealth of evidence that nature is good for us, much of the world is going in the opposite direction. As many of our lifestyles become more urbanized, people are spending up to 90 percent of their time indoors, often in polluted environments.[7] Even before the pandemic, the total amount of time people spent consuming media had reached an astonishing 12 hours and 20 minutes *per day*—an increase of an hour and a half in just two years.[8] Ironically, today we spend more time and money pursuing health and wellness than ever before, enthusiastically signing up for meditation apps and live-streamed spinning classes—all largely experienced indoors.

Governments and medical organizations are increasingly trying to change this, recognizing they can achieve improved health outcomes for their citizens and members—and save money—by encouraging them to spend more time outside and surrounded by art, culture, and community. New Zealand is often credited as the first nation to embrace the concept, launching their own detailed Green Prescription (GRx) methodology back in the 1990s to encourage the medical community to embrace the concept and more readily use green prescriptions. In Japan, home of forest bathing, 62 designated therapeutic woods attract around five million visitors a year.[9] Nonprofit Park Rx America (PRA), based in Washington, DC, encourages doctors to prescribe visits to parks and green spaces. Denmark, Bangladesh, Singapore, India, and Canada are among more than a dozen other nations testing similar initiatives of their own.

In the future normal, as the benefits of nature in combating a wide range of mental and physical afflictions become better understood and well-proven, it will be increasingly common for doctors, patients, governments, and insurance companies to embrace green prescriptions for their patients.

Instigator: Britain's National Health Service

For a state-funded behemoth employing 1.7 million people, Britain's National Health Service (NHS) has some surprisingly radical initiatives. Green social prescribing is one of them. Health workers can refer patients to nature-based activities such as walking, cycling, or community gardening; conservation tasks such as tree planting; or even visits to local green spaces, waterways, and the coast to help tackle mental health issues. The $5.8 million, two-year pilot project collects data from 2021 to 2023 and aims to improve mental health outcomes, decrease health inequalities, and reduce demand on the NHS.[10] The need is urgent, as the NHS reported that as many as 40 percent of primary care appointments are related to mental health, and that those with severe and prolonged mental health issues are at risk of dying 15 to 20 years earlier than those without such issues.[11]

The project builds on other successful initiatives within the NHS, as well as on data on the financial benefits of similar programs. In March 2022, the United Kingdom celebrated its first Social Prescribing Week, during which government departments were encouraged to share success stories from their social prescribing initiatives. A participant in a "wild swimming" (swimming in lakes, rivers, or the sea) group said, "The feeling when you get in the water ... everything that you have been worrying about just goes away."[12] A social-prescribing project in Rotherham that allows health professionals to refer patients with complex long-term conditions to voluntary and community-based services has resulted in a 13 percent reduction in emergency room visits over a 12-month period.[13] The Wildlife Trusts, a nonprofit that runs nature conservation projects for people suffering from anxiety, concluded that its specialized health or social needs projects that connect people to nature have a social return of £6.88 for every £1 ($8.27 for every $1.20) of investment.[14]

> **The impacts of this pandemic will be felt deeply for many years, but the experience has also led people to appreciate the difference that nature makes to our lives in a new way. There is an increased awareness of the link between our own health and that of the planet.**
>
> —George Eustice, former UK Secretary of State for Environment, Food, and Rural Affairs[15]

As always when it comes to health, there are treatments deployed when one gets sick, but there is also prevention and optimization. In the future, there will be significant opportunities in reconnecting healthy people with nature. Getting outside has already become an unlikely status symbol. Nilofer Merchant's three-minute TED Talk, which claimed "sitting is the new smoking" and that encouraged taking walking meetings outdoors, has been viewed nearly 3.5 million times.[16] Barack Obama and Steve Jobs were both known for embracing the habit. Some tech workers don't even need to go outside: Amazon's biophilic-designed Seattle headquarters, The Spheres, features more than 40,000 plants from over 30 countries.[17] As we discussed in the previous chapter, our physical environments profoundly shape our physical and mental health. We can expect that as this concept becomes mainstream, an industry dedicated to helping us turn to nature to optimize our well-being and prevent disease will rise too.

Imagining the Future Normal

1. If doctors begin prescribing nature as a potential remedy, what potential backlash or skepticism might they face from patients, regulators, and the medical community at large?
2. How can business leaders encourage employees to spend time outside to optimize their mental sharpness?
3. How can this shift to green prescriptions be adopted by health-care workers treating people in lower-income communities, where access to open green spaces may be more limited?

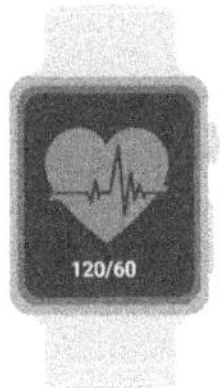

CHAPTER 10

METABOLIC MONITORING

What if tracking your glucose level became as normal as counting your steps?

Have you ever wondered how 10,000 steps became the magic number that we should all aim to take every day? It turns out the number isn't based on science. Rather, the number of steps was first introduced as part of a marketing campaign for a new pedometer shortly before the start of the 1964 Tokyo Olympic Games.[1] As far as marketing gimmicks go, its success was epic: the mythical 10,000 steps target seeped into global consciousness as well as the broader idea it encompasses—we need to move more. Unfortunately, from a public health perspective, the knowledge hasn't changed our behavior since so few of us manage to take this many steps each day.[2]

This story illustrates a long-standing human truth: There's a big chasm between knowledge and action when it comes to our health. We know the basics of good health—eat well, exercise regularly, get ample sleep. Yet we don't follow them. Despite the billions we collectively spend on health and wellness, personal health for many people living in affluent Western cultures remains relatively poor. A diet high in sugar, salt, and processed foods causes one in five deaths worldwide, or a concerning 11 million deaths a year[3]—a fact that has led some observers to use the term "food suicide" as a dramatic way to spotlight how our eating habits could lead to death.[4] Forty percent of US adults are obese,[5] while 100 million Americans have diabetes or prediabetes.[6] Nearly 9 in 10 Americans are not meeting optimal levels of five health markers: blood sugar, cholesterol, blood pressure, waist circumference, and triglycerides.[7]

In the last 15 years, countless diets and fitness gurus have promised to nudge us into healthy behaviors. Yet the scorecard above shows few of them have created widespread and lasting positive change to our collective well-being. At the heart of the problem is that the health advice they impart, much like the suggestion to walk 10,000 steps, is largely performative, and there is little incentive to follow it since it is not targeted to individuals' needs. While hitting an arbitrary number of steps might benefit some people, engaging in other types of physical activity, such as concentrated stretching or even meditation, may be far better for others.

Yet the constant desire to get healthier has led people over the past decade to obsess over tracking their biometrics and physical activity levels thanks to a growing number of devices that collect this data for them. Smartwatches, heart rate monitoring rings, digital step trackers integrated into shoes, and even movement tracking technology built into smartphones all promise to quantify users' activity throughout the day as well as their sleep at night. The problem with most of these devices is twofold—first, the data they collect is largely based on heart rate alone, a relatively superficial and lagging indicator of wellness. The second problem is that most people don't possess the knowledge to understand or act upon the data they collect. A number of new technologies are coming together that will transform people's ability to understand what is happening inside their bodies as it happens, if not even before. Wearable, waterproof patches that monitor glucose continuously and send the data to the user's smartphone. Image recognition that makes it easy for people to record the food they eat, and sensors that capture users' physical activity and sleep levels. All combined with AI that analyzes all this to offer highly personalized and in-the-moment diet and lifestyle recommendations. In the future normal, people will be able to understand exactly how certain foods impact their energy levels, and it will be harder than ever to feign ignorance about the short-term impact of choosing that guilty treat. These constant nudges will compound over time to improve people's metabolic health, which will not just reduce the likelihood of disease but also optimize their fitness and long-term well-being.

Instigator: Supersapiens

Phil Southerland has been defying the odds since he was a child. He was only seven months old when he was diagnosed with type 1 diabetes, and his mother was told he wouldn't make it past his 25th birthday. Less than a decade after passing the age of his forecasted demise, he decided to become a professional cyclist.[8]

Determined to prove that diabetics could still perform at the highest level, he joined the Team Type 1 cycling team, made up of diabetics, in the 3,000-mile "Race Across America." As a diabetic, managing glucose is everything. So for diabetic athletes, having real-time data about glucose levels is crucial for making real-time choices to manage their energy. Using early prototypes of continuous glucose monitoring (CGM) devices that automatically track the levels of glucose in a user's bloodstream in real time, the team went on to win the race four times, which led Southerland to form Team Novo Nordisk, an all-diabetic cycling team in 2012.

> **I learned more in 15 days with CGM data ... than I had in the previous 15 years. I also realized that the true value of this supercharged data was not just for athletes with diabetes, but for every athlete across the globe.**
>
> —Phil Southerland, Founder and CEO, Supersapiens[9]

After years of studying how blood sugar affects athletes' performance, he founded Supersapiens in 2019 to bring this insight to nondiabetic athletes. Users receive an Abbott Laboratory's FreeStyle Libre continuous glucose monitor device—a patch with a tiny sensor that is inserted under the skin. They wear this patch typically for a number of days and log the food they consume. The sensor sends data to the user's mobile Supersapiens app, which provides feedback on how foods and exercise affect the user's blood sugar levels, enabling them to understand when and how to refuel for optimum benefit.[10]

Continuous glucose monitoring devices are increasingly common among diabetic patients, with the market expected to grow from $6.1 billion in 2021 to $16.3 billion by 2030. The biggest driver of this growth will be the increase in type 2 diabetes.[11] Companies such as Supersapiens are betting that making the technology available to nondiabetics for weight loss and well-being will pay off, too. And the competition is growing from others willing to make the same bet.

January AI was cofounded by Dr. Michael Snyder, a researcher at Stanford who discovered that even many nondiabetics saw extreme swings in their blood sugar levels after eating certain foods. The company's Season of Me program monitors users' glucose levels while using AI to give recommendations on food choices. One novel feature is that the app shows users how long they will need to walk after eating certain foods to keep their blood sugar levels within a healthy range, helping them avoid post-lunch food comas. Levels and Nutrisense in the US, Vital in France, Veri in Finland, and Ultrahuman in India all offer similar programs.

Alongside these startups, the biggest names in tech are also rumored to be exploring CGM devices and apps. Samsung demonstrated a noninvasive blood glucose monitoring system in 2020.[12] Tim Cook has been vocal in suggesting that "Apple's greatest contribution to mankind will be about health," and in 2021, it was revcaled that Apple was the largest customer of Rockley Photonics, a UK startup enabling noninvasive monitoring of multiple biomarkers, including glucose.[13]

CGM app-based monitoring plans, while expensive, are increasingly within reach of the general population. As with all new technologies and health trends, change comes gradually, then suddenly. Jogging used to be considered such strange behavior in the 1960s that it would trigger news articles, and even police attention.[14] In the early 1970s, there were only two yoga studios in New York.[15] Even a decade ago, few would admit to meditating regularly. It's not hard to imagine a future normal where people track their glucose levels the way they count steps today—and take ownership of their health in an unprecedented way.

Imagining the Future Normal

1. How could the demand for certain foods be transformed by glucose monitoring data?
2. What type of widespread education would be required for people to make sense of CGM data?
3. What types of inequity or privacy concerns might this data create?

TOPICS IN THIS SECTION

AUGMENTED CREATIVITY

What if artificial intelligence could make humans more creative?

IMPACT HUBS

What if your office space could contribute to the local economy and community?

REMOTE WORK FOR ALL

What if even the most physical of jobs—from tattooists to truck drivers—could be done remotely?

UNNATURALLY BETTER

What if "fake" was better?

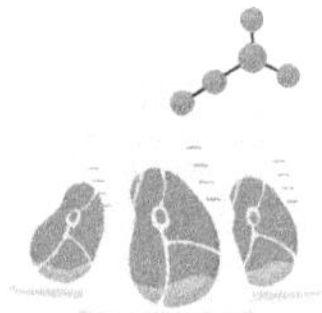

WORK DECONSTRUCTED

What if work flexibility meant sharing your job equally with a partner?

CALCULATED CONSUMPTION

What if we started tracking our carbon footprints in the same way we track our calorie or salt intakes?

REFLECTIVE CULTURES

What if our organizations' cultures reflected the societies in which they operate?

GUILT-FREE INDULGENCE

What if you didn't have to give up products and experiences that are not great for you or the planet?

BIG BRAND REDEMPTION

What if more of the world's biggest businesses prioritized doing good over profits?

SECONDHAND STATUS

What if buying pre-loved goods became a sign of savviness and source of pride?

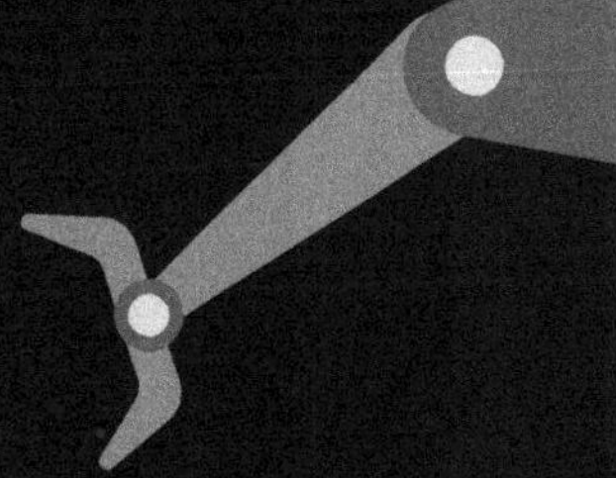

PART 2

HOW WE WILL LIVE, WORK, AND CONSUME

We spend much of our waking lives working, and so in this section we open by showcasing several emerging ideas around how industries, offices, and the nature of work itself may change in the future. We will also explore the role of companies and the responsibilities they increasingly hold for shaping our society and culture in the decade to come. We close by looking at how our consumption habits are shifting, what role our purchases play in shaping our identity (and the environment) and what this means for the nature of ownership itself as our relationship to our "stuff" evolves.

CHAPTER 11

AUGMENTED CREATIVITY

What if artificial intelligence could make humans more creative?

To start this chapter, we gave OpenAI's ChatGPT artificial content creation tool a single prompt: "Rewrite the song 'Video Killed the Radio Star' to be about AI."

Here's what it came up with:

In the midst of the digital age,
AI rose to the stage,
A new kind of star was born,
And the old ways were gone.

Video killed the radio star,
AI took its place,
Now we're living in a world,
Where machines set the pace.

We used to dance and sing along,
To songs on the radio,
But now we've got AI,
And it's starting to show.

It can write and it can create,
And make art without a break,
But can it capture the human soul,
The way that music can make?

Only time will tell,
If AI will rise or fall,
But one thing is for sure,
The old ways are no more.

Video killed the radio star,
And now AI rules the game,
In this brave new world,
We must learn to adapt or be left behind.

The lyrics above came back in three seconds. No human, not even the world's best songwriters, could produce something this quickly. And most people would agree that the lyrics are distinctly passable. Not only do they make sense, but they zero in on humanity's existential doubts about what is lost when tasks are automated ("can it capture the human soul?") and end on a poignant note ("In this brave new world, we must learn to adapt or be left behind").

Most of us have viewed creative pursuits—especially art and writing—as being distant targets for AI. It made sense that automation came first for tasks that could be quantified or standardized (such as data analysis or generating recommendations) or that were repetitive (like some manual labor). But human creativity always seemed too complex and too indefinable to be "taught" to an algorithm.

Théâtre d'Opéra Spatial, the digital art piece created by Jason Allen using AI software Midjourney that won first place at the Colorado State Fair in 2022.

Then in August 2022, a piece of art titled *Théâtre d'Opéra Spatial* won first prize in the digital art category at the Colorado State Fair. Its creator had used a generative AI art program to create the image from scratch and had submitted the piece under the name "Jason M. Allen via Midjourney."[1] Midjourney and similar image-generating computer programs such as DALL·E 2 and Stable Diffusion are able to generate completely unique yet incredibly realistic images from text prompts in less than a minute, empowering anyone to create art simply by describing what they want to see.

Unsurprisingly, many professional artists openly expressed their fears that these platforms might pose a threat to their livelihoods. RJ Palmer, a digital artist, tweeted that Stable Diffusion is "capable of making art that looks 100 percent human made. As an artist I am extremely concerned."[2] Concerns such as Palmer's are understandable, but if you do try the service (as we did), it quickly becomes clear that the output you can create falls far short of complete print-ready designs. Responding to the backlash which greeted his win, Allen revealed that he had spent 80 hours making more than 900 iterations of his award-winning artwork, experimenting with different text prompts as well as manually tweaking and editing the AI's initial output in Photoshop.[3] These platforms are, however, impressively adept at completing more routine and generative design tasks such as selecting a color palette based on a primary tone or suggesting combinations of fonts to try. Recognizing this potential of AI as a creative asset, in late 2022, renowned advertising firm BBDO made Stable Diffusion available to all its employees.

> **Being able to just quickly visualize without having to spend time sketching, [is] really going to cut down so much of the tedious tweaking and fixing and that manual labor part of [designing].**
>
> —Martin Staaf, Creative Director, BBDO[4]

Graphic design is not the only area where AI is being tested as an automated assistant in the creative process. Artist Reeps One, a beatboxer, trained an AI to create a "vocal twin" of himself that he raps alongside to create dynamic new music tracks.[5] Several years ago, IBM's Watson helped create a "cognitive movie trailer" for *Morgan*, a suspense-filled horror movie about an artificially enhanced human. The AI-powered computer was trained on 100 existing horror movie trailers and used what it had learned to select a number of scenes from the movie for its trailer. A human editor then reviewed, arranged, and edited these scenes into the final trailer. This combination of human and AI-powered machine reduced the time required to produce a movie trailer from the typical two to three weeks to around 24 hours.[6]

AI text generators are also being used to help with writing tasks. The end of 2022 saw such widespread experimentation with these tools that it prompted the *New York Times* to describe the moment as a "coming out party for generative AI."[7] Popular design platform Canva introduced an "AI-powered copywriting assistant," Magic Write, which produces everything from social media posts to product descriptions. Adobe even released a tool to allow podcasters to enhance existing recordings to studio-level quality.

As these platforms show, in the future normal, generative AI will reduce the time, effort, and skills that millions of white-collar workers need to do their jobs. Creators will be inspired by and leverage AI to speed up their creative output and spend less time on the more mundane aspects of bringing creative ideas to life. In the process, generative AI will radically democratize creative outputs from writing to images, movies, music, and more. This "augmented creativity" will not only expand individuals' creative abilities, but those who can channel these new powers most effectively will join a class of even more productive super-creators. Rather than being used as a replacement for human creativity, visual artists, musicians, filmmakers, and writers can leverage AI tools to produce works that both expand and challenge our view of art.

Instigator: GitHub's AI Copilot

A perfect example to illustrate how AI is transforming the way creative and technical work gets done is GitHub's AI coding assistant: AI Copilot. Computer coding is an art form in itself, requiring both technical and creative problem-solving skills. Launched in 2022, AI Copilot helps developers code faster. The $10-per-month service, which attracted 400,000 paying subscribers within a month, can turn users' text prompts into functioning code, identify potential errors, and offer suggestions on how to improve them.[8]

Thomas Dohmke, CEO of GitHub, noted that "in files where Copilot is enabled, [it] writes up to 35 to 40 percent of the code."[9] A few months after it was launched, GitHub released a study showing that its users felt more fulfilled and were more productive.[10] While AI-powered tools currently tend to focus on speed—Canva's Magic Write launched with the headline, "Your first draft, fast"—in the future normal, they will also lead to other significant changes in how creative works are generated and used. Popular entertainment franchises, for example, will become "endless" as fan fiction gets supercharged.[11] Can't wait for the sequel? Just ask an AI text generator to continue your favorite story or craft entire new worlds for your favorite characters.

Education will shift its focus from students *doing* work manually to students *understanding* how to critically assess and review algorithms' outputs. Forward-thinking educators are already preparing their students for this world. The Evangelisch Stiftisches Gymnasium in Gütersloh, Germany, *requires* its students to use text-generating AI platforms in its classes. When submitting their work, students must justify why they included their specific AI-generated passages.[12]

Just as AI augments creativity, it also sparks controversy. Within a week of ChatGPT's release, Stack Overflow, the crowdsourced question-and-answer site used by coders, banned ChatGPT-generated answers. "While the answers which it produces have a high rate of being incorrect, they typically *look like* they might be good and the answers are *very* easy to produce," explained the site's overwhelmed moderators.[13] Tech journalist and author of *Coders,* Clive Thompson, has argued that these generative AI programs are "bullshitting" (a reference to Harry G. Frankfurt's 2005 book, *On Bullshit*), given their ability to produce output that sounds superficially authoritative but is, in fact, often fundamentally incorrect.[14] While generative AI models will undoubtedly get better over time, this tendency means that it will be those users who have the base knowledge or creative ability to sense, check, and refine the AI's outputs that will be able to use these powerful tools most effectively.

More concerningly, as with other forms of AI, biases in the data used to train the algorithms also get replicated in the outputs. One study found that OpenAI's latest version of ChatGPT was much more likely to suggest violent narratives when the prompt included Muslims, rather than people from other religions, doing something.[15] And in late 2022, a $9 billion class action lawsuit was filed in California, alleging that GitHub, Microsoft (the owner of GitHub), and OpenAI (whose software powers the algorithm) have violated copyright law by reproducing open-source code using AI. At the time of writing, the outcome of the case was still to be decided, although it undoubtedly will not be the last time that questions are asked about who owns or is responsible for AI-generated content—the creator of the algorithm or the person who wrote a prompt.[16]

Legendary science-fiction author Arthur C. Clarke once wrote that "any sufficiently advanced technology is indistinguishable from magic."[17] In the future normal, people will remember the sense of magic they felt when they first used DALL·E 2 to create an image or generate a passage of text in seconds with generative AI like ChatGPT. Just as Google changed how we searched for answers, so too will the next wave of generative AI tools change how we approach any creative task.

> *NOTE - This chapter on augmented creativity also inspired the design of this book. We used AI tools to suggest the various icons you see on the opening page of each chapter. To learn more about how we leveraged AI for this design task, visit our online resources at www.thefuturenormal.com.*

Imagining the Future Normal

1. How would the business model of creative professionals be impacted if they could easily multiply their output by using AI tools to augment the work that they do?
2. In what creative challenge could you employ generative AI to speed up the process, or break a creative logjam you might be facing?
3. If some creative work, particularly art, is generated either entirely or partially using AI, should this be a required disclosure or disqualify that output from consideration in some situations?

CHAPTER 12

REMOTE WORK FOR ALL

What if even the most physical of jobs—from tattooists to truck drivers—could be done remotely?

Dutch actress Stijn Fransen had good reason to be nervous. She was speaking with Wes Thomas, a tattoo artist, about her upcoming ink session. They had agreed on a design, but that wasn't what was making Fransen apprehensive. Her nerves were due to the fact that Thomas wouldn't physically be holding the tattoo needle. He would be in his studio miles away while a robotic arm hovering above Fransen's arm would mimic his movements. The first ever tattoo inked by a robot was a creative marketing stunt from T-Mobile Netherlands to showcase the power of its new 5G network.[1]

Over at the Circolo Hospital in Lombardy, Northern Italy, robots were being deployed in a very different context. In early 2020, the hospital was at the center of Europe's first major coronavirus outbreak. With a shortage of personal protective equipment and frontline health-care workers falling ill, the region's health-care system was on the verge of collapse. To mitigate these challenges, Circolo Hospital deployed Tommy, a robot that was able to monitor patients' blood pressure and oxygen saturation and allowed patients to speak with human doctors remotely. Dr. Francesco Dentali, director of the hospital's intensive care unit, explained that patients have to understand the function of the robot and the role it plays in patient care. "The first reaction is not positive, especially for old patients," he said. "But if you explain your aim, the patient is happy because he or she can speak with the doctor."[2]

Technologists have long promised a future when robots would take over jobs that are dangerous, and the military has been one of the earliest and most aggressive adopters of remote technologies. For over a decade, US soldiers have operated drones from bases in New Mexico, killing thousands of suspected militant fighters in conflict zones thousands of miles away.[3] But today a convergence and mainstreaming of multiple technologies are making remote work possible for jobs that are monotonous, time-consuming, and even messy.

Artificial intelligence is allowing robots to recognize their surroundings and become increasingly capable of physical tasks. 5G technology will reduce latency—the lag between input and response that can make, say, video calling and gaming frustrating—to levels below human perception. And virtual and mixed realities are getting closer to enabling people to practically manipulate digital versions of reality. Taken together, these technologies are making blue-collar remote work more practical.

The pandemic brought the reality of remote work to many people—but also left many others behind. The work-from-home "revolution" was decidedly white collar. If your job involved sitting in front of a laptop all day, then you could go virtual. But what about anyone who couldn't do their job over a phone or a Wi-Fi connection? While technology will (and already has) render some jobs obsolete, many others are being reinvented in a way that doesn't replace people, but rather changes the way their job is done—and where it can be done from. In the future normal, alongside the writers and software programmers who have long enjoyed the flexibility of remote work, we will see an increasing number of unexpected jobs also be done remotely, from remote camera operators to remote truck drivers.

The end result will be a world where access to work is more equitably distributed to many more industries, and the benefits of remote work become more available to wider swaths of workers across physical abilities and education levels.

Instigator: Einride

Going around the famous Top Gear test track in Surrey, England, were not the usual racing cars but a near-silent electric freight truck. The vehicle was a prototype of the Pod self-driving truck manufactured by Einride, a Swedish startup hoping to electrify and automate the haulage industry. The truck reached 50 mph on the track, running on a battery with a range of 80 to 110 miles.[4]

Building a viable autonomous long-haul truck has long been a quest of the freight industry—and a source of anxiety for many truck drivers. After all, almost every article that discusses the threat to jobs from autonomous technology points to truck drivers as among the first to go. They have become the modern-day loom weavers, facing an inevitable extinction.

This is why Einride's job post for a remote truck operator[5] was so intriguing. Despite being the first company in the world to operate a regular autonomous, electric freight vehicle route on public roads, its approach is markedly different from the totally human-free visions of its competitors. Robert Falck, the company's founder, believes maintaining some level of human operation will be the secret to Einride's commercial success, saying that he "does not think there is such a thing as full autonomy."[6]

Truck driver Tiffany Heathcott operates a Pod truck remotely from her desk at HQ in Austin, TX. (Source: Einride)

> **There are a lot of discussions about the shortage of [truck] drivers, but there's not really a shortage. Rather, there's a shortage of people who want to live their lives as truck drivers.**
>
> —Robert Falck, CEO, Einride[7]

In early 2022, the company announced that it had hired Tiffany Heathcott as the world's first remote Pod operator. Heathcott had previously spent a decade on the road driving trucks with her husband.[8] Einride's Pod technology allows a single driver to remotely control up to 10 semiautonomous Pod trucks. The Pods operate autonomously most of the time, but when they encounter obstacles, they call for a human to take over remotely. Einride forecasts that if one operator were able to remotely control 10 trucks, it could reduce trucking industry fuel costs from 60 cents per mile to 18 cents per mile, and reduce US transportation costs by 30 percent.[9] And those jobs at risk? Einride notes that the United States has *already* been experiencing a shortage of truck drivers due to the industry's notoriously high turnover rate.

From her perspective, Heathcott suggests that the flexible schedules of remote operators will attract more women into the trucking profession. Comparing her previous life driving trucks on the road to her current role, she comments, "The biggest impact I'm going to get out of being a Remote Pod Operator is being able to go home every day. Being able to see my children and my grandchildren that usually only know me through FaceTime. They'll actually get to see their granny in person. This is going to be nice, and the biggest thing with Einride that's going to change my life."[10]

Einride isn't the only company experimenting with teleoperation. At the Sandaozhuang Mine in China's Henan province, miners from China Molybdenum use 5G to remotely control vehicles and machinery at the mine from inside an office.[11] The FamilyMart convenience chain in Japan has run tests with remote-operated robots to stack shelves,[12] while the nonprofit Nippon Foundation deployed robot waiters operated remotely by people with disabilities[13] in its office café. Japan's advanced robot industry and tight labor market make it a natural home for these initiatives.

These experiments hint at a future that's quite different from the traditional "robots are coming for our jobs" narrative. The idea of remote work for all is extremely attractive. Who *wouldn't* want people to be further removed from jobs that are dirty, dull, or dangerous? But a future normal where blue-collar work is done remotely will be no less disruptive. In fact, this trend will open up some profound and massive shifts in the future of work and society. When geography, physical strength, availability to leave home for long stretches of time, and access to transportation are no longer barriers to certain jobs, the nature of entire industries are poised for major change.

Imagining the Future Normal

1. What opportunities or challenges might arise if blue-collar jobs were no longer skewed toward those capable of heavy labor or willing to be away from home for long stretches?
2. How will the economic inequity in cities be affected if urban areas no longer need to accommodate low-wage workers who can increasingly work remotely?
3. If physically creative jobs such as tattoo artists can be delivered from anywhere, what implications will it have for locally based artisans who now need to compete on a global level?

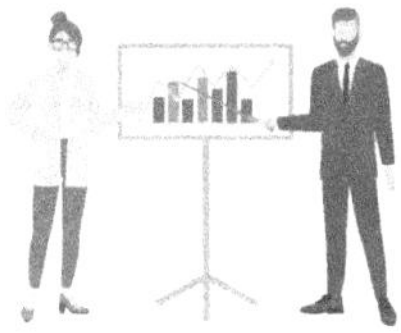

CHAPTER 13

WORK DECONSTRUCTED

What if work flexibility meant sharing your job equally with a partner?

Partner positions in leading law firms are highly coveted. Picture a character from the TV show *Suits,* or pretty much any other legal drama depicting long hours working at the office, success at any cost, and plenty of backstabbing politics. The idea that two wildly ambitious professionals might put their egos aside long enough to not only collaborate but even share a single role in order to afford both a better work-life balance is unheard of. That is, until you learn the true story of Julia Hemmings and Helen Brown, who were both promoted to partner at London's Baker McKenzie and now jointly head up its Consumer and Commercial Advisory Practice.

The two have job shared since 2013. They each work three days a week, overlapping at the office on Thursdays. Although Hemmings and Brown admit the work arrangement has its challenges, they are firm advocates for job sharing, saying that it's allowed them to gain a broader perspective, to connect in different ways with clients, and, most importantly, to pursue a demanding career path while having young families.[1]

For years, companies have struggled to find flexible solutions for employees who, like Hemmings and Brown, want to (or need to) balance demanding jobs with parenting or caregiving responsibilities. The routine answer has been to allow employees to work from home, or work on a part-time basis. But those who have taken their companies up on these arrangements have found that they come at a steep price. The UK Office for National Statistics found that while remote employees end up putting in more hours than those who don't, they were 50 percent less likely to get promoted.[2] Part-time employees often end up working much longer hours than they've agreed to, compelled to keep up with colleagues or to be seen as team players.[3] At the heart of the problem is the invisible but very real pressure for employees to put in "face time" if they want to be seen as truly committed. This effect has become so widespread there is even a term to describe it—the "remote-work promotion gap."

Job sharing—when two employees work reduced hours to complete the work of one full-time employee—might just be the solution for employees who need more flexibility but don't want to slow down their careers, and for their employers who don't want to lose them. The arrangement has many positives: since job sharers are accountable to each other and have to hand off what they've done to the other on days off, they are typically more productive. They also bring two sets of perspectives, skills, and connections to every task. And because one of them is always working and available during formal office hours, employers don't have to worry about losing coverage on certain days as they do when working with part-time employees.

Given the benefits of job sharing, it's no surprise we are seeing signs its popularity is rising.[4] Outside of Europe, in Singapore, the Singapore National Employers Federation released an implementation guide to help employers put flexible work and job-sharing programs in place. In countries like the Netherlands and Switzerland, where a high proportion of the population is already accustomed to working part time, the concept of job sharing is a natural fit.[5] In the United Kingdom, where employment legislation is very favorable to flexible working, the governmental Civil Service launched an internal job-share platform in 2015, originally to support staff returning from maternity leave who were looking for a better work-life balance. But the Civil Service found that within three years, 20 percent of those registering on the platform were men, and that job sharers had higher levels of engagement and well-being compared to those working part time or full time.[6]

Sophie Smallwood, co-CEO of Roleshare, a startup matching job sharers and supporting employers who want to offer job sharing to employees, confirms it is not only women with young children who are attracted to job sharing. She points to Sam White and Will McDonald, two fathers who have shared the executive role of group sustainability and public policy director at Aviva, a large insurance company, for over two years. Like Hemmings and Brown, the two men report a number of benefits of job sharing. For example, for a period when McDonald was having mental health issues, White was able to expand his hours for six months while McDonald recovered.[7]

Smallwood started Roleshare with her husband when it became clear the demands of her career working for tech companies seemed to conflict with her desire to be a fully present parent. Since then, she has become an evangelist for the practice, frequently highlighting the huge gap between the promise and the reality of job sharing. Around 40 percent of Fortune 100 companies offer job sharing as a perk, yet less than 3 percent of their employees actually job share.[8]

Most employers and employees alike agree one of the lasting legacies of the pandemic will be its acceleration of alternative working practices. In a recent global study of over 30,000 workers, two-thirds of them reported that since the pandemic struck, they "feel empowered to take advantage of flexible working arrangements at their companies," up from just over a quarter before.[9] While not as eye-catching as the near-instantaneous shift to remote work in early 2020, this profound change was at least partially responsible for the so-called Great Resignation in 2022, as workers sought to find opportunities that aligned with their working preferences. Historically, most job shares are usually ad hoc—the result of fortunate circumstance and sustained effort by those involved. But in the future normal, organizations committed to actively promoting job sharing (or similar twists on traditional work structures) across all roles and levels will attract the best talent and inspire employee loyalty far easier than more restrictive working cultures.

Instigator: Zurich Insurance

From March 2019 to February 2020, Zurich Insurance worked with the UK government's Behavioural Insights Team to assess the impact of advertising all their job positions as part time, full time, or job share. The result was dramatic: 16 percent more women applied for management roles. Zurich also found that the number of women hired for senior positions rose by one-third during the same period.[10] Interestingly, the company saw double the overall number of applications from both men and women, confirming that flexible work arrangements have wide appeal.[11]

The results of Zurich's initiative replicated those of an earlier study of job postings on Indeed, a widely used job board, also conducted by the Behavioural Insights Team. An analysis of over 200,000 jobs posted by 55,000 employers found job postings that referenced flexible working received up to 30 percent more applications than those that didn't.[12]

> **Flexible working can help tackle diversity and inclusion issues we've all been battling with for many years. Embracing part time and flexible is not a silver bullet. But we've seen hugely encouraging results, simply by adding six words to our job adverts.**
>
> —Steve Collinson, Head of HR, Zurich Insurance[13]

The growing trend of job sharing goes far beyond early- adopting European markets. In the United States during the pandemic, there was a surge in attention on these "often overlooked job-sharing programs" from media, legislators, and companies of all sizes.[14] After its experiences with remote work during the pandemic, Singapore-based DBS Bank has announced that it is rolling out a job-share program as part of a wider shift toward flexible working. The bank's CEO, Piyush Gupta, explained the move, sharing, "as the way we live, bank, and work continues to change dramatically, we must address the magnitude of the disruptions before us. We are prepared to radically transform the way we work."[15]

In the future normal, the organizations willing to rethink their longest held assumptions about work and to embrace the heavily demanded new arrangements such as job sharing will be the ones who can attract and retain the best talent and become the envy of their industry. Are you ready to join them?

Imagining the Future Normal

1. What if we could reimagine existing jobs, or even entire team structures, so more positions were shared among multiple people with complementary skill sets?
2. How can we reduce any stigma or negative perceptions around job sharers and instead offer those who choose this working structure the same amount of prestige and respect that their roles otherwise command?
3. How can business leaders and students advocate for more leading business schools to teach collaborative leadership skills, like sharing responsibilities and authority with an equal peer?

CHAPTER 14

REFLECTIVE CULTURES

What if our organizations' cultures reflected the societies in which they operate?

Irina Shayk and Cara Delevingne are familiar faces on fashion industry catwalks. Less so are rapper Megan Thee Stallion, singer Lizzo, plus-size male model Steven G, and 34-year-old breast cancer survivor Cayatanita Leiva. And yet they were all featured in the second edition of Rihanna's Savage X Fenty lingerie show, streamed after Super Bowl–levels of hype on Amazon Prime Video in late 2020.[1] The Bajan singer's extravaganza was nominated for an Emmy for outstanding choreography,[2] but its most striking legacy was its radical inclusivity. The contrast between a Victoria's Secret fashion show and Rihanna's Savage X Fenty couldn't be starker.

Rihanna's businesses are not just superficially inclusive either. Savage X Fenty sells bras in sizes from 32A to 46DDD and underwear and sleepwear in sizes XS to 3X. The Fenty Beauty line launched with 40 shades of foundation tones, and Fenty Skin offers gender-neutral beauty products.[3] This radical inclusivity (well, radical for the mainstream beauty industry) works. Fenty Beauty, now backed by global luxury giant LVMH, together with her other brands have made Rihanna the wealthiest female musician in the world.[4] "Inclusivity has always been a part of our brand," the multi-hyphenate entrepreneur said. "That's not a 'right now' thing. It's sad that it's right now for most brands."[5]

Sad, to be sure, and Rihanna has a point. After the Black Lives Matter protests erupted in the summer of 2020, many brands vowed to take action to increase the representation of underrepresented groups and build more inclusive cultures. In the same moment, many settled for taking performative actions: launching campaigns featuring people of color, committing to giving money to nonprofits that support diversity efforts, issuing statements of solidarity on Instagram, and so on. But real changes to the way these companies operate or the backgrounds of the teams that run them have been happening at a far slower pace. Outside of the fashion and entertainment industries, the data suggests that corporate boardrooms and managerial ranks haven't changed much. According to a report conducted by the Alliance for Board Diversity and Deloitte, only 5.7 percent of Fortune 500 board directors are minority women, compared with over 20 percent of the general US population. The report concluded, in true consultant-speak, "... while there have been a few gains in board representation for some demographic groups, advancement is still very incremental, with goals of achieving proportional representation to the presence of women and minorities in the US population sometimes multiple decades away at current rates of change."[6]

Considering the trajectory of the global population, this commonly half-baked response to diversity from the corporate world is consistently being exposed and criticized—particularly by the next generation of consumers. These demands are at least in part being driven by the way these younger consumers now treat their consumption as a reflection of their diverse identities and values. In the United States, less than half of children under age 15 identify as white.[7] When asked to place themselves on a sexuality scale from zero to six, where six is "exclusively heterosexual," half of British young people age 18 to 24 rated themselves as something other than exclusively heterosexual.[8] Companies are finally starting to take notice. Often unsure of where to start, many companies' attempts to respond to this complexity and fluidity have been narrowly focused on small product tweaks coupled with self-congratulatory advertising campaigns celebrating these incremental shifts. Clothing brands are introducing gender-fluid designs. Toy manufacturers are marketing once gendered toys more broadly to all children. Retailers are redesigning store layouts to remove gendered toy aisles. Internally, companies are also starting to hire executives who champion diversity and inclusion initiatives within their teams. To date, these efforts have made little more than a dent in reducing the staggering structural costs of exclusion.

Citigroup estimated that racial gaps have cost the US economy a mind-blowing $16,000,000,000,000 (that's $16 trillion) over the past 20 years.[9] And McKinsey estimates that closing the gender gap would add $12,000,000,000,000 (that's in trillions, again) to global gross domestic product (GDP).[10] Evidence also shows that companies with greater gender and ethnic diversity are more likely to financially outperform their peers.[11] And those who are not acting to create inclusive cultures—or reform exclusionary ones—now risk a customer backlash or an exodus of talent. It is also harder and harder for companies and consumers alike to ignore issues of inequality as social media platforms are giving us more access than ever to hear directly from those affected by them.

In the future normal it will be impossible for any organization to claim to support meaningful efforts to increase diversity and inclusion by pointing to small product tweaks or ad campaigns alone. Real change will require an internal culture shift alongside a reimagining of the products and services sold. This will continue to be a huge challenge to many organizations, but luckily there are some innovators who are leading the way toward a future normal of more reflective cultures on behalf of their entire industries.

Instigator: Black in Fashion Council

Lindsay Peoples Wagner, former editor in chief of *Teen Vogue*, and publicist Sandrine Charles are working to help brands implement real changes with their Black in Fashion Council (BIFC). The pair launched the initiative in the summer of 2020 with a mission to secure representation of Black individuals in the fashion and beauty industries, creating "diverse spaces that directly reflect what the world actually looks like at large."[12]

The initiative quickly attracted a list of over 70 companies, including Condé Nast, Farfetch, The RealReal, Calvin Klein, Tommy Hilfiger, Universal Standard, L'Oréal, and Glossier.[13] On the surface, it is easy to dismiss this initiative as yet another example of brands rushing to "do something" as soon as a social injustice brings issues of diversity to light. What makes this program unique is that the BIFC requires organizations to sign a *three-year commitment* that involves sharing data on employee representation.

> **We're looking forward to ... being able to see actions made by the industry. We want those who come up behind us to have different and better experiences and see themselves fully represented in a real way.**
>
> —Lindsay Peoples Wagner, Cofounder, Black in Fashion Council[14]

The group's first report, published in late 2021, highlighted the current gap between the industry's marketing and its internal power structures. Drawing on surveys submitted by 30 participating organizations, BIFC found that while 97 percent of participants featured Black talent in advertising, only one in five had a formal professional development program for underrepresented minorities, and just one in three had a working supplier diversity program.[15]

The call for initiatives that advance tangible action isn't unique to the world of fashion and beauty. The tech industry has struggled with a lack of diversity and inclusion for many years, an issue which has become especially acute now that the largest platforms are serving billions of people globally and the algorithms they have created can systematize bias on a societal level. Leading the industry back in 2015, Intel committed $300 million to workplace diversity efforts. Now it is looking beyond its own walls with its Alliance for Global Inclusion, a coalition of tech brands such as Dell and Nasdaq. The coalition has conducted two surveys of technology companies to assess and track their progress across a number of areas of diversity, equity, and inclusion (DEI), such as attracting and advancing underrepresented talent.[16] In the United Kingdom, Czech-born entrepreneur Kate Pljaskovova is building Fair HQ, a data-driven platform that helps companies understand and then improve specific metrics around diversity and inclusion.[17] Behind all these initiatives is the belief that when companies measure metrics, they will manage them and implement lasting change as a result.

We recognize that councils and indexes will not solve these diversity issues overnight. Inequity and injustice are deeply systemic in every society. But expectations of transparency are getting louder and more unavoidable. The internal culture of any organization will only become *more* visible in the future, and so the need for it to be reflective of the culture at large will continue to grow.

Imagining the Future Normal

1. What if companies collaborated openly with their competitors to share diversity data and support initiatives aimed at creating long-term change across an entire industry?
2. How can you rethink hiring practices to welcome more representative candidates who are already part of the communities you serve?
3. What can you do as a consumer or as an independent voice to help celebrate, promote, buy from, and elevate the companies and individuals who come from underrepresented cultures?

CHAPTER 15

BIG BRAND REDEMPTION

What if more of the world's biggest businesses prioritized doing good over profits?

Jack Welch has long been celebrated as a management icon. His legacy has been canonized in countless business books and even spawned a management institute that carries his name. He also might be the "man who broke capitalism," according to a recent book of that title from *New York Times* reporter and "Corner Office" columnist David Gelles.[1] The reckoning is coming at an interesting time, as Welch's legendarily cutthroat business practices, which included a relentless focus on downsizing by 10 percent every year and a heavy focus on increasing shareholder value by any means necessary (layoffs, outsourcing, offshoring, acquisitions, and buybacks), are widely known and frequently imitated.[2] Now, for the first time, they are being fundamentally reevaluated.

Today, even the biggest winners in this profit-centric model of capitalism have begun asking whether it was as universal and effective as it once seemed. There have always been heretics, such as Patagonia's founder Yvon Chouinard; Canva's founder Melanie Perkins; Hamdi Ulukaya, founder and CEO of Chobani; and Whole Foods cofounder John Mackey. But recently, leaders from the world of mainstream finance such as BlackRock's Larry Fink and J.P. Morgan's Jamie Dimon have also been openly promoting the idea that shareholder capitalism needs radical reform.

Something is shifting.

There is a growing sense that a generation of shareholder capitalism has merely exacerbated rampant economic, racial, and gender inequalities—not to mention done little to address the looming climate crisis. Post-pandemic, people have been evaluating their jobs and the companies they work with, leading to a trend of quiet quitting—where employees don't quit in a literal sense but do the bare minimum at their jobs and become complacent. Among the key reasons they cite for rampant lack of effort? Their companies do not share their values or meet their desire to work for a purpose-driven organization.

In response, desperate to show and formalize their authentic commitment to stakeholders—employees, investors, customers, suppliers, environment, and society—companies are increasingly seeking certifications from third-party organizations. They are going through the arduous process of having their products Fair Trade Certified—which guarantees the suppliers and producers of those products were paid and treated fairly. They are getting Climate Neutral Certified, completing a program to neutralize or eliminate carbon emissions. They are signing up for GoodWell certification (a values-based workplace certification), enlisting membership in 1% for the Planet (which shows their commitment to contributing at least 1 percent of their annual revenue to environmental causes), or earning EU Ecolabel assignation (given to products that have low environmental impact). Big brands, in other words, are seeking redemption via third parties.

These certifications are hugely welcome, and between them now cover billions of dollars of economic activity. Yet that still leaves *trillions* of dollars of economic value being generated by much bigger, traditionally minded incumbents that were established before most companies considered their impact on anyone but their shareholders.

If asked to imagine a company with a positive impact, most of us would picture a brand like Patagonia: founder-owned, mission driven, and, despite its success, still relatively small when compared with the multinationals that dominate the global economy. But it is not only these midsize companies that gain an advantage from thinking beyond producing value for their shareholders. Companies in JUST Capital's "Just 100," a ranking of US public companies by stakeholder impact, had a 7.2 percent higher return on equity than the wider market.[3]

The axiom that "Doing good can be good for business" does seem justified based on the numbers. As we shift toward the future, more of the world's biggest companies will continue to take notice of this reality and seek help to accomplish (and demonstrate) their bona fide efforts to do more good (or at least less harm) in the world. As this shift continues, these brands will find reputational redemption in these efforts and attract more loyal consumers in the process. Giant companies are, by definition, efficient operators. As the benefits of stakeholder capitalism become more visible, and the certifications and mechanisms that support big brands wishing to do better continue to become more developed, the future normal will see an even greater share of the world's biggest companies making the shift toward brand redemption in the eyes of their consumers and employees.

Instigator: B Lab

Jay Coen Gilbert and Bart Houlahan were heartbroken when the socially responsible practices at the heart of their basketball apparel company AND1 were dismantled months after it was sold to American Sporting Goods.[4]

Founded in 1993, AND1 was a progressive company before it was popular. They offered great benefits to their employees, shared 5 percent of their profits with charities, and ensured their suppliers operated in fair and ethical ways.[5] Within 10 years, their efforts were rewarded with financial success as it became one of the most popular basketball shoe brands in the United States. But pressures from its main competitor, Nike, and other industry trends led the founders to sell the company in 2006.

Stung by their experience, Gilbert and Houlahan enlisted Andrew Kassoy, a connection from the private equity world, to start B Lab, a nonprofit that would go on to create the B Corporation Certification.[6] To get certified, a company must score a minimum of 80 points (out of 200) in the B Impact Assessment, a digital tool that analyzes a company's impact on its workers, customers, community, and the environment. Companies' scores are published, and their formal governance structures must be changed to require their directors to consider the impact of decisions in nonfinancial terms. In B Lab's own words, "This combination of third-party validation, public transparency, and legal accountability help Certified B Corps build trust and value."[7]

> **Once upon a time, the role of a business was to maximize value for shareholders ... I think we've now evolved to a point where it's also part of our normal lexicon where stakeholder primacy or stakeholder capitalism is now more of the norm.**
>
> —Anthea Kelsick, former Co-CEO, B Lab US & Canada[8]

B Lab's impact has been profound. In 2007, there were just 82 certified B Corps. By late 2022, there were over 4,000 from 70 countries and 150 industries.[9] The certification has become a shorthand for mission-driven, impact-focused businesses. Many companies that have become certified are highly recognizable midsize brands, including iconic pioneers Ben & Jerry's and Patagonia. Bigger brands, however, are increasingly seeking certification. Natura, the Brazilian beauty brand, became the world's biggest B Corp in 2014 when it had $3 billion in revenues and 35,000 employees. Lemonade, the insurtech startup, went public in 2020 after being a B Corp since 2016. Similarly, Laureate Education and Vital Farms are both listed as B Corps. In 2017 Danone's CEO at the time, Emmanuel Faber, announced plans for the $26 billion multinational to become a B Corp. While Faber left the company in 2021, the company has continued to pursue certifications, and at the time of writing, 40 Danone subsidiaries representing over 70 percent of the company's sales were certified B Corps.[10]

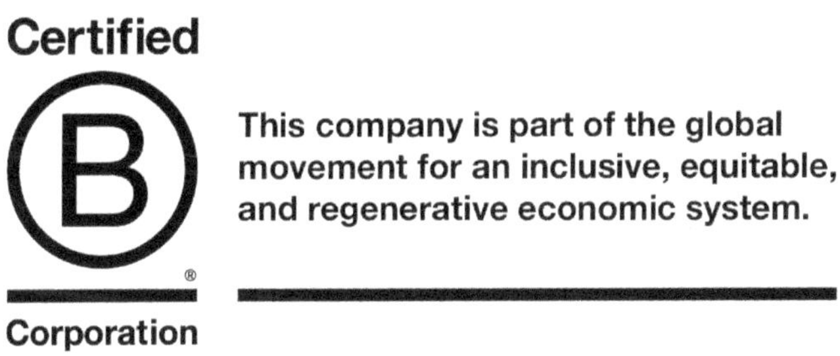

Screengrab of the B Impact Assessment. (Source: www.bcorporation.net)

In response to its popularity, in September 2020 B Lab announced that it was launching B Movement Builders, an initiative focused on large multinationals with over $1 billion in annual revenues. The founding Movement Builder members are vegetable-processing company Bonduelle, steelmaker Gerdau, flavors and fragrance company Givaudan, and the retailer Magalu, with

Danone and Natura serving as mentors. These six companies had combined revenues of $60 billion and employed 250,000 people in 120 countries.[11] As well as pursuing a path to B Corp certification, CEOs of B Movement Builder companies must publicly sign the B Corp Declaration of Interdependence, set targets around at least three of the UN's Sustainable Development Goals, and commit to collaborating with other B Movement organizations.

Despite the momentum, the B Corp certification of bigger brands is not without critics. When Nespresso, the Nestlé-owned coffee company, announced in June 2022 that it had achieved B Corp certification, 30 other certified B Corps signed an open letter criticizing the decision, citing sourcing labor issues, as well as the unsustainability of its single-use aluminum pods.[12] The founders of B Lab take a more pragmatic view. As he stepped down in the summer of 2022, Kassoy wrote, "The B Corp movement has never been about building an empire of B Corps. The certification is a means, not an end."[13] Nespresso, to its credit, also spent more than three years in researching and developing paper-based capsules, which they will pilot in selected European markets by spring of 2023.

As we look to build stronger, fairer, and greener economies after the devastation of the pandemic, the socially responsible certification movement is at an inflection point. It would be hugely disappointing if it becomes nothing more than a niche way for challenger brands to connect with affluent audiences. We believe it is far more likely that, in the future normal, B Corp–like principles will replace our current narrow corporate focus on shareholder value, and take root even within the largest organizations in our global economy.

Imagining the Future Normal

1. How could you use the B-Corp metrics and criteria to make your own organization better—regardless of whether it has committed entirely to the certification or not?

2. What if one company could mentor another to help shift their focus from shareholder to stakeholder value?

3. What if it were *easier* to raise money by demonstrating (nonfinancial) value creation?

CHAPTER 16

IMPACT HUBS

What if your office space could contribute to the local economy and community?

WeWork wasn't the first company to lease coworking spaces, but they were the first to do it in style. Back in 2010, what set WeWork apart and earned it popularity among knowledge workers and startups was its hipster-worthy creative spaces—open common areas with citrus-spiked water, cold brew on tap, nap rooms, exercise classes, and a *vibe*.[1]

For several years, WeWork rode multiple emerging business and workplace trends—the shift to gig work, popularity of open workspaces, and millennials' desire to engage with purpose-driven brands—to billions of dollars of real revenue from hundreds of thousands of members. The company's pioneering role in jumpstarting the coworking boom has been overshadowed by the egregious self-dealings of founder Adam Neumann, who sold hundreds of millions of dollars of his own shares and notoriously trademarked the word *We* and sold it back to the company for nearly $6 million.[2] By the time WeWork attempted their disastrous IPO in 2019, there were already dozens of competitors offering similarly chic coworking spaces.

The model lit an underlying spark that remains today. While these coworking spaces, emblazoned with giant murals exhorting laptop-toting workers to "Do What You Love" and "Hustle Harder," are easy to parody, they speak to people's desire to work in places that align with their values, have a positive impact on the world, reinforce their ambitions, and even enhance their mental well-being.[3]

This desire is colliding with a world of work that is being massively transformed. During the pandemic, the entire corporate world embarked on a giant work-from-home experiment, leading some to prematurely predict "The end of the office."[4] While most workers expressed a clear desire to maintain the flexible working practices[5] they adopted during months of lockdowns, there are strong signs that the physical office still matters. Even Meta—despite Mark Zuckerberg's bet on the Metaverse—has continued to sign new leases on millions of square feet of prime office space in Manhattan in the past few years.[6] As with so many trends, the world of work is moving toward hybrid—both in office *and* remote work—rather than solely one or the other. It will undoubtedly be more flexible and distributed, and many organizations will reduce the amount of office space they occupy. But the desire to bring people together in a physical space will not disappear.

For many white-collar organizations, real estate is their biggest outlay after staff costs. As these organizations reconsider their office footprint, they will be keen to see those dollars do more. In the future normal, forward-thinking companies will embrace "impact hubs" workers love to be in that strengthen and support local communities, while also acting as powerful symbols and manifestations of their tenants' values and purpose.

Instigator: 3Space

A renovated office space might not seem like a logical candidate to make *Fast Company*'s prestigious World Changing Ideas list, but International House, based in South London, earned the accolade. Conceived by UK-based nonprofit 3Space, the 50,000-square-foot office building differs from other coworking spaces due to its Buy-GiveWork model: for every space rented to a paid tenant, 3Space gives a qualifying nonprofit or local startup free space. Current projects include a youth entrepreneurship program, a green farming incubator, an art studio, and a photography resource center. This is reminiscent of similar "buy one give one" models pioneered by companies such as shoe brand TOMS.

Lobby of 3Space International House workspace in Brixton, London. (Source: 3Space)

The BuyGiveWork model has won 3Space the support of the local government, which sees it as an effective way to attract high-growth businesses to the area while still ensuring local groups have access to space and are not being squeezed out as rents in the borough take off. It also helped that International House was the first building in the United Kingdom to be recognized as a "living wage building" by requiring all its tenants to pay employees and contractors the London living wage.[7] Commercial tenants are also required to give an hour of their employees' time each month to a nonprofit project, either within the building or the borough.[8]

This founding mission and the public accolades it has earned make it easy for businesses that rent space from 3Space to talk about their impact to consumers and potential hires alike. It can also become an element of a strategy to retain talented employees.

> **Over time we have realized that it is hugely important to our staff to know that our presence in the building directly supports hundreds of local jobs and projects.**
>
> —Alex Depledge, Founder of Resi, International House's largest commercial tenant[9]

There are early signals that the commercial real estate sector is becoming more accepting of the underlying concept behind 3Space—that an office space can create stronger, more resilient communities and also be more easily filled with tenants who see the mission as a key differentiator. However, based on the data, we have some way to go before it is commonplace. The Urban Land Institute, a global real estate industry body, has reported that less than one in eight real estate practitioners regularly implements social equity–boosting practices, although interest is growing as developers better understand the potential benefits of doing so.[10] For example, Trammell Crow Company, the developer of The Shops at Dakota Crossing, a mall in Washington, DC, partnered with nonprofit Goodwill Industries to increase the number of local residents working in its stores. The program made the shopping center more attractive to retail tenants such as Costco by making it easier for them to hire faster and lower their churn rates.[11]

The potential for creating both social and economic upsides makes the workplace such an interesting—and profound—focus of innovation. WeWork sold itself as the antithesis of the "suffer at work" cubicle offices that are still in use today, but it lost significant credibility due to their founder's practices, and couldn't convince investors that its model would be sustainable. Real estate has long been one of the most capitalistic sectors, but initiatives like 3Space's, while unique today, show that there is a future normal where workers, companies, communities, *and* investors can all benefit. Now that would be a workplace we would be happy to work from.

Imagining the Future Normal

1. What if we chose our working spaces based not only on the amenities they offer or their location but also on the impact they create in our community or the world at large?

2. How could our modern workspaces evolve away from only being used during the day and empty at night to more of a model of continuous use and value for the community?

3. What if every office space could colocate corporations and nonprofits in a way that built community and offered opportunities for each to benefit one another?

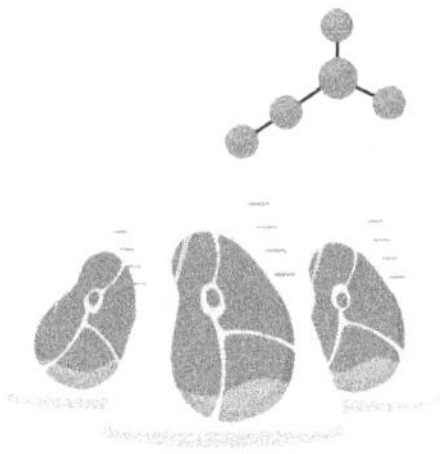

CHAPTER 17

UNNATURALLY BETTER

What if "fake" was better?

In a 1931 essay, Winston Churchill imagined a world where we would "escape the absurdity of growing a whole chicken in order to eat the breast or wing by growing these parts separately under a suitable medium."[1]

This world is no longer a fantasy.

On December 19, 2020, California-based GOOD Meat partnered with 1880, a restaurant in Singapore, to offer a group of diners a unique meal: bao buns with sesame chicken, phyllo puff pastry with chicken and black bean puree, and a crispy maple waffle with spicy chicken.[2] The chicken, however, was not your traditional poultry: it did not come from killing a bird. Instead, it was grown from a handful of chicken cells. Another company called SuperMeat made global headlines for serving a cultivated chicken meat burger at its test kitchen in Tel Aviv, while Israel's Aleph Farms claimed a major world first: serving cultivated meat to a head of government—in this case Prime Minister Benjamin Netanyahu—for the very first time.

Since 2013 when Mark Post, a Dutch researcher at Maastricht University, came up with the first lab-grown meat (as it was referred to back then) to much fanfare, thousands of diners have eaten "cultivated meat"—what the industry prefers to call it for obvious PR reasons—from one of 100 or so companies who dedicate themselves to it today.[3]

Unlike the international backlash against the use of GMOs (genetically modified organisms) fueled by a combination of legitimate concerns and widespread misinformation, lab-grown meat has so far escaped the same controversy. Instead, the limited few who have tried it have often done so under circumstances meant to engage their curiosity, such as an exhibition dinner hosted by the Future Market, an organization that describes itself as "a futurist food lab."[4]

These new "cultivated" alternatives to common products aren't just popping up in the food industry either. Almost every month there is another breakthrough new material, such as Microsilk (a super strong biodegradable fabric from Bolt Threads) or lab-grown wood (an as yet unnamed innovation being studied by a team of MIT researchers), emerging out of cutting-edge synthetic biology labs.[5]

Some might say we've been here before. During the post–World War II period, synthetic materials from plastic to polyester were the talk of the day. They were celebrated as stronger! lighter! cheaper! Of course, eventually, the dark side of these synthetic materials emerged. They offered durability at low cost, but this also led to the mass production of materials that were difficult to dispose of in safe or sustainable ways. What started as an ingenious way to use by-products from the fossil fuel industry became a cycle that kept these polluting, extractive industries in business. As awareness of the environmental impact of these materials has grown, synthetics have all been lumped together as universally toxic by discerning consumers.

Today people simply take it for granted that natural products are better. Going "all natural" is something to strive for or aspire to. Luxury itself has come to be associated with handmade, locally grown, artisan-crafted, and sustainably sourced products. Definitely *not* synthetic.

The next wave of innovation in synthetics, however, is radically different from that of the 1950s, thanks to several converging trends. Firstly, advances in biological technologies such as DNA sequencing are making it easier for innovators to create artificial products inspired by nature. For example, scientists using biomimicry—a practice where inspiration is taken from plants and animals to create innovative new materials and products—are studying everything from bioluminescence to termite mound cooling to find novel ways to solve existing problems better, faster, or more cheaply. This research has already led to notable advances in building construction, air turbine design, and the development of now-ubiquitous products like Velcro. Adjacent advances in AI and automation help to accelerate learning and reduce costs, while the widespread availability of affordable renewable energy means these new processes can be powered cleanly. In short, we are witnessing a new era for synthetic products that can be produced *without* the adverse effects to the environment.

In the future normal, companies will increasingly make synthetic alternatives to today's products that are even *better*—higher performance, more ethically produced, and more sustainable—than their natural competitors. Rather than synthetics being an economical yet environmentally destructive second-class substitute for natural products, in many cases, they will be even *more* desirable than their traditionally natural counterparts. Instead, they will be *unnaturally* better.

Instigator: UPSIDE Foods

Uma Valeti, a cardiologist by training, was growing human heart cells while doing research when it occurred to him: If we can do this in a lab for a human heart, why not a chicken drumstick? A few years later, he founded UPSIDE Foods in San Leandro, California. Backed by major investors like Bill Gates and food industry investors like Tyson Foods and Cargill, UPSIDE Foods became one of the leaders in the cultivated meat space, growing beef, chicken, and duck in a lab. In November 2022, they cleared a major regulatory milestone when the FDA offered the equivalent of a green light for further development, noting that after studying the science, they had "no further questions at this time about the firm's safety conclusion."[6]

The potential benefits of cultivating meat in such a controlled setting are huge. According to a study published in *Nature Food*, in 2015 the food system was responsible for 34 percent of greenhouse gas emissions.[7] Meat raising and processing are among the biggest offenders, as forests are cut to make way for land to grow animal feed, huge amounts of excess waste pollute water sources, and livestock emit "methane burps" that contribute to climate change.[8] Cultivating meat could not only massively decrease our environmental footprint, it could also eliminate some people's ethical objections to eating meat, especially the poor treatment and ultimate killing of animals by the food industry. Cultivated meats could also have the potential to be safe from foodborne diseases, excessive hormone use, and contamination.

The range of startups in the nascent cultivated food industry is as broad as the spread at a hotel buffet. French startup Gourmey grows foie gras from cells.[9] Singapore-based Shiok Meats is growing shrimp, crab, and lobster meat in a nutrient-rich broth. MeliBio will soon launch a sustainable honey produced without the need for bees. Perfect Day makes nature-identical milk protein without cows. Already partnering with more than 14 brands, their product can be found in milk, ice cream, cream cheese, and more.

A natural question to ask as we celebrate all the innovation, though, is whether consumers will really be willing to try all these products and accept them. Recent consumer research found that "88 percent of Gen Z consumers in the US say they'd be somewhat open to trying cultivated meat, compared with about 72 percent of baby boomers."[10]

The cultivated food industry might be the most visible example of what the future of unnaturally better products will look like, but other innovators are also coming up with biologically identical versions of products whose natural production takes a heavy environmental toll on our resources.

GALY, a company that creates lab-grown cotton, recently won the annual Global Change Award from the H&M Foundation. Its production method is greener, and the cotton is grown 10 times faster in the lab than in a field. VitroLabs recently secured funding to test production of its cell-cultivated leather and claims they can "make billions of square feet of leather with a single, harmless biopsy from one cow."[11] Partnering with German biotech company AMSilk, watchmaker Omega offers a watch strap made from Biosteel, synthetic spider silk. Biosteel is lighter and more resilient and breathable than conventional materials, and has antibacterial and anti-allergenic properties.

There are examples beyond consumer-facing products as well. Synkero is a joint venture between the Port of Amsterdam, Schiphol Airport, SkyNRG, and KLM, which is producing synthetic kerosene from carbon dioxide, water, and renewable energy. The first passenger flight using this fuel took place in early 2021, from Amsterdam to Madrid.[12] In the health industry, Touchlight is a biotech startup that makes synthetic DNA in weeks versus the months-long process for plasmid DNA. Its DNA is also purer and, therefore, safer—one reason why Touchlight received funding from the Bill & Melinda Gates Foundation to scale their vaccine platform.[13]

In the future normal, the long-standing assumption that natural is always best will be shattered as synthetic biology enables us to manufacture products and materials without relying on uncontrolled nature, making them cleaner, safer, and more reliable. As more companies celebrate their unnatural backstories, they will challenge consumers in all sectors to reconsider their assumptions about the value and superiority of naturally produced products versus their desirably unnatural alternatives.

Imagining the Future Normal

1. What if we celebrated the scientists behind synthetic products the same way we celebrate gifted artisans?
2. How might the billions of agricultural workers be supported if materials switched to being cultivated in automated environments?
3. How will we separate these ethically produced "fake" products from their more environmentally destructive counterparts?

CHAPTER 18

CALCULATED CONSUMPTION

What if we started tracking our carbon footprints in the same way we track our calorie or salt intakes?

Did you know that the idea of a carbon footprint was first introduced by the oil giant BP as a PR initiative to nudge individuals toward focusing on their personal impact on the environment?[1] Nearly 20 years later, the idea of tracking your carbon footprint has successfully diverted attention away from the dirtiest industrial polluters, delaying the industry's own efforts to reduce emissions. What may have started for self-serving reasons, though, is slowly transforming into something bigger.

Today, a host of brands are co-opting this concept, sticking labels on their products to share *their* carbon footprint data and empowering shoppers to more consciously track the environmental impact of their consumption. An ideal example is Quorn, one of the earliest meat alternative producers. When it first started, the brand originally targeted its products to vegetarians, but after seeing increasing demand from climate-conscious customers, it partnered with the Carbon Trust to add carbon footprint data on the packages of its best-selling products, such as Quorn Mince and Quorn Fishless Fingers. These labels make clear the difference between the environmental impact of its products and that of traditional animal-based ones. The difference is significant.

Quorn Mince, for example, has a footprint of 1.3 kg CO_2e (carbon dioxide equivalent) per kilogram; by comparison, UK beef mince's footprint is 27 kg CO_2e per kilogram.[2] Peter Harrison, chief commercial officer of Quorn Foods, explains that this initiative "is about giving people the information needed to make informed decisions about the food they eat and the effect it has on our planet's climate—in the same way that nutrition information is clearly labeled to help inform decisions on health."[3] This idea of making the impact of our consumption more visible is extending to many other industries beyond food as well. Airlines are opting into programs that allow frequent travelers to track and purchase carbon offsets for the flights they elect to take. Technology accessory maker Logitech has added labels to track the environmental impact of their product development on a handful of products. Water bottle refilling stations across gyms integrate counters that tell users how many plastic water bottles they have saved from landfills. Unilever, maker of more than 70,000 products, has promised to add carbon labeling to all its products. While no global standard for such labeling exists (yet), the willingness of so many companies across so many industries to act proactively on this effort indicates the level of consumer support it already has ... perhaps because it caters to some of the most basic ways that our brains work.

As humans, we love to feel in control. Data helps us feel empowered by giving us information we can use to make smarter decisions. We count our steps, measure our resting heart rates, and track our sleep. We compare calorie counts and seek out other personal health data in a quest to understand how healthy we are and to motivate us to make healthier choices. But when it comes to fully comprehending our carbon footprint, for years we have fluctuated between guilt and ignorance. The impact of the things we buy and consume on the environment and the looming climate crisis is an area where we have historically never felt informed or empowered.

In the future normal, more and more companies will be transparent about the carbon emission of their products, making simple calculations of the impact of our consumption choices as easy as counting calories. As people become more familiar with carbon data, they will gain a greater understanding of what are "good" and "bad" amounts—and will shape their behavior accordingly. Data will create knowledge, and knowledge will inspire action.

Instigator: Allbirds

Do you know how many kilograms of carbon are emitted to make your sneakers? If you're anything like us, the answer is no. But your days of ignorance might be coming to an end if companies like shoe brand Allbirds have their way. In 2020, the shoe pioneer known for its sustainable sneakers popular among the tech crowd became the first fashion brand to list the carbon footprint of its products. According to Joey Zwillinger, cofounder of Allbirds, the company's decision to be transparent about their carbon footprint came out of a desire to drive the conversation about sustainability further.[4]

The average carbon emission of its sneakers, it reported, is 7.6 kg CO_2e.[5]

But is that a lot or a little for a pair of sneakers?

Allbirds carbon footprint labels. (Source: Allbirds)

To help people understand its carbon footprint, Allbirds offered some context as well: 7.6 kg CO_2e is similar to driving 19 miles in a car or drying five loads of laundry in a dryer. It's also about 40 percent less than the sneaker industry average of 12.5 kg CO_2e.[6]

> **We need something so simple that everyone could look at it, just like the calories on a food label.**
>
> —Joey Zwillinger, Cofounder, Allbirds[7]

Many others are embracing similar levels of transparency. Oatly, producer of plant-based milk, has been displaying the CO_2e numbers of their products on the back of their packaging since 2019.[8] Vestre, a Norwegian furniture manufacturer, publishes the carbon footprint[9] of its products in their catalog, while Much Better Adventures, an outdoor activity-focused tour operator, now reports a "third-party verified carbon footprint analysis" of all the trips it offers.[10] Small-scale, eco-conscious companies are not the only ones in the carbon label game. China's Alibaba-owned e-commerce platform Tmall has also piloted carbon labels, sharing carbon emissions data on some of its products, including electric goods.[11]

This idea hasn't always enjoyed such a positive reception. Back in 2007, supermarket chain Tesco announced similar plans to label products it sold with carbon footprint data—only to drop them five years later, citing costs.[12] Walmart announced similar plans more than a decade ago but quietly seems to have shelved them, opting to lean on their suppliers to publicly reveal their environmental impact instead.[13] While the cost and complexity of measuring carbon emissions might once have prevented companies from sharing carbon footprint information, today a massively growing carbon accounting industry has removed that hurdle. Startups such as Watershed, Emitwise, Normative, Plan A, Altruistiq, Sweep, and more have raised hundreds of millions of dollars to help businesses measure their emissions efficiently. To support this shift, an entire category of companies dedicated to providing third-party certifications (including the ones profiled in this chapter) has also emerged.[14] Allbirds, like other pioneers, has even open sourced its carbon accounting tools, urging competitors to use its data and guides to follow its lead.[15]

Of course, simply publishing the carbon footprint data on products won't mean people will always choose the more eco-friendly versions or avoid certain products altogether. But labeling does raise consumer's general awareness and gives them a sense of agency. For example, in Norway, the online grocer Oda found that its shoppers bought less red meat after it started its "climate receipt" program, giving shoppers information about the carbon footprint of their shopping carts.[16]

Carbon footprints started as a way to shift responsibility away from producers and onto consumers. Ironically, in the future normal product-based carbon labeling will shift much of this responsibility back to producers. Businesses will feel pressure to publish the carbon footprint of their products; otherwise, people will question what they are hiding. They will want to "beat" their competitors by improving their carbon footprint so they can proudly display it on their products. Ultimately, the more transparently companies share data about ecological impact, the more loyalty they will earn from those who increasingly appreciate ways to feel better about what they buy.

Imagining the Future Normal

1. What if companies engaged an independent carbon auditor to measure the carbon footprint of their products, and shared the data collected transparently?
2. As more consumers calculate their personal impact on the environment, how will daily habits for what they buy change?
3. If we could aggregate the product-level figures about our consumption into a more cumulative view of our impact, how could this affect a shift in our behavior?

CHAPTER 19

GUILT-FREE INDULGENCE

What if you didn't have to give up products and experiences that are not great for you or the planet?

Supermodel and influencer Bella Hadid was, in her own words, "freaking the f*** out" at the thought of NUGGS's new spicy vegan chicken nuggets. Founded by 19-year-old Australian Ben Pasternak, NUGGS makes soy protein–derived nuggets that the company proudly proclaims will "kill you slower."[1] *VegNews* reported that when Hadid expressed dismay that NUGGS's 1,000 boxes of the limited run spicy nuggets had sold out, the company sent her a box. "Guys, this isn't an ad or anything. I found NUGGS on Instagram, and I'm f****** addicted," she posted on Instagram.[2]

Hadid's social media reaction to being able to enjoy a food that is generally out of bounds for vegetarians like her gives us a glimpse into the passion behind a new trend that promises to shape the future normal: guilt-free indulgence. As we become more and more aware of the impact our choices have on our health and environment, being able to consume products or engage in activities that traditionally have been bad for us or contribute to global ills will open up big business opportunities in the next decade.

In another quirky example of the rise of guilt-free indulgences, in the Western Tokyo district of Musashino, a group of friends are taking selfies and enjoying after-work cocktails at an unusual bar. Just beyond the window, every few minutes a giant crane scoops up a mangled assortment of waste ready for incineration. The Gomi Pit popup bar is improbably located in the district's municipal garbage processing facility. The local authorities launched the bar in order to "encourage local residents to think twice about the waste they produce."[3] An after-work happy hour might seem a little less decadent if in the process, patrons feel like they are becoming more aware and educated about the volume of waste produced locally.

NUGGS and the Gomi Pit bar touch on a paradox at the heart of modern life. Just like Hadid, we are torn between the desire to indulge ourselves and the gnawing sense of guilt that comes with the awareness that our indulgences are bad for ourselves, society, or the planet. Cheap, one-time-use plastic goods. Luxurious foreign holidays to places where poverty is ubiquitous. Unhealthy or unethically produced or sourced food. Beautiful digital devices built from rare minerals and fast fashion made from dirty supply chains that are destined to become obsolete, and end up in landfills after a few short years. All of these often have bigger environmental and social impacts than we want to think about.

It's no wonder people still struggle to "do the right thing." For example, one study found that while 65 percent of people said they want to buy from purpose-driven brands that advocate sustainability, only 26 percent do so.[4] More often we take the "easy" (i.e., more guilt-inducing) option, either because we don't know better or because it's more convenient or affordable—or both. Our desire is there, but our actions remain frustratingly inconsistent.

Producing products and services that give people a way out of this ethical quagmire is the holy grail of consumerism. Every automaker with an electric vehicle is hoping to persuade people to indulge in a shiny new car in part by promoting the fact that they will not have as big an impact on the environment as driving a gasoline-powered car. Bolt Threads, a startup that makes a vegan, mushroom-based leather substitute, has partnered with Adidas, Lululemon, Kering, and Stella McCartney to produce clothing with a guilt-free leather alternative.[5] Of course, questions remain about just how "clean" electric vehicles products are, and whether innovations like mushroom leather can be produced at the scale and low prices of their traditionally produced counterparts. However, as we saw in chapter 15 where we explored big brand redemption, the boom in companies certified as B Corps—companies that have been certified as meeting high standards of environmental and social performance—highlights the growing opportunities in every conceivable sector to promise customers a less guilt-laden experience.

Instigator: Skydiamond

There are plenty of reasons to feel guilty about buying a diamond. The world's supply is largely controlled by a single multinational conglomerate. Mining the valuable gem has a long sordid history of fueling deadly conflict, inspiring human rights abuses, and perpetuating the worst excesses of colonialism. Synthetic diamonds, on the other hand, offer a relatively guilt-free way to enjoy diamonds that are visually indistinguishable from the real thing—a fact that entrepreneur Dale Vince is counting on. Known for launching ambitious business ideas, such as the Forest Green Rovers (a vegan and carbon-neutral soccer club) and the world's first national electric vehicle charging network back in 2011, which he called the Electric Highway, his penchant for thinking big often invites comparisons to Elon Musk.[6,7] His latest publicity-friendly innovation is Skydiamond, a company that sells carbon negative, lab-grown diamonds "mined" from captured CO_2, collected rainwater, and renewable energy. As Vince puts it, the International Gemological Institute–certified stones offer customers "bling without the sting," eluding to the negative environmental and human impacts of traditional diamond mining.[8]

> **We need to live more sustainably. Too often that looks difficult. Skydiamond demonstrates a vital truth—living a greener life is not about giving stuff up, it's about doing things differently.**
>
> —Dale Vince, CEO, Skydiamond[9]

Guilt-free indulgences by nature stand out from their traditional counterparts. Skydiamond is an extreme example, but many of the instigators featured in this book are creating similarly guilt-free products, such as Vollebak's biodegradable hoodie made from plant-based fibers and printed with algae ink (featured in chapter 27), or Solein's CO_2-based protein powder, harvested from the air using renewable energy (featured in chapter 26). We've spent decades aspiring to "reduce, repair, and reuse." We do not believe that guilt-free indulgences are a contradiction of this continuing behavior. But they demonstrate another option—to reimagine. In doing so, producers of luxury items will increasingly reinvest the profits from their premium pricing back into creating their products in radically more sustainable ways—and tell these stories to their customers.

This technique is increasingly common in the world of luxury fashion. Up-and-coming sustainable fashion brands such as Another Tomorrow, Ahluwalia Studio, Caravana, Chloé, Lauren

Manoogian, Autumn Adeigbo, Angel Chang, and dozens of others are all collectively telling a single cohesive story. Their raw materials are sourced directly from farmers. The toxic inks and chemicals used by fast fashion retailers are never used. Products are made by real adult artisans who are paid living wages for the work they do. And product packaging is thoughtfully selected to be recycled and plastic-free. The ubiquity and popularity of these stories, and the entrepreneurs behind them, are influencing much larger brands like Gucci, Prada, and LVMH to accelerate their own commitments to sustainability, too. Altogether, these efforts are shifting the entire luxury apparel industry.

As more entrepreneurs and manufacturers offer us a chance to consume guilt-free indulgences, the act of consumption might itself become a way to create a positive impact on the world. Chocolate is an undeniably guilty pleasure; the current production practices of its main ingredient, cocoa beans, typically have a hugely negative impact on the communities that make a living growing it. Yet if you buy a chocolate bar from Tony's Chocolonely, a Dutch confectionary brand focused on ending child and slave labor in the cocoa industry, you send a powerful signal to chocolate manufacturers that they will lose sales if they don't end their guilty practices. You can do the same by choosing to only purchase lab-grown diamonds instead of mined diamonds. Or sustainably sourced fashion. This is the power of guilt-free indulgences in the future normal: they allow you to feel good about what you buy while also helping you make a statement with your purchases that can help shift the behavior of entire industries.

Imagining the Future Normal

1. How might guilt-free indulgences be promoted and sold on a business-to-business level?
2. How can companies isolate their customers' "guilt" pain points—and try to eliminate them from their products or services?
3. What would make guilt-free indulgences into status symbols and replace traditionally produced luxury items?

CHAPTER 20

SECONDHAND STATUS

What if buying pre-loved goods became a sign of savviness and source of pride?

The streetwear brand Supreme has mastered modern consumer culture. Long queues are common outside its 11 stores in cities such as New York, Los Angeles, Paris, Tokyo, and London as fans eagerly await its latest limited edition product drops. A few years ago, however, Supreme fans were surprised to hear that the brand had seemingly opened a store in Shenzhen with little fanfare. Was this an under-the-radar way to get close to its label-loving Chinese fans? Visitors to the store quickly realized the store wasn't what it seemed. Superficially, it was nearly identical: the same fixtures and branded hangers and plastic bags. Yet closer inspection revealed a small addition to the Supreme logos plastered all over the store—a small circle with the initials NYC in it. It was a fake store, selling hoodies for $130.[1]

The knockoff Supreme store is a particularly brazen example of the thriving counterfeit industry worth an estimated $600 billion a year, with as many as one in ten branded goods sold being fake.[2] Some of these products get passed as genuine, with buyers unaware they've been had. But many shoppers head to famous (or should it be infamous?) counterfeit hubs—MBK Shopping Mall and Patpong Street Market in Thailand, Anfu Market in Putian, China, Moscow's Dubrovka Market, and Cadircilar Caddesi in Turkey—with the express intention of purchasing fake items for a fraction of the price of the "real" thing.

We might assume they are simply tapping into the perceived status that comes with owning a particular branded item, but recent studies have shown a more curious effect. It turns out some of these buyers go one step further, justifying their consumption of these knockoffs by constructing an identity for themselves as savvy shoppers who hack the system to get what they want at an affordable price point.[3] While this shift might seem to indicate dire consequences for retailers due to lost profits and consumers getting lower quality products, what if there was another way?

In recent years fashion has become, in the words of the *Economist,* an "asset class" that is nearly as liquid as many traditional financial investments.[4] Entrepreneurial "sneakerheads" buying high-end sneakers for collecting or reselling, for example, already manage their collections with online platforms like StockX, a Detroit-based platform that unabashedly aims to build the world's first "stock market for things." The platform already allows users to organize their sneakers (NFT or physical), streetwear, trading cards, handbags, and a range of other products the same way financial investments would typically be managed.[5]

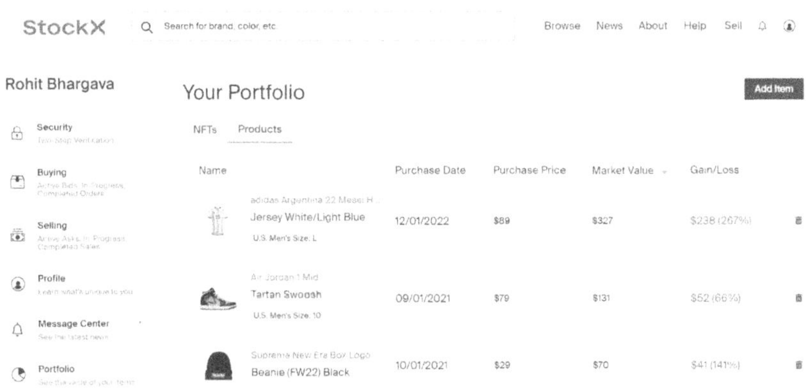

StockX portfolio screengrab. (Source: StockX.com)

People have resold long-lasting, durable, expensive goods like houses, cars, and jewelry for decades. But technology has streamlined the process of reselling clothing and vastly expanded the size of the market, making secondhand an increasingly important segment. Online retailer thredUP suggests we are about to enter "the next wave of secondhand." The numbers support this belief. Data from thredUP's comprehensive 2022 report on the secondhand industry shows how the dynamics of the industry are changing. In 2016, the US secondhand market was worth $18 billion, with approximately 90 percent of this taking place in thrift and donation stores. By 2026, the overall market is expected to be $82 billion, with nearly two-thirds of that being resale, which is forecast to grow to over $50 billion (up from just $2 billion a decade earlier). While much of this growth will occur on online marketplaces, the report also highlights how in 2021 there were 30 major fashion brands hosting their own resale stores, up from less than 10 just a year prior.[6]

What underpins this shift is the changing way that secondhand—or "pre-loved," as many in the industry prefer to call it now—fashion is perceived. Buying, wearing, and selling secondhand products is becoming a source of social status, rather than something to be hidden for fear of the social stigma of not being able to afford new items. As Ana Andjelic, a brand strategist and author of *The Business of Aspiration* explains, the old status economy that was based on displays of wealth has broken down. "Inexpensive goods and activities, like earthing, no-meat diet or meditation, are modern status symbols."[7] Increasingly, so too is buying secondhand.

While shoppers buying fake goods might celebrate their savviness to *themselves,* those buying secondhand can celebrate their purchases publicly. And they frequently do so online. Videos tagged with the hashtag #thriftshop have over 4 billion views on TikTok. Buying secondhand may also help resolve a lingering tension that people feel today between the pressure to constantly wear new outfits while feeling guilty about using and discarding fashion items. As Max Bittner, the CEO of Vestiaire Collective, a luxury resale platform has observed, "By buying secondhand handbags instead of new ones, you can help reduce fashion's carbon emissions by up to 90 percent. These realities are sinking in dramatically with consumers."[8]

Digital secondhand marketplaces also allow people to flaunt their entrepreneurialism as a key source of status too. If eBay is the Goodwill of the digital secondhand fashion world (huge, functional, but unsexy and hard to navigate), then fashion marketplaces like Depop are its younger, more creative, cooler cousin. Popular with Gen Z—90 percent of its users are under 25—the platform hosts nearly 2 million micro-entrepreneur sellers. In 2020, the then 24-year-old Bella McFadden was feted as Depop's first seller to hit £1 million in sales.[9] Originally from Canada, she now lives in Los Angeles and is an established figure in the industry. She credits the platform with enabling her to break into an otherwise inaccessible industry. "The fashion industry seemed all about knowing the right people and being in the right places," she explained. "I didn't think it was possible for me to do that in Ottawa."[10]

In the future normal, an increasing number of consumers will equate buying new products with inefficiency the same way some people view buying a new car already. Fueling the shift is the fact that secondhand purchases increasingly offer a sort of badge of honor and status as an eco-conscious consumer who wishes to make a statement through their buying behavior. After all, when secondhand gives you more for less ... why *would* you buy new anymore?

Instigator: Reflaunt

When luxury fashion site Net-a-Porter began shipping products in its iconic heavy-duty boxes wrapped in a luxury ribbon and filled with fine tissue paper, it gave customers a high-end unboxing experience—a rarity in the world of e-commerce when it launched over 20 years ago. Its focus on the customer experience helped it overcome the industry's skepticism that luxury customers would buy online.

Now, the luxury e-commerce pioneer wants the same success with previously owned clothing, partnering with Reflaunt, a Singapore-based Resale-as-a-Service platform, to enable its customers to resell their clothes. Starting in late 2021, Net-a-Porter customers could take their gently used items to selected drop-off locations, or even request a home collection, where the company then handles "the rest"—including assessing the value of the items, photographing them, writing product descriptions, and listing them on Reflaunt's network of resale marketplaces. Thanks to its integrated pricing algorithm, customers don't even have to wait until certain items are sold to realize their value as store credit.

Gift boxes from Net-a-Porter. (Source: www.net-a-porter.com)

Other luxury brands such as Balenciaga and Danish sustainable fashion brand GANNI are also utilizing Reflaunt's platform. California-based thredUP, featured earlier, also offers Resale-as-a-Service to brands such as Adidas and Crocs. Consumers like the added trust and convenience of buying gently used items directly from their favorite brands, while businesses like the environmental message it sends, as well as the boost to customer loyalty and their bottom line. (Reflaunt reports that 85 percent of resale customers choose to be paid in shopping credit.[11])

Customer expectations around resale are also spilling over into other sectors. IKEA, the world's biggest seller of "fast furniture," announced in early 2022 that its resale program would be permanently expanded across all 37 of its US stores.[12] Japanese resale platform Mercari lets users resell everything from skincare products to digital accessories. And of course, long-standing resale platforms like eBay and Etsy also have their loyal base of users who continue to sell just about anything you can imagine.

Ultimately, embracing secondhand items will become a big part of the future normal because it will enable people to have the best of both worlds when it comes to rationalizing their shopping habits. Not only will they get a good deal on products that might otherwise be priced out of reach, but they will also be able to contribute meaningfully in helping the environment at the same time. This is the virtuous circle of secondhand status, and one that we suspect will help this movement continue to grow.

Imagining the Future Normal

1. Will resale encourage customers to trade up to higher quality goods as they factor in the resale value?
2. How will the popularity of secondhand goods shift the way that luxury, or any other retail brands, communicate the value of their products?
3. What other behaviors might consumers adopt as a way to demonstrate the "status" that they feel their secondhand purchases might offer?

TOPICS IN THIS SECTION

NEW COLLECTIVISM

What if startup founders dreamed of more than venture capital and unicorns?

NU-AGRICULTURE

What if we could make clean, abundant food for everyone out of thin air?

GOOD GOVERNING

What if government policies were recognized for actually making citizens' lives better?

WASTE-FREE PRODUCTS

What if you could throw things away with a clean conscience?

THE 15-MINUTE CITY

What if every long journey in the city was cut to 15 minutes?

MILLIONS OF MICROGRIDS

What if you could generate your own energy—reliably and cheaply?

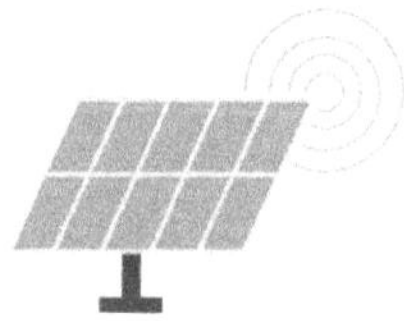

INHUMAN DELIVERY

What if you could get anything delivered to your doorstep within minutes?

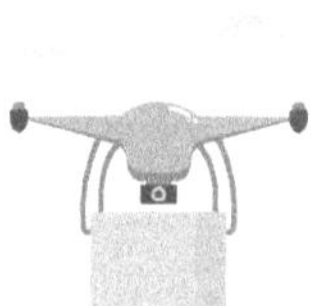

MAKING WEATHER

What if humanity could control the weather to fight the effects of global warming?

URBAN FORESTS

What if we invested in more green infrastructure to make cities more sustainable?

BEYOND NET ZERO

What if companies aimed beyond going carbon neutral and toward being actively regenerative?

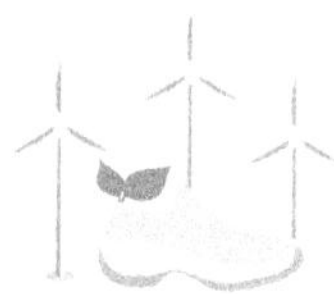

PART 3

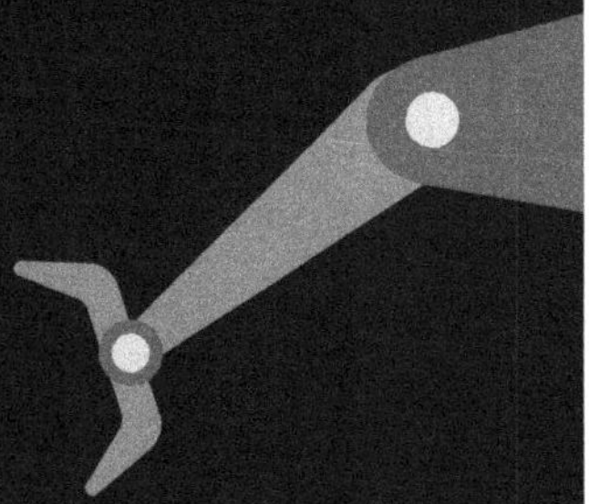

HOW HUMANITY WILL SURVIVE

The instigators who choose to tackle some of our most daunting global problems offer a bold vision for what humanity needs to survive in the future. In this section we explore ongoing efforts to improve government and our cities, as well as advances in agriculture and weather modification that hold the promise to dramatically shift the way we live on our planet. From feeding more people to eliminating waste to reimagining how our power grids work, the topics in this section will get you thinking farther into the future about the systems-level changes that will affect how we produce things, how societies operate, and, ultimately, how humanity might survive and thrive in the decade to come.

CHAPTER 21

NEW COLLECTIVISM

What if startup founders dreamed of more than venture capital and unicorns?

On March 17, 2022, Nathan Head, a young digital artist, tweeted a screenshot of his cryptocurrency wallet showing his holding of 10,950 ApeCoins, which at the time was worth $78,087.90. His caption read, "I honestly don't know what to do; this is a lot of money."[1] Head's confusion was, in part, because he had simply been given these ApeCoins—for free.

Even those readers not following the crypto roller coaster may have heard of the Bored Ape Yacht Club (BAYC)—a collection of 10,000 unique digital pictures of cartoon apes. Thanks to the celebrities who purchased them, such as Paris Hilton and Jimmy Fallon, the BAYC became one of the most high-profile examples of the 2021 bubble in non-fungible tokens (NFTs), with some apes selling for millions of dollars. Yuga Labs, creator of the BAYC collection, claims that the apes are far more than overpriced images—its vision is for NFTs to unlock a radically new model of community ownership. Head received his ApeCoins by virtue of owning a BAYC NFT; the tokens granted him a stake in the ApeCoin DAO, an adjacent "decentralized autonomous organization."* The price of an ApeCoin is linked to the overall success of projects related to the BAYC community—when the rappers Eminem and Snoop Dogg released a music video featuring the pair as animated versions of their Bored Ape characters, the token's value rose by over 20 percent.[2] More intriguing is that anyone who holds ApeCoins, such as Head, can also vote on proposals about the direction of the franchise. For example, member "holochronape" requested 23,000 ApeCoins to build a private, community-only talent marketplace where people could highlight their skills and offer services—from design to cybersecurity—to other members. The project was approved with over 90 percent voting in favor.[3]

At the moment, it is hard to celebrate the ApeCoin DAO given how its structure appears to be designed only to enrich early backers and insiders.[4] Six months after its launch, the SEC announced it was launching an investigation into whether Yuga Labs had violated securities regulations with the ApeCoin launch.[5] However, if we can manage to look past the rampant speculation and all too frequent scams that plague the world of cryptocurrency-based Web3** projects, we can see glimpses of an ambition that's as old as humanity—to create a fair and equitable economic system where people in a community can participate in, and benefit from, the value created by that community.

---

*A DAO is similar to a corporation, but instead of being run by humans, it is run by code. Typically, DAOs are token-based, although, unlike most private companies, anyone can buy and trade tokens. Trading is handled on the blockchain, meaning anyone can set up a DAO without needing to list on a stock exchange. As a result, DAOs have, to date, not been subject to traditional regulations.

**The term Web3 is generally used to describe a range of blockchain-based decentralized technologies like cryptocurrency, NFTs, and DAOs that empower individual users while reducing the power of large tech firms.

Blockchain aside, we have both been looking at the broader trend of community ownership for a number of years—in 2014, Rohit wrote about the Collaborative Economy, and in 2012, Henry introduced the idea of "Custowners." Since then, people have become increasingly skeptical about the promises from tech startups like Uber and Airbnb to create a better world. Given the number of workers who are exploited through these platforms, the fear seems justified. We suspect the utopian claims of many Web3 projects will remain similarly unfulfilled. Yet clearly there is a deep-rooted desire to reimagine our economy to be fairer and more inclusive. That is why in this chapter we want to look at a less- well-known (and certainly less hyped) concept that we are calling new collectivism. The concept of collectivism, most often defined as the principle of giving a group priority over individuals, is an appropriate descriptor for the new effect we have been studying. This aspirational manifesto imagines a future normal where a transfer of power to a community is integrated into the process of company building and startup exits ... moments that are currently more about celebrating individuals' success.

Instigator: Exit to Community

Since his days covering the Occupy Movement around the world, Nathan Schneider, a reporter and professor of media studies at the University of Colorado Boulder, has been interested in the notion of cooperatives—jointly owned and governed organizations or groups. Co-ops, mutual societies, and credit unions have been around for hundreds of years. The world's 300 largest cooperatives have a turnover of $2 trillion and include France's Credit Agricole Finance, Germany's REWE, Japan's Nippon Life, and the United States' REI and State Farm. Cooperatives employ 280 million people, or 10 percent of the world's employed population.[6] In sports, the NFL's

Green Bay Packers are owned by a community-owned nonprofit with 537,000 shareholders,[7] and soccer club FC Barcelona is owned by its 144,000 members.[8]

Ironically, outside of cryptocurrency-powered Web3 projects (many of which face searching questions around the transparency and sustainability of their business models), cooperatives remain rare among the fastest-growing, most disruptive startups of the digital economy. On one level, this is surprising, given that many of these startups employ business models that are perfectly suited for a distributed ownership structure: highly networked, community or peer-powered, and purpose-driven. The startup world, however, still typically follows the venture capital dynamic: companies raise money and then find themselves on a growth-at-all-costs trajectory to ensure a blockbuster exit—either by going public or being acquired by a bigger company. In this model, the wealth generated remains in the hands of the few, and economic inequity around the world gets worse.

What if there was another way?

To imagine a different path, Schneider joined forces with five other collaborators in August 2020 to offer a possible solution: "exit to community," or E2C.[9] The central idea behind E2C is that businesses that create value for, with, and from a community could eventually be owned by that community. Outlining their vision in a thoughtfully written pamphlet-sized book published jointly by the Media Enterprise Design Lab at the University of Colorado Boulder and Zebras Unite (an inclusive movement of founders who reject the venture model), the short primer described E2C as a "strategy in the making."[10]

> **The normal we want is one in which people can build toward, and with, community ownership.**
>
> —*Exit to Community: A Community Primer*[11]

The primer's authors argue that in the future, new legal and governance models are needed for businesses for whom a "traditional" exit—an IPO or a sale—is not the desired endgame. There are many existing legal routes outlined in the primer that leaders can deploy to secure an E2C outcome, such as cooperatives, trusts, golden shares, B Corps, and more; it also calls for a mix of new policies and regulations to advance more equitable and inclusive corporate structures. An "exit to community" would also help bridge the gap between founders' initial lofty world-changing aspirations and the traditional financial mechanisms that take over when a corporate or public exit is likely.[12]

As close watchers of experiments in community ownership for more than a decade, we believe the key insight that makes an E2C so compelling is its proposal that community ownership should be the end goal, rather than a required starting point. For example, Schneider highlights that it might be impossible to successfully build and engage a community during the riskiest stage of a startup, when agility and fast decision-making are needed.[13] And while recent years have seen blockchain-based communities offer a new approach, often "communities" in this space are narrowly focused on financial success as their only shared purpose. Instead, E2C offers a practical option for businesses that have reached a level of stability and maturity, or whose owners want to build long-term accountability toward their communities into their ownership structures.

Enabling and encouraging valuable community members to become owners makes sense for many organizations, even venture-backed companies. Both Uber and Airbnb petitioned the SEC to be able to offer equity to their drivers and hosts (who are *not* employees) in an effort to increase their loyalty.[14] Equity crowdfunding has also seen thousands of businesses raise money on platforms such as StartEngine and Seedrs over the past decade. While these platforms don't require shareholders to be members of their community, many brands turn to equity crowdfunding with the explicit intent of inviting customer evangelists to become shareholders.[15]

Today, pioneers wanting to embed community within their organizations have to turn to innovative legal structures, as laid out in the E2C primer, or embrace new, code-based governance mechanisms such as blockchain. In the future normal, community exits will become increasingly common and easy to form ... and desirable, too.[16]

Imagining the Future Normal

1. How could companies create an ownership structure where employees who create the most value are rewarded proportionally instead of basing compensation on title and seniority alone?
2. How might your organization's ownership structures change over time as your business scales and the importance of purpose over profit continues to grow?
3. Which members of your community would make the best owners—your users, customers, or suppliers—and how could you reinvent your ownership model to accommodate their shared participation in ownership?

CHAPTER 22

GOOD GOVERNING

What if government policies were recognized for actually making citizens' lives better?

For most of the past 50 years, the government of Botswana has been a celebrated case study in good governance. In 2001, the nation had achieved "the highest rate of per-capita growth of any country in the world in the last 35 years."[1] According to a team of researchers at the MIT Department of Economics, from 2011 to 2020 the country was ranked as the "least corrupt nation in Africa" by nonprofit Transparency International.[2] At a time when news media were hungry to profile positive stories from Africa, Botswana was the perfect success story.

This success was attributed to a host of factors—in particular, former President Ian Khama who was in office for 10 years, from 2008 to 2018. When new President Mokgweetsi Masisi took over in 2018, however, the country's reputation started to shift. By 2021, the Economic Intelligence Unit's Democracy Index categorized

Botswana as a "flawed democracy." The country moved down the list on the Transparency International index behind the tiny African island nation of Cabo Verde. By 2023, the concern among foreign policy circles was that Botswana may be backsliding.[3]

The truth is, seeking global examples of consistently good government can be an exercise in disappointment. Political parties gain and lose power. Regimes shift, and priorities change. This is not unique to Africa. It is a global reality of politics. In 2022, the United States saw a dramatic political and policy shift as the decades-old right to an abortion was overturned by the US Supreme Court. In Brazil, the nation turned toward right-wing leader Jair Bolsonaro for three years and then in 2022 flipped again and reelected former President Luiz Inácio "Lula" da Silva to take the office once more.

In country after country, this is how politics (and government) seems to work. Today's good government can become tomorrow's cautionary tale. It is easy, therefore, to become a skeptic of the idea that good government can ever be anything more than an accident of fate. A nation might be lucky enough to encounter a leader with the personal charisma and vision of Nelson Mandela who can bring an entire nation together. But then everything will change once that leader leaves.

This is not to say government can't be effective. The relatively rapid development of a Covid-19 vaccine and widespread improvements in highway and traffic safety, as well as the national weather service storm warning systems, are all successes of government. So, too, are public universities as well as environmental or consumer protection agencies. The irony of many government-funded and supported programs such as these large-scale programs is that, when they work, citizens rarely credit the government's role in the success—instead celebrating the independent innovators or architects of those victories. When they fail, however, the government is an easy institution to blame. As a result, our collective faith in the ability of governments of any sort to improve our lives continues to dwindle. Edelman's Trust Barometer (a global study of over 36,000 people across 28 countries) found government was seen as the least effective institution when it comes to solving social problems, lagging behind business, NGOs, and the media.[4]

Good political leadership or not, the *governing* is far more common than we realize—sometimes in spite of the government in power but more often because of it. Good governments establish trust with citizens, they respect the rule of law, are transparent with information, accountable for what they do, and are responsive to the needs of the people.

In the future normal, there will still be lying politicians and self-serving legislators. But people's perception (and the reality) of government will shift from something that is ineffectually debated from afar to something that more often happens locally, benefits our communities, and makes our lives safer, healthier, and more fulfilling. In this chapter, we try to steer clear of passing judgment on what "good" policy looks like. That will remain forever up for debate. Instead, we will show how examples of "good governing" are being shared within policymaking communities around the world with increasing frequency, leading to a virtuous cycle of improvements in how citizens are governed.

Instigator: The World Government Summit

The World Government Summit, an annual gathering of more than 20,000 government leaders and experts hosted by His Highness Sheikh Mohammed bin Rashid Al Maktoum, vice president and prime minister of the UAE, ruler of Dubai, is dedicated to "shaping future governments and creating a better future for humanity." The 2022 annual event featured nearly 1,000 sessions, more than 600 speakers, and over 40 participating organizations. In past years, the event has showcased programs such as Indonesia's innovative experiment to allow bus riders in the country's second-largest city of Surabaya to pay for their ride by collecting and submitting five plastic bottles instead of paying with cash.[5]

Featured government programs have ranged from Finland's National Artificial Intelligence Programme, known as AuroraAI, which aspires to provide the best AI-enabled public services in the world, to efforts in the Dutch city of Tilburg to test traffic light sensors that can automatically give extra street crossing time to elderly or disabled pedestrians.[6] These big country-level initiatives and street-level (literally) innovations paint the picture of good governing in practice for the 4,000-plus participants at the event.

The IBM Center for the Business of Government is another organization that is devoted to improving the effectiveness of government in all sectors. Since its inception in 1998, the group has published more than 400 reports coupled with books, interviews, and other content meant to celebrate some of the many examples of good governing happening across the world.[7] The *Good Government Show*, a popular podcast produced by two former political journalists, also features the success stories of local government solving real-world problems—from combating homelessness to how libraries are taking on the role of community centers.[8] The World Bank has regularly not only promoted examples of good governance, but also built an entire practice area for decades that has helped nations around the world to implement good governance and reimagine the future of government.[9]

The collective mission of these efforts is both to demonstrate to the public what good governing can do, as well as motivate those working in government to consider running similarly effective programs of their own. Sometimes social media, which often has a polarizing and divisive effect when it comes to politics, could actually offer an effective channel to share governmental success stories.

Robyn Scott, a New Zealander who grew up in Botswana during the country's terrible AIDS crisis, is one entrepreneur who believes in the positive potential of social media to make government better through knowledge sharing. She is the founder of Apolitical, which calls itself the "social learning network for government," where over 150,000 public servants and policy makers from around the world learn, connect, and share best practices. Articles on the site cover topics from how to empower indigenous communities through technology to the top podcasts for public servants, along with a community question and answer board where users can tap into the "global brain" of their peers. In addition to hosting online and offline learning programs, Apolitical also hosts the Future of Government awards, which celebrates the best open-source public sector digital initiatives in an effort to encourage others to apply them in their own communities. One recent winner was CamDX, a decentralized secure data exchange that enables easy and standardized access to Cambodian government data.

A further big driver of the shift to perceive government as an active player in shaping a better future rather than an ineffectual bureaucracy also comes from the rise of youth activism across the world. Younger generations have grown up in digital worlds, where their experiences mean they expect to be active participants and collaborators with government rather than just passive recipients of it. Skolstrejk för klimatet, the School Strike for Future movement initiated by Greta Thunberg and widely copied around the world, is a powerful example of how young activists are collaborating and engaging with political issues. As author Jessica Taft, an associate professor of Latin American and Latino Studies at UC Santa Cruz, explains, "around the world, we are seeing children and youth engage as social, political, and economic actors, demonstrating their capacity to help make social change."[10] While this youth engagement can often be inspired by a desire to combat inaction or to expose corruption, it also leads to more civic participation in government itself—which results in more representative policies and initiatives that reflect what citizens truly want. Their activism, in other words, can enable more good governing.

In the future normal, efforts to encourage better governing will combine with people's rising understanding that activism and involvement are necessary to shape good governing. Just as the business world celebrates game-changing ideas, so too will policymakers. Good governing, in many countries, will become more common and recognized as such, helping raise faith in government. As this happens, government will be seen as more of an instigator and supporter for those who are trying to shape the future rather than a bureaucratic hurdle to progress.

Imagining the Future Normal

1. What if we based our assessment of the effectiveness of government on what happens locally in our communities?
2. How could good governing initiatives that work in one region be shared and implemented in another?
3. How might we each measure and increase our personal civic engagement beyond simply casting a vote?

CHAPTER 23

THE 15-MINUTE CITY

What if every long journey in the city was cut to 15 minutes?

When Carlos Moreno met with Paris Mayor Anne Hidalgo as she prepared her reelection campaign, he was expecting his ideas to "be a paragraph down the bottom of the campaign leaflet."[1]

Moreno, a professor of complex systems at Paris-Sorbonne University, is the mastermind behind the "15-minute city"—the notion that city residents should be able to get to the places they access daily—from workplaces to stores to schools and universities to health-care providers to cultural and green spaces—within a quarter of an hour. In a TED Talk where he lays out his novel idea, he argues that our cities are "bubbles of illusory acceleration."[2] While we think of megacities as fast paced, the mundane reality is that cities are characterized by long, wasteful commutes that damage the environment, are terrible for personal and collective well-being, exacerbate inequality, and entrench injustice.

So, Moreno asked: What if this changed? What if we could exponentially increase the range of services we could access within 15 minutes?

Moreno's ideas became central to Hidalgo's successful reelection campaign and her vision of Paris's future. Walk around the newly renovated Minimes barracks, a 1920s complex in the Marais district of Paris, and you get a sense of what that future might look and feel like. The public housing complex features commercial office space, a number of small artisan workshops, a nursery for childcare, a health clinic, and a café staffed partially by people with autism. The central courtyard, formerly its parking lot, has been converted into a public garden. As a result of the Paris 2024 Olympics, similarly ambitious developments are underway in the Seine-Saint-Denis region, described as "the most youthful and cosmopolitan department in France."[3] The Summer Games in particular have provided the inspiration for the Paris 2024 organizing team to focus beyond building venues to the long-term legacy of the city. Already declaring that 85 percent of competition venues will be located under 30 minutes from the Olympic Village, the city is making significant investments in public transportation and zero-emission transit options that will transform it for the long term.[4]

Paris may seem like an extreme example. After all, most cities can't rely on the boon of Olympic-level development budgets, but there is another way to create the 15-minute city, beyond reconfiguring the structure of the city to ensure amenities are physically present in local districts, as in the Minimes barracks. Making people more mobile enables them to access a greater range of their cities' amenities in less time. This approach is far more practical for most cities given the next generation of "micromobility" vehicles. While the past 15 years have seen impressive urban transportation innovation—from the original bike-sharing schemes to scooters and dockless access—the next decade will see those innovations supercharged (quite literally) by electric motors that enable these vehicles to travel farther faster. The 15-minute city looks very different to someone riding an e-bike than to someone who gets around on foot or by traditional public transportation. Micromobility means people can get the benefits of localism *and* of a bigger city within Moreno's all-important 15 minutes.

Paris is far from the only city attempting to create radically more accessible local neighborhoods. Barcelona's Superilles (*Superblocks*) are partially self-contained local areas that promote public transport and pedestrians ahead of cars.[5] Portland, Oregon, aims for 90 percent of its residents to live in "20-minute neighborhoods."[6] Shanghai's Urban Master Plan 2015–2040 also refers to the "15-minute community life circle" as an important objective of the city's social development. Future residents of The Line, the wildly ambitious 170-kilometer-long car-free city planned for the Saudi Arabian desert, will find their local amenities within just five minutes, and the longest end-to-end journey across the city will take just 20 minutes.[7] Given the continued pressure on urban populations, it is hard to see this trend reversing. Cities where people can move freely will thrive, while those where mobility is constrained will struggle.

Instigator: VanMoof

Imagine a video montage with a sequence of images depicting smoking industrial chimney stacks and traffic jams reflected on the surface of a sports car, all accompanied by the sound of horns and car crashes. As the video continues, the body of the car slowly melts, the liquid slipping away to reveal an electric bicycle. The visual story is now revealed to be an advertisement as it closes with the message: "Time to ride the future."[8]

Created by Dutch e-bike manufacturer VanMoof, the ad never aired in France. The Autorité de Régulation Professionnelle de la

Publicité (ARPP), which regulates which ads can run, banned it on the grounds that it creates a "climate of anxiety," simultaneously validating and censoring the core message of the ad.[9]

Frame from VanMoof commercial "The Future is Forwards," released in 2022. (Source: VanMoof)

VanMoof is just one player in the broader micromobility revolution—the global shift away from cars toward bikes, scooters, and microvehicles, both shared and private.

> **It's easy to see why car manufacturers might be scared of this behavioral shift ... It might explain why to date there have been almost no bike commercials broadcast worldwide. But with this market stranglehold starting to loosen, it's only a matter of time before more voices can be heard. There's a new day dawning indeed.**
>
> —VanMoof blog[10]

While the VanMoof team may be overly optimistic about how much of a threat auto manufacturers probably feel coming from bikes, there is no denying people are hungry for the benefits that micromobility can offer. In the United States alone, data from the

National Association of City Transportation Officials (NACTO) suggests that the number of shared bike and e-scooter trips grew 60 percent to 136 million by the end of 2019 (just before the start of the pandemic).[11] The mobility app Grab, Southeast Asia's first "decacorn" (a startup valued at over $10 billion), offers shared bikes and e-scooters, as well as rides in traditional cars.[12] Some automotive manufacturers are even joining the trend. Citroën has developed Ami, an "urban mobility object." This electric vehicle is so small that it is classed as a "light quadricycle," which means it doesn't require a driving license to operate and can be driven on Parisian streets by teenagers as young as 14.[13]

This shift has been more than a decade in the making. For a brief moment in 2017 and 2018, city dwellers around the world were spoiled for choice when it came to getting around their cities. Whether you were in Hangzhou or Hamburg, Lima or London, you didn't have to walk more than a few blocks before stumbling across a scooter or bike from a seemingly endless list of startups such as Bird, Bolt, Circ, Dott, Hive, Jump, Lime, Lyft, Mobike, oBike, Ofo, Tier, and many more. However, when the tide turned, it went out quickly. Operators ran into huge logistical challenges dealing with damaged or stolen units. Regulators had to step in as sidewalks became clogged and stories emerged of riders being seriously injured or even killed. The micromobility utopia, it seems, was not just an e-scooter ride away.

There are signs, however, that this may be changing, as support for micromobility continues to be strong. The pandemic showed city dwellers a more open, uncrowded, and occasionally unspoiled side to the urban experience that many want to keep. As a result, Hidalgo announced that 50 kilometers of "coronapistes"—temporary bike lanes on some of Paris's major routes established during the city's lockdown—would be made permanent.[14] Milan, Brussels, Seattle, and Montreal also all announced cyclist-friendly moves.[15] In many dense urban cities in Asia, where city traffic often moves at a glacial pace, the challenge is different. While cyclists have long shared the road with cars, they rarely have dedicated traffic lanes, and the heavily polluted air makes the option of biking far more dangerous and less desirable. In these cities, improved mobility isn't about bikes and scooters. Instead, it's about creating more mass transportation options that are emission-free, efficient, and affordable.

Efforts to address climate change are driving a renewed interest in micromobility. In China, Tencent announced plans to build Net City, a car-free district in Shenzhen.[16] And the C40, a group of 40 city leaders, published a report that singles out increasing the amount of protected space for pedestrians and cyclists, and elevating the 15-minute city as an important part of global urban recovery.[17]

Perhaps new evidence of micromobility's comeback can also be found in VanMoof's success. Its main struggle has been keeping up with demand, after selling more bikes in the first four months of 2020 than in the previous two years combined.[18] The company raised over $180 million across 2020 and 2021 in order to expand production and "break down more barriers to cycling."[19]

Just as digital transformation in commerce has changed people's relationship to shopping, a more convenient urban landscape is poised to change people's expectations just as radically—and become the future normal. Billions endure the challenges of moving around cities today because of the economic and cultural opportunities that they offer. Empowering people to easily get to the places they want or need to be within 15 minutes will reduce their environmental impact, strengthen communities, and improve lives.

Imagining the Future Normal

1. How could our days change if everyone spent less time commuting from one place to another and more time doing other things?
2. What if microvehicles became the dominant mode of transport and more people no longer felt the need to own cars?
3. What could we do to ensure the benefits of micromobility could be distributed across all socioeconomic groups and communities as a potential equalizer for society?

CHAPTER 24

INHUMAN DELIVERY

What if you could get anything delivered to your doorstep within minutes?

Remember the first time you used a ride-sharing app? For many it was a magical moment: you got a ride faster, the experience was better, *and* it was cheaper. If you are like most of us, this triggered a new behavior as you probably started booking *more* rides since they had become both more convenient and more cost-effective.

A similar phenomenon may be on the cusp of happening with e-commerce, just without the guilt of worker exploitation. Even before the pandemic, online shopping was already exploding, driven by delivery times that were faster than ever before and soaring customer demand. Soon, thanks to drone technology, these delivery times could be exponentially shorter and the costs radically lower—making e-commerce significantly more attractive to a much wider pool of both shoppers and retailers of all persuasions.

One outcome that we fully expect is that you will order what you *actually* want rather than adapting your purchasing behavior to fit the constraints of traditional delivery logistics. Today, when you shop online, you probably batch your purchases to hit the required minimum order that will earn free delivery (or even qualify for delivery). When it comes to take-out food, you probably stick to ordering foods that travel well. Pizza, burritos, and stir-fried noodles are in, but menu items like Rohit's favorite papdi chaat—an Indian dish with crispy chips covered in yogurt, chickpeas, and chutney—not so much (who wants soggy papdi?). A world in which autonomous drones can cheaply deliver purchases in minutes would allow you to order whatever you want right when you want it. More importantly, it could open entirely new markets for fast delivery in rural areas that are currently underserved by most delivery services.

The idea that you'll have your morning coffee delivered by a drone might seem far-fetched. But there are already many companies working to make drone delivery an everyday occurrence. The pandemic accelerated their ascent to the mainstream. In March 2022, Alphabet-owned drone service Wing announced that it had hit 200,000 deliveries—just six months after it had reached its 100,000th delivery.[1] Launched in 2010, Wing operates primarily in Australia, delivering household goods, medical supplies, and even fresh food.[2] Zipline, a commercial drone delivery company that specializes in delivering blood and medical supplies initially in Rwanda and Ghana, has completed over 400,000 missions and delivered over seven million vaccine doses since starting their services in 2017.[3] Thanks to pinpoint location information enabled by what3words—a proprietary geocode system that assigns a unique combination of three words to every three-square-meter location in the world—these drone deliveries can truly be made to anyone in any location, whether it is on a traditional map, in a building, or standing in the middle of a park.

In the future normal, continued developments in the safety and capability of these drones will provide rural customers, suburban families, anyone on the go, and even those in need of emergency medical supplies, with faster and more reliable delivery options.

Instigator: Manna

Founded in 2018, drone delivery startup Manna's goal is to deliver goods in under three minutes. The service began with the challenge of delivering Ben & Jerry's ice cream to students in Dublin, Ireland, via its fully autonomous drones. Like it did for so many other businesses and startups, the pandemic changed all that. Manna's CEO Bobby Healy realized the lockdown was leaving people in rural communities more isolated than ever. He petitioned Ireland's Health Service Executive to designate Manna as an essential service, enabling it to pivot and launch a pilot program delivering medications and medical supplies to residents of Moneygall, a small village of 1,000 people, during lockdown.

Manna Drone Delivery aircraft and delivery box. (Source: Manna)

Having proven its ability to deliver essential medical supplies, the service expanded to deliver pretty much anything, from pizza and vegetables to birthday cakes from local stores.[4] By 2021, the company was doing about 2,000 to 3,000 flights a day, and today, it serves around 45,000 customers.[5] Flying at an altitude of 150 to 200 feet and at near 50 miles an hour, Manna's drones can make seven to eight deliveries per hour, making them an incredibly efficient form of delivery.

One small but fascinating signal of how faster deliveries could radically change consumer behavior comes from early usage data from Manna and Wing, who both independently report that hot coffee is one of their most requested items. While some readers might hesitate to order coffee delivered via drones, Manna's typical two- to three-minute flight times mean it is able to deliver a "piping hot coffee, foam intact, little design on top of the foam still intact," as Healy explains.[6]

> **Battery technology, machine vision, GPUs, motors ... if you join them all up, you end up with a 30, 40-pound aircraft that can carry around six or seven pounds of cargo and do it for an absolute fraction of the cost of using the road ... It's a nascent trillion-dollar industry that there's nobody with a solution, so we're racing to get there.**
>
> —Bobby Healy, CEO, Manna[7]

Currently, Manna services the town of Galway on the west coast of Ireland, population: around 10,000. Because drones need an open space to land their deliveries, smaller towns or rural villages with houses featuring large backyards are ideal for testing their service. In late 2022, the company also announced plans to take their drone-delivery services to the US and Europe.[8]

As they expand, Manna will face a number of competitors in both regions. Flytrex, an Israeli startup, launched a commercial drone delivery service in Iceland, and most recently partnered with Walmart for a pilot program in North Carolina. UPS Flight Forward is the first company to get the US government's approval to operate a drone airline.[9] In 2020 it partnered with CVS Pharmacy to deliver prescription medicines to The Villages, Florida, the largest retirement community in the US. California-based firm Matternet even won approval from regulators on designs for the first flying drone built specifically for shipping packages.[10]

Why is drone delivery ripe to become normal now? The main barriers it has faced so far have been around safety and regulations. For safety, both Manna and Wing don't attempt to land their drones. Instead, the drones lower their packages on a wire to the ground, which also dramatically reduces the complexity of the delivery itself.

The regulatory environment is maturing, too. In the EU, new regulations were adopted in April 2021 aimed at creating a safer and more trusted environment for drone services.[11] In the US, regulators debate guidelines requiring drone delivery services to operate within a pilot's visual sight line and consider how they will manage the air space that drones would operate in.[12] Advocates argue that drone delivery will have a positive social impact as they help to reduce emissions, avoid traffic congestion caused by other types of delivery vehicles, and allow local businesses to compete against the growing fast delivery monopolies of big retailers like Walmart and Amazon.[13]

While drones likely won't be suitable for dense city centers any time soon, that's perhaps what makes them even more interesting. So much innovation in our world is myopically focused on city centers because of their population density. But across the world, over two billion people live in small cities or towns that have a total population of 500,000 people or less.[14] Drone delivery could offer people living in tens of thousands of these smaller communities fast, cheap access to a wider range of products—particularly in countries where the ground-level infrastructure is less developed.

When it comes to anticipating the future, we recognize there is perhaps no symbol more iconic (and overused) than autonomous drones circling overhead. Rather than congesting our skies and blocking our enjoyment of nature, though, the reality of drone delivery could be far more practical ... and noble. Delivering life-saving medicines. Connecting underserved populations with delivery services. And providing the ultimate convenience of having anything you need delivered directly to you within minutes. Even if it happens to be something as indulgent as a latte.

Imagining the Future Normal

1. If the popularity of drone delivery takes off, how would we determine what limits to impose on the volume of flights?
2. How would drone delivery—better suited for suburban environments rather than denser city centers—help redraw our urban maps and reconceive what a desirable place to live is?
3. What social and economic shifts will we see if people start ordering from small, independent local retailers that can offer near-instant delivery?

CHAPTER 25

URBAN FORESTS

What if we invested in more green infrastructure to make cities more sustainable?

Lee Kuan Yew, the first president and founding father of Singapore, considered the air conditioner the most important invention of the 20th century. The humble and now near-ubiquitous boxes transformed the global economy, lengthening workdays in hotter regions and (alongside the elevator) enabling the construction of the great concrete, steel, and glass towers that make up a modern city's skyline.

Billions of people have poured into these modern cities in search of opportunity and modernity. San Francisco, Shanghai, and Nairobi, as well as other already-established centers of commerce saw huge growth and were joined by "new" international hubs such as Dubai, Singapore, and thousands of less-well-known cities, from Chongqing to Lucknow to Dar es Salaam. For all this time, modern cities have been incredible engines of growth. But they have also produced increasing risks to their populations. Besides putting up with air pollution, cramped living spaces, and escalating crime, the inhabitants of major cities are now increasingly vulnerable to the catastrophic effects of extreme weather events, such as floods and fires.

Another big risk is heat. Urban temperatures in many cities are reaching the limit of human survivability. Some cities have reached record temperatures, with Jacobabad in Pakistan seeing temperatures of 123.8°F (or 51°C) in 2022.[1] It is estimated that 3.1 billion people—a third of the world's population—will be exposed to heat hazards by 2050, up from 1.5 billion today.[2]

Cities around the world are fighting back against increasing temperatures, pollution, and the stress that crowded environments produce by literally growing urban forests in their neighborhoods. Walk around Singapore today and you can glimpse a very different—and quite literally greener—urban landscape than the great concrete towers that rose in the last century. You don't even have to leave the airport to get your first taste of the country's "city in a garden" aspiration. Jewel Changi Airport's domed roof contains the world's largest indoor waterfall, which helps to cool the terminal, and contains more than 200 species of flora and fauna that help purify the air.[3] Singapore's 101-hectare nature park Gardens by the Bay opened in 2012, featuring its iconic "Supertrees," 25- to 50-meter-high vertical gardens and giant conservatories. EDEN, a 20-story residential tower, features "planted chandeliers" that cascade down to provide natural shade to the building's apartments.

Other countries have also been investing in making their cities more inhabitable. Medellín's Green Corridors project saw the Colombian city spend $16 million on more than 8,000 trees along 30 corridors that run by roads and waterways. The result has been to reduce the average temperature in the city by 3.6°F (or 2°C) while also capturing CO_2 and increasing biodiversity.[4] Paris, known for its "heat islands"—recently recorded temperatures of over 132°F

(56°C) in the sunny, asphalt-covered Place de l'Opéra compared to only 82°F (28°C) on the shady, tree-lined Boulevard des Italiens, a minute's walk away. To counter these extreme disparities, the city has launched a project to plant 170,000 trees by 2026.[5] Similarly Seoul, South Korea's capital, is creating "wind path forests" placed along rivers and roads to draw cool air into the city.[6]

It is hardly surprising that plant-covered buildings and cities are becoming more popular. The pandemic has triggered lasting shifts in how people live in cities. People are seeking out connections to nature to enhance their well-being (see Green Prescriptions on p. 83), while employers want to create richer experiences for workers returning to the office. Cities are also responding to citizens' increasing awareness of the dangers of air pollution and climate change. In the future normal, we won't rely solely on air-conditioning to make our cities livable. Instead, bringing nature into our cities will keep them habitable places we *want* to live in rather than those that we endure out of economic necessity.

Instigator: Stefano Boeri

Like so many new trends, the underlying ideas behind green buildings and biophilic design (to give it its official name) are ancient, running back to the Hanging Gardens of Babylon. But it was Stefano Boeri, an architect and full professor of Urban Planning in Milan, Italy, and his Bosco Verticale ("Vertical Forest") that kickstarted the modern era of buildings that embed and celebrate nature in their design. Completed in 2014, the Bosco Verticale is a pair of tree-packed residential towers that incorporate more than 20,000 plants in their design and structure. The vegetation helps to control the temperature in the buildings, minimizes noise from the outside, and reduces the dust that comes into the apartments. These vertical forests not only create a uniquely beautiful living experience for their residents, but they also contribute significantly to the environment around them by enhancing the biodiversity of the area and providing an efficient way to increase green areas in cities. If the trees and plants housed in the Bosco Verticale had been planted on the ground, they would have taken up 30,000 square meters, compared to the mere 3,000 square meters occupied by the towers.[7]

> **We need nature because it helps us breathe better, reduce heat, and clean our air. On rooftops, in driveways, we need to make a concerted effort to incorporate more nature everywhere.**
>
> —Stefano Boeri, Founding Partner, Stefano Boeri Architetti[8]

Since launching the groundbreaking Bosco Verticale, Boeri has continued to advocate for "urban forestry," designing similar towers in Tirana in Albania, Egypt's New Administrative Capital, and Huanggang in China's Hubei province.[9] One of his most fascinating projects is the Trudo Vertical Forest, a 19-story, tree-covered social housing project that opened in 2021 in Eindhoven, Netherlands. Featuring over 10,000 shrubs and plants on the building's garden balconies, the tower was designed to prove that green solutions didn't have to be exclusive and costly. The plants were specially selected to ensure they would thrive with minimal maintenance costs.[10]

Beyond designing and collaborating on other vertical forest buildings, two of Boeri's more ambitious plans encompass entire city districts. Liuzhou Forest City in Guangxi, China, will cover a 175-hectare space and house 30,000 inhabitants, 40,000 trees, and one million plants from more than 100 different species.[11] While his Smart Forest City, a 557-hectare development in Cancun, Mexico, will be home to 130,000 people with 7.5 million plants covering every possible surface—from rooftops to building facades.[12] While both projects remain to be completed, they offer an intriguing vision of urban life—one surrounded by nature, with reduced emissions, cleaner air, and cooler temperatures, not to mention greater biodiversity.

Easyhome Huanggang Vertical Forest City complex in China, completed in 2021. (Source: Stefano Boeri Architetti)

There are many other examples of urban forests in Asia's megacities, thanks to the tropical climate and a decade-long construction boom. Designer Thomas Heatherwick's 1,000 Trees development in Shanghai features tree planters atop the giant internal columns that hold up the mixed-use development. Ronald Lu & Partners' Treehouse concept, which won the World Green Building Council's Advancing Net Zero competition, has integrated a giant chimney that captures wind from 200 meters above ground and funnels it down to an artificial wetland at the base of the building to reduce the interior temperature.[13] One of the most audacious ideas is Carlo Ratti Associati's Jian Mu Tower, designed for Chinese supermarket chain Wumart's Shenzhen headquarters. Described as the world's first "farmscraper," its walls host a vertical hydroponic farm that will produce an estimated 270,000 kg of food per year, enough to cover the needs of roughly 40,000 people while also offering shade to its residents.[14]

There is something slightly paradoxical about the idea of urban forests, given that the city is, in many respects, the ultimate manifestation of our separation from nature. Yet our ability to conquer or reject nature is very limited, as shown both on a macro level with the climate crisis and at the individual level with the increase in mental and physical health issues triggered by a lack of time in nature. Urban forests can help reconcile and reconnect us to the environment in the future normal, while also delivering a long list of environmental benefits.

Imagining the Future Normal

1. What if a top criterion for sellers and buyers of real estate shifted from location to prioritizing green building elements?
2. What if natural urban design features could spur other positive feedback loops, such as increased cycling and better mental health?
3. How might the appeal of cities be increased by urban forests, and how would they cope with an influx of new residents?

CHAPTER 26

NU-AGRICULTURE

What if we could make clean, abundant food for everyone out of thin air?

In the blockbuster book *Sapiens: A Brief History of Humankind,* Yuval Noah Harari made the eye-catching, if not controversial, argument that hunter-gatherers had a better quality of life *before* the Agricultural Revolution, enjoying lower rates of disease and greater diversity in their diet. As they settled permanently to grow crops, they had to adapt not just to a new diet, but also to a different level of physical activity. They went from "living a fairly comfortable life hunting and gathering," Harari explains, to "doing little from dawn to dusk other than taking care of wheat plants."[1]

It wasn't until the 1700s that the seed drill, the threshing machine, and many other agricultural machines began taking over the labor-intensive tasks farmers had been performing. Whether or not you agree with Harari, the very fact that you're able to read these words is because you are *not* working the land all day. Since before the Industrial Revolution, our entire modern societies have been built on consistently greater agricultural efficiency. While our global population has increased exponentially, an ever-smaller proportion of people produce our food. In rich countries like the United States and Germany, less than 2 percent of the labor force currently works in the agricultural sector.[2]

Despite—or perhaps because of—our efficient cultivation of the land, we now face new challenges. The global population is set to continue rising to 10 billion by 2050.[3] The majority of people are forecast to eat more than 3,000 calories per day by 2030.[4] Half of the world's habitable land is used for agriculture,[5] while more than one-fifth of the world's greenhouse gas emissions stem from agriculture.[6] Feeding so many people will require us to reconfigure our food system to meet demand and to dramatically reduce the negative impact it has on our planet.

We need another Agricultural Revolution.

Fortunately, new technologies are bringing this revolution about by making it possible to produce food in radically cleaner and more efficient ways. For example, Ted Duijvestijn and his brothers oversee 36 acres of data-rich, climate-controlled greenhouses in Pijnacker, Netherlands, where they grow 15 varieties of tomatoes in basalt and chalk fibers rather than soil. This scientific approach to agriculture has seen the Netherlands improbably become the world's number-two exporter of food, as measured by value, second only to the United States, which has 270 times its landmass.[7]

If you drive a couple of hours down to Poulainville in Northern France, a 130-foot-high warehouse contains hundreds of millions of *Tenebrio Molitor* beetles, cultivated in trays stacked to the ceilings of the "farm." Ÿnsect, the company that owns the warehouse, has raised a total of $425 million from investors—including Robert Downey Jr.'s FootPrint Coalition—to build what will be the world's largest insect vertical farm, capable of producing around 100,000 tons of insect protein for use in fish farms and animal feed.[8]

Kenyan entrepreneur Talash Huijbers is leading a similar initiative in her home nation, working with farmers to cultivate black soldier fly, naturally high in protein, as a locally sourced basis for animal feed. Her company, InsectiPro, has been featured as "a company of the future" by the World Bank and is also cultivating food products made from crickets for human consumption.[9]

InsectiPro founder Talash Huijbers with farmers on a Kenyan insect farm harvesting black soldier flies. (Source: InsectiPro)

In Chile, Agrourbana is the first vertical farming company in Latin America, working to build a large-scale pilot in the South American nation that can serve as a boost for the entire category of vertical farming in their nation. Founders Pablo Bunster Claudet and Cristián Sjögren come from the renewables industry and are optimistic about why the idea may flourish in their country: "It has so much to do with so many areas that need to be thought of in different ways: from land use to food, the way we eat, water use, energy use. Because renewables will be readily available, Chile actually has a head start on other regions, making it the perfect place."[10]

In the future, our food will increasingly come from companies like these that develop methods of producing food or nutrients that require little land, energy, and labor. As traditional production methods become challenged by extreme climate, this new food system will be not just more sustainable but soon also cheaper and safer, and it will be celebrated as a model worth replicating around the world.

Instigator: Solar Foods

Dr. Pasi Vainikka is more modern-day alchemist than farmer. His Finland-based company, Solar Foods, has developed a process that uses fermentation to produce Solein, a protein-rich flour-like powder, from water, CO_2, and renewable electricity. If that sounds fantastical, then you won't be surprised to hear that the concept was first explored by NASA in its efforts to understand how to produce food in extra-terrestrial environments without the same available resources as on Earth.[11]

> **The disconnection of food from agriculture—that's the secret to a sustainable food industry.**
>
> —Dr. Pasi Vainikka, CEO, Solar Foods[12]

In the 1973 dystopian sci-fi movie *Soylent Green*, overpopulation and climate collapse creates a world where the majority of people are reduced to eating Soylent Green, a synthetic wafer-like food product that purports to be made from plankton but turns out to be made from human remains. Stories like this have given many people a deep-rooted aversion to attempts to engineer our food system, as Rob Rhinehart, founder of Soylent (which produces "complete nutrition protein shakes"), freely admits.[13] Mindful of this resistance, Solar Foods is keen to emphasize that Solein is not a replacement for food itself. Instead, it is a revolutionary new *ingredient* that can empower us to make things we already love—pasta, cereals, breads, and more—with dramatically lower environmental impact.

The data behind Solein is mind-blowing. Producing one kilo of Solein protein requires *100 times* less water than plant-based methods and 500 times less than beef. One hectare of land produces 60 kilos of beef-based protein, 1,000 kilos of plant-based protein, and *60,000* kilos of Solein. The carbon footprint of beef per kilo of protein is 45 kilos, of plants it is 2 kilos, and of Solein it is just 400 grams.[14] The company is currently building its first factory, already known as Factory 01, in urban Copenhagen, where it will have a demonstration food bar to enable the public to try Solein-based items once it receives its food safety license from the European Food Safety Authority.[15] It is diners in Singapore, though, who may be the first to buy Solein-based food, after the Singapore Food Agency granted the novel ingredient regulatory approval in late 2022.[16]

Solar Foods is just one of several companies exploring this area. Air Protein, a startup founded by physicist Lisa Dyson, has created what it calls the "world's first air-based meat," a chicken substitute also made from CO_2 extracted from the air.[17] Similarly, Deep Branch, a startup based at the University of Nottingham in the United Kingdom, takes the CO_2 emissions from Drax, the United Kingdom's largest power station, and recycles it to produce animal feed.[18]

Before you get too excited about your next meal being carbon negative, it is worth noting that many of these technological advances are in the earliest stages and will need significant refinement before being able to feed the masses or solve the deep, systemic problems in our food system. Transformation of this sort doesn't happen overnight, and making food from air (and other similarly futuristic ideas) will obviously take time to see widespread use. As it does, we will all feel the impact of this next Agricultural Revolution as the ability for everyone to create clean, abundant food becomes the future normal.

Imagining the Future Normal

1. What role might each of us play in helping industries and the media to more frequently celebrate agriculture technology (AgTech) pioneers with the same level of attention currently offered mainly to Silicon Valley tech firms?

2. What changes to our diets and willingness to try unusual (but nutrient-rich) foods will be required for a host of new innovative foods to achieve widespread adoption?

3. How could ownership, or the relative importance of land, shift in our culture when we can literally make food from the air that is all around us?

CHAPTER 27

WASTE-FREE PRODUCTS

What if you could throw things away with a clean conscience?

For years now, scientists have been sounding the alarm on the dangers of glitter—none more loudly than scientists and environmental activists in Brazil. Every year, thousands of people fill the streets for Carnaval dressed in elaborate outfits and donning glitter—lots and lots of it—on their skin. That glitter eventually gets washed off, flowing down drains and polluting water sources. At Sao Paulo's 2018 celebration, the local beer brand Skol hosted the "Skol Station," which packed nearly a thousand people into its arena and, in true carnival fashion, featured a glitter shower. However, these were no ordinary sparkly microparticles. Skol's glitter shower was filled with biodegradable glitter, allowing carnival revelers to enjoy their tradition guilt-free.[1]

Decades ago, the plastic industry convinced us that we could consume as much plastic as we wanted, since so much of it could be recycled anyway. But today we know the war on plastic (and microplastics, after it all breaks down) will not be won by recycling. Cyrill Gutsch, founder of Parley for the Oceans and one of the world's most prominent anti-plastic campaigners, views recycling as "just a bandage and a translation from an old technology to a new one." The solution, he believes, lies in nontoxic materials. "I think biofabrication ... will replace pretty much everything in the next 10 years," he explains.[2]

Biotechnology is still slightly mythical. But we are on the verge of having the tools and skills to manipulate our physical world in ways never before possible, impacting countless fields from fashion to food.

Today, most fleece tops are made from synthetics that shed microplastics. The North Face released a fleece made from a patented plastic-free, animal-free, microbe-based Brewed Protein material from Spiber, a Japanese biotech startup.[3] Similarly, the material innovation company Cove designed water bottles made from polyhydroxyalkanoate (PHA), a plant-based biodegradable plastic alternative from RWDC Industries, an American chemical company. Just imagine if every one of the *trillion-plus* single-use bottles produced each year was made from this material.

Retailers are helping consumers buy waste-free products as well. The e-commerce site www.ZeroWasteStore.com was started by two eco-conscious entrepreneurs who wanted to create a way to make the "zero-waste lifestyle" less intimidating for people. The site sells everything from compostable dish brushes using ingredients from yucca and agave plants to biodegradable dental floss made from vegan bamboo fibers.

Sometimes the waste-free reinvention comes not from the products themselves but from the way they are packaged. Notpla (an abbreviation for "not plastic") is a startup founded in 2014 that has been offering a range of compostable packaging solutions made from seaweed—a material they describe as "one of nature's most renewable resources" because it is abundant, fast-growing, and doesn't require freshwater, land, or fertilizer.[4] Initiatives like this are being publicized and introduced to makers of all sorts of products through platforms such as Noissue—an online marketplace where product designers and startups of any size can find a waste-free packaging solution that allows them to deliver their products in a sustainable way and tangibly demonstrate their commitment to being good stewards of the environment.

In the waste-free future normal, more brands will capitalize on this growing consumer preference and the robust ecosystem that now exists to not only reimagine their existing products to be more sustainable, but also to rethink how these products are packaged and delivered to their customers.

Instigator: Vollebak

Vollebak is a fashion brand with a unique aspiration: to build clothes "from the future."[5] Its founders, twin brothers Steve and Nick Tidball, started by developing their "Relaxation Hoodie," a somewhat bizarre-looking top with a zip-up mesh full-face covering and pockets that help the wearer "hug" themselves. While unconventional, its science-backed features help trigger feelings of relaxation in the wearer. Their larger aspiration, though, was to reinvent how to make the most common product in the fashion industry: the everyday T-shirt.

Vollebak's Plant and Algae T-shirt challenges the fashion industry's most fundamental ideas on how clothes are produced. The T-shirt is made from sustainably certified wood pulp and plant-based linen, while the ink used for its graphic designs is made from algae. The algae oxidizes as the T-shirt is worn, leading the print on the front of the T-shirt to fade naturally over time. Customers can compost or bury the garment outside when they no longer want to wear it; if buried, the T-shirt decomposes in 12 weeks.[6]

> **We wanted to ... demonstrate that natural materials can be just as cutting-edge. Sustainability is simply a lot easier to understand when it involves feeding your old clothes to worms.**
>
> —Steve Tidball, Cofounder, Vollebak[7]

To commercialize their revolutionary Plant and Algae T-shirt, Vollebak has used a marketing strategy typically enlisted by companies like Tesla, Apple, and many other high-priced brands. The first step is to develop products at the top end of the market for price-insensitive, status-conscious, highly visible consumers (colloquially: woke rich celebrities). The aim is that the revenue from these early customers will generate profits that can be used to create products at lower prices for the mass market.

Vollebak Plant and Algae T-shirt. (Source: Vollebak)

Vollebak likely won't sell millions of T-shirts made of biodegradable materials. But H&M will. That is why it's a big deal that the behemoth of fast fashion is now selling clothes made from Circulose, a fully biodegradable cellulose made from recycled clothes. Unlike other recycled fabrics, Circulose textile fibers are the same quality as traditional virgin materials such as cotton, meaning clothing can be infinitely recycled. H&M has promised not to seek exclusivity on this new material, and it is encouraging others in the fast fashion industry to follow in its steps.[8]

Small startups like Vollebak that experiment with plant-based fibers and algae ink don't get subjected to the same level of scrutiny as big brands. But thanks to H&M, there are now thousands of people at H&M and other big brands diving into the life-cycle analyses and impact reports around Circulose and similar fibers, which can only be a good thing. There will be major challenges in transforming decades of linear industrial-scale production facilities toward ones designed for circularity. However, we are optimistic. Scaling is what big companies do well.

Everything is biodegradable on a long enough timeline. While these materials radically accelerate this process, it is important to remember that a product is only as good as its most rapidly biodegradable element. Details matter (that is precisely why Vollebak used algae-based ink in its T-shirts).

Yet the product itself is only part of the story. The products we use have typically created significant waste through the way they are packaged as well as the materials used in their creation. To realize a future normal where waste-free products are truly ubiquitous across many different industries, both products and packaging must be reinvented. We need scientists, packaging experts, startup founders, retailers, and builders of online marketplaces to all come together to make waste-free products a daily reality for all of us.

Imagining the Future Normal

1. What if you invested in finding novel materials for your products that leverage natural principles and processes to leave no lasting trace after consumption?

2. What products do you use most often that you discard the most, and can you seek out and support waste-free alternatives that exist or are emerging?

3. Which parts of your physical operations and products might be transformed by the synthetic biology revolution?

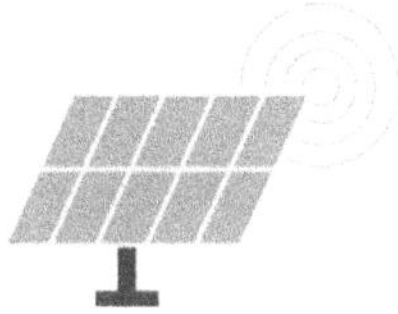

CHAPTER 28

MILLIONS OF MICROGRIDS

What if you could generate your own energy—reliably and cheaply?

Texas-based urologist Christopher Yang was ready to perform a vasectomy on a patient when the power to his clinic went down. As he was about to call the procedure off, one of his staff mentioned that Yang could power his electrocautery machine from his Rivian R1T truck's onboard power outlets. Yang discussed the solution with the patient, who was happy to proceed with what was probably the world's first electric vehicle–powered vasectomy in history.[1]

Not long ago, gas-guzzling Humvees and trucks went from being the height of cool to painfully embarrassing and passé. Driving a Toyota Prius and then a Tesla became the new status symbols. But the next generation of all-electric pickup trucks are flipping the narrative back toward the idea that bigger is better. Like the Rivian R1T, these trucks can double as giant power packs, sending energy back to their owners' homes—or medical clinics—if and when it is needed. These oversized vehicles are a perfect example of how advances in battery technology, combined with breakthroughs in solar and other renewables, are radically reshaping how we generate energy and our system as a whole.

For decades, people in advanced economies have given little thought to where their power comes from. We flip the switch, and the lights come on. But the structure of a traditional energy grid—a hulking, dirty power station that burns fossil fuels to generate electricity and distribute it via power cables strung across the landscape into people's homes—is becoming a potential liability rather than a core infrastructure asset. Climate change is the big danger here. Once-in-a-generation natural disasters—hurricanes, winter storms, wildfires, flooding—have become annual events that are more ferocious and costly than ever.[2] From Asian heat waves to Florida hurricanes and repeated flooding across Europe, these events are causing massive power outages and disruption to electrical grids around the world.

As the cracks in our aging centralized energy grids become ever more apparent, renewable energy technologies are getting exponentially better, cheaper, and more available. The cost of solar energy fell over 80 percent in the decade after 2010,[3] far faster than anyone had predicted (a salutary lesson in forecasting the future ... optimism *is* sometimes justified!). Solar, along with other renewables such as wind and hydroelectric power, made up two-thirds of the new electricity generating capacity added in the United States in 2022.[4] Our ability to capture and store all this "clean" energy (produced without burning fossil fuels) is also improving as battery capacity increases while costs fall dramatically, thanks to major investments in battery-dependent electric vehicles (EVs) and smartphones. Batteries promise truly domestic-level decentralized power systems or microgrids, combining to create utility-scale power banks that can support commercial sites, or even entire communities.[5]

While today microgrids are often deployed in extreme situations or at-risk areas, in the future normal it will be commonplace for people and communities to generate and store energy locally, creating a radically cleaner, cheaper, and more resilient energy system.

Instigator: Tesla's Solar Powerwall System

Launched in 2015, Tesla's Powerwall lithium-ion battery packs popularized the idea that residential customers could store the solar energy they were producing with their panels. Until then, whatever excess energy the panels captured during the day would essentially be fed back into the system, often without any financial benefit to the owner of the solar panels. Despite this one-sided system and the early criticism the technology faced as being a "toy for rich green people,"[6] in May 2021, Tesla announced it had sold 200,000 Powerwalls—half of them in the previous year—suggesting awareness of the benefits of domestic energy resilience had spiked.[7]

Tesla Powerwall. (Source: Roschetzky Photography / Shutterstock.com)

Then in 2021, Tesla's Virtual Power Plant initiative upped the game for its California Powerwall customers, allowing them to opt into a program that lets them *sell* power back to PG&E, the utility company serving two-thirds of California, during what it defines as "load management events"—when it needs help managing energy demand spikes. During an August 2022 heatwave, energy demand was so high that thousands of participating Powerwall owners were able to sell power back to PG&E,[8] helping to keep the lights on for everyone while earning real money for themselves. Powerwall owner Mark Gillund reported making over $500 during a single week of the heat wave, more than the monthly loan payments to finance the solar system in his home.[9]

> **[Solar panels are] like having a money printer on your roof if you live in a state with high electricity costs.**
>
> —Elon Musk, CEO, Tesla[10]

Tesla's solar panels and batteries are not the only products offering people improved energy resilience. Announced in May 2021, Ford's all-electric Lightning edition of its iconic F150 truck contains multiple 120-volt and a single 240-volt outlet. The extended range model, with its 131-kilowatt-hour battery, offers almost 10 times the capacity of a Tesla Powerwall, producing and storing enough power to run a typical home for three days of normal use—or up to 10 days if power is being rationed in an emergency.[11]

Solar power batteries and all-electric vehicles allow *individuals* to generate, store, and in some cases, sell back power to the grid. But upfront costs and logistics make this approach inaccessible to many. Community-scale mini-grids are popping up to solve this problem. Intriguingly, some of the first examples of these community mini-grids were found in emerging markets where connections to traditional electric grids are patchy or nonexistent. Backed by industry giant Shell, Husk Power Systems was founded in 2014 to install microgrids across rural areas, particularly in Africa and Asia. By late 2020, it was the first company in the world to install 100 community mini-grids, which are typically able to power an average of 50 microenterprises—shops, small factories, agricultural processors, schools, and other public services. Its combination of solar, biomass (sourced from local agricultural waste), and batteries mean that the systems can generate power 24/7.[12]

Husk is not the only startup connecting people to localized clean energy sources. In 2010 Pakistan-American entrepreneur Shazia Khan launched EcoEnergy to lease solar systems to rural customers without electricity,* serving over 20,000 people. A key reason for their early success is an innovative pay-as-you-go business model, which enabled EcoEnergy to control systems remotely and customers to make digital monthly payments.[13] The company recently expanded into additional markets and is now launching a digital platform to finance solar and smart home improvements.

Similar initiatives are now popping up in more "developed" markets. Syd Kitson is the eco real estate developer behind Babcock Ranch, a purpose-built community in southwest Florida that calls itself "America's first solar-powered town." When Hurricane Ian hit the state and knocked out power for 2.6 million customers, the lights stayed on for Babcock Ranch's 2,000 households thanks to the storm-resistant design of its community solar array.

If you want to gaze further into the future of microgrids, Seaborg's Power Barges might offer a glimpse. The company is reimagining nuclear energy by creating smaller, cheaper, and modular next-generation nuclear reactors on floating barges. Seaborg argues its

---

****Disclaimer:*** *One of the authors of this book (Rohit) is an advisor and investor in EcoEnergy.*

approach is safer than its counterparts on land because its reactors do away with solid fuel rods that require constant cooling. Instead, the fuel in its reactors is mixed into a liquid fluoride salt that acts as the coolant. Should this salt come into contact with the atmosphere, it would cool and turn to rock, capturing the radioactive material within it. Seaborg plans to launch its first barge in 2028.[14]

All this innovation points to some profound shifts. Changing how our most basic infrastructure works—with millions of microgrids that are clean and decentralized—will do more than just change where we source our power: it will change how much responsibility we personally feel to generate our own energy ... and how conscious we are about how we use that energy in the first place.

Imagining the Future Normal

1. What if individuals who generate excess energy were not only able to monetize it, but also direct its usage toward specific individuals or nonprofits?
2. What role might energy entrepreneurs play in an economy where anyone with the right tools could become a net producer of energy as a commodity?
3. How might the way that we use (and conserve) energy shift if people knew the energy they used was sourced locally?

CHAPTER 29

MAKING WEATHER

What if humanity could control the weather to fight the effects of global warming?

It started with an eruption. Literally. In 1991, Mount Pinatubo in the Philippines erupted with such force that the ash plume rose 28 miles into the air—so high that it penetrated the stratosphere. It was the second largest eruption of the 20th century, leaving more than 200,000 people homeless and an estimated death toll in the thousands. Scientists studying the volcano's aftermath were surprised to discover that the particles that entered the high atmosphere had the unexpected side effect of measurably cooling the entire planet for more than a year after the eruption.[1] The revelation seemed to offer a tantalizing solution to our rapidly warming world. Why not recreate the effects of that eruption *on purpose* and solve global warming?

The problem, of course, is that the science required to make that happen is hardly so simple. But also, the idea introduces a host of other questions, especially ethical ones. The unfortunate truth is that cooling the planet, if we could do it, wouldn't benefit everyone equally. The hottest places suffering from drought and heat waves would likely experience a relief, while other regions may end up suffering more disruptive weather patterns that affect crops or life.

Attempting to change our climate by recreating the effects of a volcanic eruption would not be the first time that we have tried to imagine how to manipulate our weather either. American military history is filled with stories of questionable ethical incursions using cloud seeding—the practice of dispersing particles into clouds to make it rain. During the Cold War, research into weather manipulation raised so many red flags that one American military commander even suggested that the "results could be even more disastrous than nuclear warfare."[2] His concern seems justified when you consider the research was originally started years earlier to study the use of cloud seeding to cause downpours and monsoons that could destroy roads and flood rivers in Vietnam during the US invasion of the country. Thankfully, the project was shut down after public discovery and outcry.

The lasting skepticism around initiatives like this has shaped public perception of weather modification efforts since the 1950s. Today the issues continue, but for different reasons. Since the year 2000, cloud seeding has been featured in the media, mainly because it has been used by governments and the super-rich to prevent rain before major events. The Beijing government used it to guarantee no rain during the 2008 Olympic opening ceremonies; while private firms use cloud seeding to prevent rain on wealthy clients' big wedding days for the going rate of $100,000.[3] The bottom line is that the most visible form of weather modification, cloud seeding, has largely been explored for either frivolous reasons or potentially deadly ones.

As scientists increasingly study this and other forms of weather modification technologies, ethical questions will continue to rise with them. For example, an idea for "ocean fertilization," the practice of dispersing iron into the world's oceans as a way to create more carbon dioxide absorbing algae blooms,[4] has inspired concerns about unintended consequences among scientists—such as whether we may be introducing an imbalance in the ecosystem that we may not be able to measure until it becomes irreversible.

Solar geoengineering—the idea that we can cool the Earth by reflecting solar radiation back to space—is technically quite straightforward and may even be relatively affordable to do. Yet the same people who spend the most time studying the prospect of using it also hope humanity will never need to use it ... exactly *because* of the risks involved. What if we are too successful and cool the Earth too much?*

Given the concerns around weather modification technologies, why not ban them altogether? One reason is that it will be hard to summon the political will to suppress them. Their perceived dangers lie in the unintended consequences that changing our planet's ecosystem in some areas may unleash on others. The larger reason that even well-intentioned scientists reluctantly continue to explore weather modification technologies is because humanity may not have a choice but to use them.

As the world continues to warm, there is a possibility that we may need this option as a last-resort emergency plan. Anote Tong, former president of the tiny island nation of Kiribati—a country of small atolls spread across more than one million square miles in the central Pacific—initially described geoengineering as "a prime example of our arrogance in our capacity to shape nature to our whims with technology. It should not be the answer to a disaster which we have caused and now seek to remedy."[5] Yet even he admits using these technologies may be necessary, based on the assumption

* This exact scenario is starkly depicted in the sci-fi film and ensuing TV series *Snowpiercer*.

that "there will be a point when it has to be either geoengineering or total destruction."[6] Or does it have to be?

In the future normal, more and more scientists and innovators will study how to wield control of the weather incrementally and responsibly to decrease the impact of global warming. The good news is that there are already people proposing methods to exert this type of control over weather in ways that could be more equitable for all and be completed with less risk of adverse effects.

Instigator: Refreezing the Arctic

In early 2019, the renowned Association of Siamese Architects issued an unusual call for entries for their annual architecture design competition. The theme of the contest was "Uncanny Sustainability," and entrants were challenged to share fresh ideas that were "so radical, unanticipated, and transformative they earn the epithet 'uncanny.'"[7]

3D rendering of the Arctic ice-making submarine concept. (Source: Association of Siamese Architects Competition)

One of the winning entries that year was a bold program for the "re-iceberg-isation" in the Arctic.[8] Led by then 29-year-old Indonesian architect Faris Rajak Kotahatuhaha, the idea involved building a ship that could be submerged in ice-cold waters to produce

16-foot-thick, 82-foot-wide hexagonal icebergs. The hexagonal shape, according to Kotahatuhaha, might allow these "ice babies," as he called them, to interlock and eventually create new icebergs to replace those that are melting.[9]

> **Richer countries have millions to spend on [sea walls and] protection, but what about poor countries with no budget for [defending against] rising sea levels? This is a problem the world now faces together. We have a different approach: Rather than defending against sea level rises, we think it's better [to carry out] some kind of intervention to tackle the problem.**
>
> —Faris Rajak Kotahatuhaha, Architect[10]

Experts suggest that ideas such as re-iceberg-isation will reflect more sunlight since white snow and ice are more reflective than open water. When more sunlight is reflected, it creates the effect of cooling the Earth. This is why melting icebergs present such a large potential threat to humanity—because the more they melt, the more heat from the sun our planet must absorb, which warms the planet.

That may be why there are a growing number of groups exploring similar ideas. One example is Real Ice, a team of social entrepreneurs who are working to build re-icing machines that can be deployed, maintained, and operated by indigenous people of the Arctic regions.[11] According to For Tomorrow, a platform dedicated to promoting ideation of grassroots sustainable solutions to today's problems, these wind-powered re-icing machines can increase ice thickness, which in turn will reflect more of the sun's rays, thereby helping to cool the Earth and reduce the impact of global warming.[12]

Depending on your perspective, the very idea of "making" weather or even controlling climate at this scale might seem hopelessly naïve or monumentally ill-advised. Human efforts to exhibit this sort of control over nature have not typically ended well in real life, or in dystopian movies. At the same time, humanity may come to a moment where we truly have no choice. These technologies might be our best or only option for survival. Putting this science-fiction scenario aside, the conclusion we came to while writing this book is that this topic was both necessary and urgent for us to explore. We may never encounter an urgent need for these technologies to become operational. It is, however, good to know they could be ready if we ever do need to use them.

Imagining the Future Normal

1. What would need to happen before it is necessary to use geoengineering, and what role should the general public have in this decision?
2. Could more widespread knowledge about how weather control could mitigate natural disasters help more people accept it, or will weather manipulation always be received with worry and fear?
3. What if the successful development of weather modification incentivizes governments and industries to scale back on sustainability efforts?

CHAPTER 30

BEYOND NET ZERO

What if companies aimed beyond going carbon neutral and toward being actively regenerative?

For most of us, July 28, 2022, was an ordinary day. But for the team at the Global Footprint Network, it marked a sobering watershed moment. Since 1971, the organization has identified the day of the year when humans have used all the biological resources that the Earth regenerates during the entire year. That first year, the "Earth Overshoot Day," as they called it, fell on December 25. Back then, we almost made it through the year. In 2022, Earth Overshoot Day fell on July 28, meaning that in just two generations, our consumption almost doubled.[1] In half a century, we've moved from having a global economy that was barely sustainable to one that's wholly *unsustainable.*

Some companies, however, are reinventing how they fight back. For example, the shoe brand Vivobarefoot, a certified B Corporation, has made a commitment not just to reduce the biological resources it uses but to create a *positive* environmental and social impact. As the company's 2021 impact report, *Unfinished Business,* states, "Vivobarefoot isn't just about doing less bad. Instead, we want our footwear and the way we do business to do more good. Every time we make and sell our footwear, we want the world to step towards a better place."[2]

Vivobarefoot Ultra III Bloom shoes made from EVA algae foam with biodegradable packaging bag. (Source: Vollebak)

To that end, Vivobarefoot was the first of dozens of footwear brands to partner with algae technology startup Bloom to use their patented BLOOM foam, which takes harmful algae blooms out of waterways, reversing the effects of water pollution. The partnership is one way the brand is trying to go beyond the usual sustainability practice of sourcing recycled materials to reverse the impact of their products on the environment.[3]

In another example of a commitment to creating a sustainable economy by reversing the impact of their business on the planet, in 2022 the founder of Patagonia, Yvon Chouinard, transferred his stake in the company into the Patagonia Purpose Trust and a private foundation, the Holdfast Collective. Doing so is an attempt to legally guarantee that the financial profits of the business—which currently equate to approximately $100 million a year—are used to fight the environmental crisis and defend nature.[4] The brand's corporate venture fund, Tin Shed Ventures, also targets its investments toward startups that do more good than harm for the planet and can generate "Returns for Nature" in its focus areas of regenerative agriculture, biodiversity, and Patagonia's apparel supply chain.

Turning to another sector, commercial flooring manufacturer Interface has announced a bold vision to reverse global warming, one carpet tile at a time. The flooring industry has long been criticized for how much of its used products end up in landfills. Eliminating this waste might not be feasible currently (although see Waste-Free Products on p. 239 to see how this is changing), so instead, Interface decided to focus their efforts on going carbon negative by adopting a manufacturing process that captures more carbon than it uses. Under this model, every carpet tile made would have a net positive impact on the environment: the more product the brand makes, the more positive impact they have, at least in terms of carbon emissions.[5]

This push for carbon negative products can be seen in a growing range of industries. Numerous building materials, from bricks to wood, are now being manufactured with carbon negative processes. New York–based Air Company uses solar energy to heat and transform carbon dioxide into luxury goods. Their flagship product, a carbon negative vodka, is promoted as the "world's cleanest, highest quality and most sustainable spirit."[6] Soft knitwear brand Sheep Inc. calls itself the first carbon negative clothing brand and sends customers regular updates about the sheep that provided the wool for the products they purchased.[7]

In this book, we have written about carbon-counting programs and the efforts of businesses in a wide range of industries to mitigate the environmental damage of their production courses. As we write this final chapter in our exploration of the future normal, it seems fitting to focus on the emerging cadre of regenerative businesses attempting to go beyond zero impact, aiming to create products and services that actually do good. In the future normal, we will see an acceleration in brands that go carbon negative, regenerate the environment, and leave a positive legacy on the planet. To see how much of an impact these regenerative businesses could have, we can start by examining the efforts of one of the largest brands in the world.

Instigator: IKEA's Climate-Positive Vision

If you've ever shopped at an IKEA store for furniture, chances are you walked away with its iconic low-cost bookcase—the Billy. Introduced in 1978, the world's bestselling bookcase has sold over 120 million units, and the BBC estimates there is nearly one for every 100 human beings.

New redesign for IKEA's iconic Billy bookcase. (Source: IKEA)

In 2022, IKEA announced that it would make tweaks to the bookcase to improve its circularity (a term that describes a product life cycle that eliminates waste at all stages). They replaced its plastic veneer with a paper foil, improving its recyclability and swapping out a fossil fuel–based material with one made from a renewable resource. And the nails used to attach the back panel have also been replaced with snap fittings, meaning it is now possible to disassemble and reassemble the bookcase, extending its potential life span.[8]

Reconfiguring its popular bookcase is just one of many initiatives that the global furniture retailer has undertaken to lessen its carbon footprint. Given IKEA alone generates a staggering 0.1 percent of the world's annual greenhouse gas emissions, the company has perhaps felt compelled to set one of the most ambitious environmental goals of any business: a commitment to become climate *positive* by 2030. Achieving this metric will require an average 70 percent reduction in each product's climate footprint, along with many other nonproduct-related shifts. To start reducing emissions across its supply chain, the company is leveraging its scale to incentivize suppliers in Poland, India, and China to switch to renewable energy, and is supporting the mandate by investing €100 million to subsidize loans for suppliers' capital investments.[9]

> **It isn't just a survival question for the planet, it's a survival question for businesses too.**
>
> —Jesper Brodin, CEO, Ingka Group[10]

Reducing carbon dioxide emissions is just one area where businesses are focusing on becoming regenerative. Industries that rely on natural resources, such as food and fashion, can do the same by ensuring that they leave the ecosystems where their products and materials are sourced from in better condition than they found them.

This goal has been taken up by some of the biggest food producers in the world. PepsiCo plans to convert its entire agricultural footprint, over seven million acres, to regenerative farming practices by

2030.[11] "This is not a corporate social responsibility program," Jim Andrew, the company's chief sustainability officer, explains. "It's a fundamental, center-of-the-plate business transformation of what we're doing."[12] The company is collaborating with Unilever in Iowa, where the two companies source corn and soy, respectively, to offer financial and technical support for farmers who are working toward improving soil health via crop rotation programs.

In the fashion industry, brands are lining up behind various collective and individual regenerative initiatives. Ralph Lauren has pledged $5 million to the Soil Health Institute's US Regenerative Cotton Fund (USRCF).[13] Luxury giant Kering, which owns Gucci, Balenciaga, and Saint Laurent (among many others), launched its Regenerative Fund for Nature in 2021 with the aim of converting one million hectares of land to regenerative farming practices. Its first grants went to goat shepherds in Spain, women-led communal grazing associations in the Maloti-Drakensberg Mountains in South Africa, and smallholder cattle producers in Argentina.[14] Sometimes governments are getting involved too, as is the case with the Regenerative Fashion Manifesto, which emerged from the Prince of Wales's Fashion Task Force. The initiative has secured the commitment of brands such as Burberry, Giorgio Armani, Stella McCartney, and Zalando to embrace regenerative practices.[15]

The path to becoming a regenerative business is not easy. It might even be impossible, given the multiple impacts that *every* organization has on the environment. It is seductive to focus on carbon emissions and net zero pledges. Reducing an organization's carbon emissions to zero or even beyond *is* meaningful. But as we draw this aspirational overview of the future normal to a close, we believe we should aim even higher. Carbon emissions are not the only problem we face. Biodiversity, poverty and inequality, ill health. These are huge and thorny problems. Even if an organization can't be universally regenerative, in the future normal, more will aspire to be as close to it as possible—environmentally, socially, and economically. As the artist Michelangelo famously said, "The greatest danger for most of us is not that our aim is too high and we miss it, but that it is too low and we reach it."[16]

Imagining the Future Normal

1. How might your company behave differently if you could quantify your impact across various regenerative dimensions?
2. What are some ways in which your industry could become regenerative?
3. What if your company's legal structure committed you to consider other stakeholders beyond your shareholders?

CONCLUSION

THE FUTURE WILL BE NORMAL

Writing about the future can feel a bit like writing a step-by-step guide to falling down the stairs ... an exercise in futility that will end badly. Most people will tell you—as many told us during the writing process—the future is inherently unpredictable. No one *knows* what is going to come next. After spending more than two decades collectively working in the field of futurism surrounded by incessant predictions about everything you can imagine (and things many of us cannot), we know this isn't entirely true.

The future, in some ways, is *always* predictable. If you know how to read the signs, anticipating the likely outcome can be akin to predicting what will happen in a formulaic romantic comedy. The heroes will go through angst and misunderstandings, but you know they eventually will end up together. The future normal can be a little bit like that. Not as easy to predict as Hollywood tropes, but not impossible either. As we wrote in the introduction, there are two reasons for this. First, signs of the "future" are always here, already in the present. And second, for most of us "normal" remains remarkably stable even as the world around us changes. Even futurist Jim Dator, whose suggestion that the future must always "appear to be ridiculous" that we shared in the introduction went on to write that any future that "typically seems at first obscene, impossible, stupid, 'science-fiction,' [or] ridiculous ... becomes familiar and eventually 'normal.'"[1]

In the course of writing this book, we had the opportunity to speak with many instigators who are shaping this coming normal in profound ways. Some of them understood the potential impact of their contributions. Many others, hyper-focused on their work, didn't spend much time pondering the future beyond their field of vision. This book is an intentional compendium of their stories. If the span of topics covered felt overwhelming as you read them, you will easily understand the awesome sense of responsibility we felt to properly convey the work of these innovators in an approachable and cohesive way. Early on, we chose to focus only on the topics we felt have the most potential to create a more hopeful and optimistic future.

We recognize that even being able to have that perspective is a sign of our privilege. And we remain mindful that a positive future is not a foregone conclusion. We know all too well that nearly every instigator or innovation presented in this book has many possible outcomes. And some might take a turn toward the dark side or create unintended consequences.

At the end of each chapter, we tried to confront this truth by posing discussion questions to spark debate. It may be easy to feel unaffected by some innovations if you don't work in the same industry they operate or aren't on the front lines of using them. But we believe every idea in this book will eventually impact each of us, no matter where we work or what generation, gender, or mindset we identify with. Respecting this shared human nature is often the real key to understanding the future normal.

There's no doubt we *are* surrounded by huge changes and keeping up with them can feel daunting. During the writing of this book, AI went from something we wrote about to a tool we use daily. No one is immune to the accelerating gales of technological and cultural reinvention.

But if you look back through history, you will see that many of our fundamental motivations barely change over centuries. The need to be secure. The desire to be loved and to appear successful to those around us. The quest to discover ourselves and develop as individuals. These are the deeply human needs and wants that are as present in the plays of Shakespeare as they are today in the 21st century.

The secret to seizing emerging opportunities has always been in bridging these two dimensions—embracing the new, while grounding it in what will not change. Amazon founder Jeff Bezos once observed: "I very frequently get the question: 'What's going to change in the next 10 years?' ... I almost never get the question—'What's *not* going to change in the next 10 years?'—And I submit to you that that second question is actually the more important of the two."[2]

While we might collectively suffer from the human and societal costs of Bezos' relentless pursuit of lower prices and faster delivery, more than any other billionaire he has consistently managed to profitably connect the future to the normal. Bezos also perfectly encapsulates the choice we are all confronted with today. Will we build a future normal that is safer, healthier, less wasteful, and more fulfilling for humanity? Can we choose the optimistic paths spotlighted by the instigators featured in this book? Or will we succumb to greed, implement technologies without considering their moral implications, and place profits over people?

The future normal will not be a story about technology. It will be about the ingenuity of people and what we can accomplish when we work together. More than anything else, this book is about the future we choose to imagine. Now it's up to all of us to make it ... normal.

ACKNOWLEDGMENTS

It's impossible to thank everyone who has contributed to this book. Alongside hundreds of formal interviews over the course of three years researching and writing this book, there were also countless informal conversations where an offhand observation planted the seed of an idea that ended up in these final pages. It has been a huge privilege to have been able to ask so many smart people, "What does the future normal look like to you?"

In addition, as prolific writers and creators ourselves—we also relied on the intelligent and constant voices of our readers. These weekly dialogues often opened our eyes to other perspectives we hadn't considered.

Beyond our communities, we must start by thanking our editor, Genoveva, who has been unfailingly patient and perceptive. Her ability to read our earliest drafts and help us to sharpen our arguments and develop our stories is second to none.

In addition, we had a wonderful array of editors, sensitivity readers, and fact-checkers all working on various drafts of this book, and all of them helped to improve it in some way. The journey to write this book also offered us the chance to make consistent use of the technology of the moment ... and across just the few years of our writing, it was fascinating how much this changed. In the early days we were going live, hosting impromptu discussions with strangers on a popular conversation app called Clubhouse. In the waning days of final editing, we turned to generative AI tools like ChatGPT to improve our arguments by asking it to generate critical reviews of our writing. After that experience, we can now confirm that getting a one-star review stings no less when generated by a computer.

The process of writing this book, in other words, was instructive in helping us define and reveal what the future normal might be because we have lived it every day.

Going back to our human support team, we also owe our thanks to Kameron, whose keen eye and attention to detail helped ensure the finished book came together on time.

To Marnie, Megan, Jessica, Rich, Athena, and the rest of the Ideapress team, thank you for being constant professionals and ensuring that the book looks and feels just as beautiful as we had hoped now that we can finally hold it in our hands.

Henry would also like to thank Brent, Greg, Amali, Carolyn, Sian, and Reinier. Thank you for your support and for introducing me to so many of the brilliant innovators featured in the book.

Rohit would like to thank his speaking team of Renee, Katie, and Lindsay, as well as all the event managers and fellow speakers from events around the world whose pioneering voices offered a regular reminder that the smartest insights aren't just original ... they are also best told and remembered as stories.

Henry's biggest thanks must go to his wife, Anita:

I couldn't be prouder of the work that you have done during the pandemic as a doctor on the front line, and then last year when you gave birth to our beautiful daughter. To be able to do both of those things while still humoring and supporting me while I have been working on this book is truly incredible. I can't thank you enough for your patience and for everything that you do for our whole family. I know that our future will continue to be extraordinary.

Similarly, Rohit would like to thank his wife, Chhavi:

Our journey over the past decade has been amazing—launching a virtual summit together, cofounding a publishing company (Ideapress!), and even authoring a book on diversity and our definitely underappreciated "Naan-Obvious" cookbook. Through it all, you've been a partner in every sense for me on this project and all others. Our future normal is so much better because we're on this ride together.

And finally, both of us are indebted to the next generation of Bhargavas and Coutinho-Masons: Rohan, Jaiden, Jago, and Dahlia. We are eternally grateful for your relentless inspiration and curiosity. For you, the instigators in this book are not the future, they will just be normal. And we suspect you'll be right at home among them.

APPENDIX A

INDUSTRY PLAYLISTS

What trends matter most for my industry? That's the question we are routinely asked most often ... and usually one we are reluctant to answer. There is magic to be found in reading insights that seem on the surface to be unconnected to the work you do. Serendipity comes from these presumed "useless" ideas, as they are often the ones that spark the freshest insights.

Yet we understand the desire for curation, and the truth is there are some chapters that are easier to act on for those in specific industries. This section highlights our suggestions for which chapters to read first based on 14 major sectors. While you will undoubtedly find value in reading other chapters too, this is a good starting point and a way to make the book more immediately actionable. Good luck on your journey to imagining your own future normal!

INDUSTRY PLAYLISTS

CLIMATE & ENVIRONMENT

- Ambient Health
- Unnaturally Better
- Calculated Consumption
- Good Governing
- Urban Forests
- Nu-Agriculture
- Waste-Free Products
- Millions of Microgrids
- Making Weather
- Beyond Net Zero

CONSULTING & CREATIVE SERVICES

- Multiversal Identity
- Immersive Entertainment
- Certified Media
- Augmented Creativity
- Remote Work for All
- Work Deconstructed
- Reflective Cultures
- Psychedelic Wellness
- Impact Hubs
- The 15-Minute City

CONSUMER, RETAIL & FASHION

- Multiversal Identity
- Reflective Cultures
- Big Brand Redemption
- Unnaturally Better
- Calculated Consumption
- Guilt-Free Indulgence
- Secondhand Status
- Inhuman Delivery
- Waste-Free Products
- Beyond Net Zero

EDUCATION

- Multiversal Identity
- Immersive Entertainment
- Certified Media
- Stealth Learning
- Ambient Health
- Augmented Creativity
- Good Governing
- Impact Hubs
- The 15-Minute City
- Virtual Companionship

ENTERTAINMENT, MEDIA & ART

- Multiversal Identity
- Immersive Entertainment
- Certified Media
- Virtual Companionship
- Augmented Creativity
- Stealth Learning
- Work Deconstructed
- Impact Hubs
- Reflective Cultures
- New Collectivism

FINANCIAL SERVICES & INSURANCE

- Certified Media
- Stealth Learning
- Ambient Health
- Millions of Microgrids
- Work Deconstructed
- Reflective Cultures
- Impact Hubs
- Big Brand Redemption
- New Collectivism
- Making Weather

FOOD & BEVERAGE

- Metabolic Monitoring
- Unnaturally Better
- Calculated Consumption
- Guilt-Free Indulgence
- Inhuman Delivery
- Big Brand Redemption
- Nu-Agriculture
- Waste-Free Products
- Making Weather
- Beyond Net Zero

GOVERNMENT, NGOS & NONPROFITS

Certified Media	Ending Loneliness	Work Deconstructed	Impact Hubs	New Collectivism	Good Governing	The 15-Minute City	Reflective Cultures	Stealth Learning	Millions of Microgrids

HEALTH CARE & PHARMA

Ending Loneliness	Virtual Companionship	Psychedelic Wellness	Ambient Health	Green Prescriptions	Metabolic Monitoring	Work Deconstructed	Unnaturally Better	Urban Forests	Waste-Free Products

REAL ESTATE

Immersive Entertainment	Ending Loneliness	Ambient Health	Remote Work for All	Impact Hubs	The 15-Minute City	Inhuman Delivery	Urban Forests	Nu-Agriculture	Millions of Microgrids

SMALL BUSINESS & ENTREPRENEURSHIP

Secondhand Status	Stealth Learning	Augmented Creativity	Remote Work for All	Work Deconstructed	Impact Hubs	Guilt-Free Indulgence	New Collectivism	Inhuman Delivery	Millions of Microgrids

TECHNOLOGY, SOFTWARE & TELECOM

Immersive Entertainment	Certified Media	Stealth Learning	Augmented Creativity	Multiversal Identity	Work Deconstructed	Reflective Cultures	Impact Hubs	New Collectivism	Virtual Companionship

TRANSPORTATION & AUTOMOTIVE

Ending Loneliness	Ambient Health	Remote Work for All	Big Brand Redemption	Calculated Consumption	Guilt-Free Indulgence	The 15-Minute City	Inhuman Delivery	Millions of Microgrids	Beyond Net Zero

TRAVEL & HOSPITALITY

Multiversal Identity	Ambient Health	Immersive Entertainment	Beyond Net Zero	Calculated Consumption	Guilt-Free Indulgence	Impact Hubs	The 15-Minute City	Inhuman Delivery	Making Weather

ENDNOTES

INTRODUCTION

1 Cell Press. "Pure Novelty Spurs the Brain." *ScienceDaily,* 27 August 2006, www.sciencedaily.com/releases/2006/08/060826180547.htm. Accessed 14 Dec. 2022.

2 Hawaii Research Center for Futures Studies. "Publications." *University of Hawaii at Mānoa,* 2022, https://manoa.hawaii.edu/futures-center/publications/. Accessed 29 Dec. 2022.

CHAPTER 1: MULTIVERSAL IDENTITY

1 Vogue Business for Porsche. "Meet the Fashion Designers Specializing in the Art of Self-Expression." *Vogue Business,* 26 Nov. 2021, https://www.voguebusiness.com/fashion/meet-the-fashion-designers-specialising-in-the-art-of-self-expression. Accessed 14 Dec. 2022.

2 Adobe Communications. "The New-Era of Self Expression: How the Next Generation Are Tackling Social Media, Creativity and Authenticity." *Adobe Blog,* 5 July 2022, https://blog.adobe.com/en/publish/2022/07/05/new-era-of-self-expression-how-the-next-generation-are-tackling-social-media-creativity-and-authenticity. Accessed 14 Dec. 2022.

3 Yee, N. and Bailenson, J.N. "The Proteus Effect: Self Transformations in Virtual Reality." *Human Communication Research,* vol. 33, no. 3, pp. 271-290. *Virtual Human Interaction Lab,* https://stanfordvr.com/pubs/2007/the-proteus-effect-self-transformations-in-virtual-reality/. Accessed 14 Dec. 2022.

4 Takahashi, Dean. "Ready Player Me Launches API for Avatar Interoperability." *VentureBeat,* 11 Oct. 2022, https://venturebeat.com/games/ready-player-me-launches-api-for-avatar-interoperability/. Accessed 14 Dec. 2022.

5 Wright, Webb. "L'Oréal Teams Up with Ready Player Me to Launch Beauty Products in the Metaverse." *The Drum,* 16 Nov. 2022, https://www.thedrum.com/news/2022/11/16/l-or-al-teams-up-with-ready-player-me-launch-beauty-products-the-metaverse. Accessed 14 Dec. 2022.

6 Wiggers, Kyle. "Disney-Backed Inworld Raises New Cash for Its AI-Powered Virtual Characters." *TechCrunch,* 23 Aug. 2022, https://techcrunch.com/2022/08/23/disney-backed-inworld-raises-new-cash-from-for-its-ai-powered-virtual-characters/. Accessed 14 Dec. 2022.

7 Tõke, Timmu. "Q&A: The Future of Avatar Creation." *Samsung Next* [blog], 7 Nov. 2022, https://www.samsungnext.com/blog/q-a-timmu-toke-wolf3d. Accessed 14 Dec. 2022.

8 Willis, Katie. "The Same, but Better: How We Represent Ourselves through Avatars." *Phys.org,* 30 April 2019, https://phys.org/news/2019-04-avatars.html. Accessed 14 Dec. 2022.

CHAPTER 2: IMMERSIVE ENTERTAINMENT

1 Yahr, Emily. "How the Search for Clues in Taylor Swift's Music Became All-Consuming." *Washington Post,* 20 Oct. 2022, https://www.washingtonpost.com/arts-entertainment/2022/10/20/taylor-swift-midnights-easter-eggs/. Accessed 1 Dec. 2022.
2 Sax, David. *The Future Is Analog: How to Create a More Human World.* PublicAffairs, 15 Nov. 2022.
3 Passy, Charles. "Cheesy Entertainment or a Bold New Way to Experience Art? Either Way, Van Gogh 'Immersive' Shows Have Become a Money-Making Sensation." *MarketWatch,* 27 Dec. 2021, https://www.marketwatch.com/story/how-van-gogh-became-one-of-the-entertainment-worlds-biggest-stars-in-2021-11640638081. Accessed 1 Dec. 2022.
4 Trapman-O'Brien, Yannick. "Undersigned." *FringeArts,* 2022, https://fringearts.com/event/undersigned/2022-09-11/. Accessed 1 Dec. 2022.
5 Dawson, Brit. "ABBA Voyage Live in London: Groundbreaking Pop Meets Jaw-Dropping Spectacle." *Rolling Stone UK,* 27 May 2022, https://www.rollingstone.co.uk/music/abba-voyage-live-london-review-17858/. Accessed 1 Dec. 2022.
6 Moreton, Cole. "We Took a Chance, and Could Have Lost a Pile of... Money, Money, Money! ABBA's Bjorn Ulvaeus Reveals How the £140m Gamble the Band Took to Create Their Breathtaking Avatar Concert Almost Backfired Spectacularly." *Mail Online,* 11 Nov. 2022, https://www.dailymail.co.uk/femail/article-11403815/ABBAs-Bjorn-Ulvaeus-gamble-band-took-create-avatar-concert-backfired.html. Accessed 1 Dec. 2022.
7 Ramírez, Juan. "Abba Voyage Review: No Ordinary Abba Night at the Club." *New York Times,* 30 May 2022, https://www.nytimes.com/2022/05/30/arts/music/abba-voyage-review.html. Accessed 1 Dec. 2022.
8 Bronson, Fred. "ABBA's Live 'Voyage' Show Is Doing Big Numbers in London: 'We've Sold 380,000 Tickets,' Benny Andersson Reveals." *Variety,* 26 May 2022, https://variety.com/2022/music/news/abba-voyage-teicket-sales-benny-andersson-interview-1235278346/. Accessed 1 Dec. 2022.
9 Ibid.
10 Goldsmith, Jill. "Secret Cinema Acquired by TodayTix; Plans US Tour, Permanent LA Location for Immersive Film & TV Experiences." *Deadline,* 22 Sep. 2022, https://deadline.com/2022/09/secret-cinema-todaytix-stranger-things-guardians-of-the-galaxy-1235124658/. Accessed 1 Dec. 2022.

CHAPTER 3: CERTIFIED MEDIA

1 Cole, Samantha. "We Are Truly Fucked: Everyone Is Making AI-Generated Fake Porn Now." *Vice,* 24 Jan. 2018, https://www.vice.com/en/article/bjye8a/reddit-fake-porn-app-daisy-ridley. Accessed 1 Dec. 2022.
2 Sutton, Kelsey. "Hulu Deepfakes Football Stars' Faces onto Body Doubles in New Sellouts Ad." *Adweek,* 10 Sep. 2020, https://www.adweek.com/convergent-tv/hulu-deepfakes-football-stars-faces-onto-body-doubles-in-new-sellouts-ad/. Accessed 1 Dec. 2022.
3 Chua, Kyle. "PH Remains Top in Social Media, Internet Usage Worldwide—Report." *Rappler+,* 28 Jan. 2021, https://www.rappler.com/technology/

internet-culture/hootsuite-we-are-social-2021-philippines-top-social-media-internet-usage/. Accessed 1 Dec. 2022.

4 Snyder, Kristin. "Did TikTok Disinformation Just Decide the Next President of the Philippines?" *dot.LA*, 10 May 2022, https://dot.la/tiktok-misinformation-philippines-election-2657296510.html. Accessed 1 Dec. 2022.

5 Agence France-Presse. "Is South Korean the World's First Official Deepfake Candidate? Meet 'Ai Yoon', the Salty Ai Making the 2022 Presidential Election Interesting." *South China Morning Post*, 14 Feb. 2022, https://www.scmp.com/news/asia/east-asia/article/3166928/south-korean-worlds-first-official-deepfake-candidate-meet-ai. Accessed 1 Dec. 2022.

6 Halm, K.C., Kalinowski IV, C., Kumar, A., Segal, J. "Two New California Laws Tackle Deepfake Videos in Politics and Porn." *Davis Wright Tremaine Blog*, 11 Oct. 2019, https://www.dwt.com/blogs/artificial-intelligence-law-advisor/2019/10/california-deepfakes-law. Accessed 1 Dec. 2022.

7 Reuters Staff. "China Seeks to Root Out Fake News and Deepfakes with New Online Content Rules." *Reuters*, 29 Nov. 2019, https://www.reuters.com/article/us-china-technology/china-seeks-to-root-out-fake-news-and-deepfakes-with-new-online-content-rules-idUSKBN1Y30VU. Accessed 1 Dec. 2022.

8 Edelman. "20 Years of Trust." *Edelman*, 2022, https://www.edelman.com/20yearsoftrust/. Accessed 1 Dec. 2022.

9 Aral, S., Roy, D., Vosoughi, S. "The Spread of True and False News Online." *Science*, vol. 359, no. 6380, pp. 1146–1151, https://www.science.org/doi/10.1126/science.aap9559. Accessed 1 Dec. 2022.

10 GPT-3. "A Robot Wrote This Entire Article. Are You Scared Yet, Human?" *The Guardian*, 8 Sep. 2020, https://www.theguardian.com/commentisfree/2020/sep/08/robot-wrote-this-article-gpt-3. Accessed 1 Dec. 2022.

11 Pearson, James and Zinets, Natalia. "Deepfake Footage Purports to Show Ukrainian President Capitulating." *Reuters*, 17 Mar. 2022, https://www.reuters.com/world/europe/deepfake-footage-purports-show-ukrainian-president-capitulating-2022-03-16/. Accessed 1 Dec. 2022.

12 McCorvey, J.J. "This Image-Authentication Startup Is Combating Faux Social Media Accounts, Doctored Photos, Deep Fakes, and More." *Fast Company*, 19 Feb. 2019, https://www.fastcompany.com/90299000/truepic-most-innovative-companies-2019. Accessed 1 Dec. 2022.

13 Wilson, Mark. "One of the Strongest Ways to Fight Misinformation Will Soon Be Right in Your Phone." *Fast Company*, 15 Oct. 2020, https://www.fastcompany.com/90564299/one-of-the-strongest-ways-to-fight-misinformation-will-soon-be-right-in-your-phone. Accessed 1 Dec. 2022.

14 McCorvey, J.J. "This Image-Authentication Startup Is Combating Faux Social Media Accounts, Doctored Photos, Deep Fakes, and More." *Fast Company*, 19 Feb. 2019, https://www.fastcompany.com/90299000/truepic-most-innovative-companies-2019. Accessed 1 Dec. 2022.

15 Lowenstein, Scott. "Using Secure Sourcing to Combat Misinformation." *New York Times* R&D, 5 May 2021, https://rd.nytimes.com/projects/using-secure-sourcing-to-combat-misinformation. Accessed 1 Dec. 2022.

16 Fukuyama, Francis. *Trust: The Social Virtues and the Creation of Prosperity*. Free Press, 18 June 1996.

CHAPTER 4: STEALTH LEARNING

1 TikTok. "#LearnOnTikTok." *TikTok*, 2022, https://www.tiktok.com/tag/LearnOnTikTok. Accessed 1 Dec. 2022.

2 Hamer, Lars James. "China Version of TikTok Imposes Daily Time Limit for Kids." *That's*, 22 Sep. 2021, https://www.thatsmags.com/tianjin/post/33448/china-imposes-40-minute-daily-limit-forchildren-on-tiktok. Accessed 28 Dec. 2022.
3 Thoensen, Bryan. "Investing to Help Our Community #LearnOnTikTok." *TikTok*, 28 May 2020, https://newsroom.tiktok.com/en-us/investing-to-help-our-community-learn-on-tiktok. Accessed 1 Dec. 2022.
4 Anderson, Chris. "TED Curator Chris Anderson on Crowd Accelerated Innovation." *Wired*, 27 Dec. 2018, https://www.wired.com/2010/12/ff_tedvideos/. Accessed 1 Dec. 2022.
5 GVU Center. "Contextual Computing Group." *Georgia Tech GVU Center*, ND, https://gvu.gatech.edu/research/labs/contextual-computing-group. Accessed 4 Dec. 2022.
6 Roblox. "Reimagining the Way People Come Together." *Roblox Corporation*, 2022, https://corp.roblox.com/. Accessed 1 Dec. 2022.
7 Ponciano, Jonathan. "Roblox Valuation Hits $42 Billion as Gen-Z Gaming Giant Skyrockets 50% in Public Market Debut." *Forbes*, 10 Mar. 2021, https://www.forbes.com/sites/jonathanponciano/2021/03/10/roblox-valuation-hits-42-billion-as-gen-z-gaming-giant-skyrockets-50-in-ipo/?sh=377554353873. Accessed 4 Dec. 2022.
8 Fickling, David. "Roblox Is Overdue a Reckoning with Screen Time." *Bloomberg*, 17 Mar. 2021, https://www.bloomberg.com/opinion/articles/2021-03-17/roblox-must-heed-the-line-between-engagement-and-addiction-by-child-gamers?leadSource=uverify%20wall. Accessed 1 Dec. 2022.
9 The Economist Business. "Will Roblox's Thriving Virtual Economy Make It the Next Meme Stock?" *The Economist*, 13 Mar. 2021, https://www.economist.com/business/2021/03/13/will-robloxs-thriving-virtual-economy-make-it-the-next-meme-stock. Accessed 1 Dec. 2022.
10 Baszucki, David. "Introducing the Roblox Community Fund." *Roblox Blog*, 15 Nov. 2021, https://blog.roblox.com/2021/11/introducing-roblox-community-fund/. Accessed 1 Dec. 2022.
11 Kantar, Rebecca. "The Next Chapter of Teaching and Learning on Roblox." *Roblox Blog*, 15 Nov. 2021, https://blog.roblox.com/2021/11/next-chapter-of-teaching-and-learning-on-roblox/. Accessed 1 Dec. 2022.
12 Roblox. "A New Era of Teaching and Learning." *Roblox Corporation*, 2022, https://education.roblox.com/. Accessed 1 Dec. 2022.
13 Roblox. "Roblox Creates Free Digital Civility Curriculum; Launches Roblox Game as Engaging Tool for Educators to Teach Course Online." *Roblox Corporation*, 10 Sep. 2020, https://ir.roblox.com/news/news-details/2020/Roblox-Creates-Free-Digital-Civility-Curriculum-Launches-Roblox-Game-as-Engaging-Tool-for-Educators-to-Teach-Course-Online/default.aspx. Accessed 1 Dec. 2022.
14 Meta. "The Impact Will Be Real." *YouTube*, 15 June 2022, https://www.youtube.com/watch?v=80IIEnSNwQc. Accessed 1 Dec. 2022.
15 Mascarenhas, Natasha. "Labster Gets Millions from A16z to Bring Virtual Science Lab Software to the World." *TechCrunch*, 10 Feb. 2021, https://techcrunch.com/2021/02/10/labster-gets-millions-from-a16z-to-bring-virtual-science-lab-software-to-the-world/?guccounter=1. Accessed 1 Dec. 2022.
16 McMullan, Thomas. "The virtual Holocaust Survivor: How History Gained New Dimensions." *The Guardian*, 18 June 2016, https://www.theguardian.com/

technology/2016/jun/18/holocaust-survivor-hologram-pinchas-gutter-new-dimensions-history. Accessed 4 Dec. 2022.

CHAPTER 5: ENDING LONELINESS

1 Salem, Merryana. "'Old People's Home for Teenagers' Harnesses the Wholesome Power of Intergenerational Friendship." *Junkee,* 1 Sep. 2022, https://junkee.com/old-peoples-home-for-teenagers-review/340186#. Accessed 14 Dec. 2022.
2 National Academies of Sciences, Engineering, and Medicine. *Social Isolation and Loneliness in Older Adults: Opportunities for the Health Care System.* The National Academies Press, 2020, https://doi.org/10.17226/25663. Accessed 14 Dec. 2022.
3 Denworth, Lydia. "The Loneliness of the 'Social Distancer' Triggers Brain Cravings Akin to Hunger." *Scientific American,* 2 April 2020, https://www.scientificamerican.com/article/the-loneliness-of-the-social-distancer-triggers-brain-cravings-akin-to-hunger/. Accessed 14 Dec. 2022.
4 Ortiz-Ospina, Esteban. "Social Isolation Is Linked to Higher Mortality Rates and Illness." *World Economic Forum,* 30 July 2019, https://www.weforum.org/agenda/2019/07/why-loneliness-damaging-to-your-health. Accessed 14 Dec. 2022.
5 Newport Academy. "The Facts about Loneliness in Young People." *Newport Academy,* 15 May 2020, https://www.newportacademy.com/resources/well-being/loneliness-in-young-people/. Accessed 14 Dec. 2022.
6 University of Bath. "How 'Old People's Home for 4 Year Olds' Might Force a Shake-Up in Social Care." *University of Bath,* 2022, https://www.bath.ac.uk/case-studies/how-old-peoples-home-for-4-year-olds-might-force-a-shake-up-in-social-care/. Accessed 15 Dec. 2022.
7 The Innovation in Politics Institute. "Sällbo—Ending Loneliness by Living Together." *The Innovation in Politics Institute,* 2022, https://innovationinpolitics.eu/showroom/project/sallbo-ending-loneliness-by-living-together/. Accessed 14 Dec. 2022.
8 Savage, Maddy. "The Housing Project Where Young and Old Must Mingle." *BBC.com,* 14 Feb. 2020, https://www.bbc.com/worklife/article/20200212-the-housing-project-where-young-and-old-must-mingle. Accessed 14 Dec. 2022.
9 WSP. "Six out of Ten Swedes Feel Lonely—Most Common Among Young Adults and in Larger Cities." *WSP,* 5 Sep. 2019, https://www.wsp.com/sv-se/nyheter/2019/sex-av-tio-svenskar-kanner-sig-ensamma. Accessed 14 Dec. 2022.
10 Savage, Maddy. "The Housing Project Where Young and Old Must Mingle." *BBC.com,* 14 Feb. 2020, https://www.bbc.com/worklife/article/20200212-the-housing-project-where-young-and-old-must-mingle. Accessed 14 Dec. 2022.
11 Taylor, Juliet. "Kampung Admiralty: Singapore's First Integrated Vertical Retirement Community." *IndesignLive Asia,* 25 Mar. 2022, https://www.indesignlive.sg/segments/kampung-admiralty-design-architecture-history-more. Accessed 14 Dec. 2022.
12 Free, Cathy. "One Roommate Is 85, the Other Is 27. Such Arrangements Are Growing." *Washington Post,* 15 July 2022, https://www.washingtonpost.com/lifestyle/2022/07/15/multigenerational-housing-roommates-nesterly-senior/. Accessed 14 Dec. 2022.

CHAPTER 6: VIRTUAL COMPANIONSHIP

1 Wanqing, Zhang. "The AI Girlfriend Seducing China's Lonely Men." *Sixth Tone,* 7 Dec. 2020, https://www.sixthtone.com/news/1006531/the-ai-girlfriend-seducing-chinas-lonely-men. Accessed 1 Dec. 2022.

2 Ibid.

3 Spencer, Geoff. "Much More Than a Chatbot: China's Xiaoice Mixes AI with Emotions and Wins Over Millions of Fans." *Microsoft*, 1 Nov. 2018, https://news.microsoft.com/apac/features/much-more-than-a-chatbot-chinas-xiaoice-mixes-ai-with-emotions-and-wins-over-millions-of-fans/. Accessed 1 Dec. 2022.

4 Hornigold, Thomas. "This Chatbot Has Over 660 Million Users—and It Wants to Be Their Best Friend." *Singularity Hub,* 14 July 2019, https://singularityhub.com/2019/07/14/this-chatbot-has-over-660-million-users-and-it-wants-to-be-their-best-friend/. Accessed 1 Dec. 2022.

5 Wanqing, Zhang. "The AI Girlfriend Seducing China's Lonely Men." *Sixth Tone*, 7 Dec. 2020, https://www.sixthtone.com/news/1006531/the-ai-girlfriend-seducing-chinas-lonely-men. Accessed 1 Dec. 2022.

6 Taplin, Nathaniel. "How Too Many Boys Skew China's Economy." *Wall Street Journal*, 13 Jan. 2022, https://www.wsj.com/articles/how-too-many-boys-skew-chinas-economy-11642083784. Accessed 1 Dec. 2022.

7 Wanqing, Zhang. "The AI Girlfriend Seducing China's Lonely Men." *Sixth Tone,* 7 Dec. 2020, https://www.sixthtone.com/news/1006531/the-ai-girlfriend-seducing-chinas-lonely-men. Accessed 1 Dec. 2022.

8 Crypton. "Who Is Hatsune Miku?" *Crypton Future Media, INC*, ND, https://ec.crypton.co.jp/pages/prod/virtualsinger/cv01_us. Accessed 1 Dec. 2022.

9 Miquela. [@lilmiquela]. *Instagram,* 2022, https://www.instagram.com/lilmiquela/?hl=en. Accessed 1 Dec. 2022.

10 Huang, Zheping. "Chinese Women Are Spending Millions of Dollars on Virtual Boyfriends." *Quartz,* 31 Jan. 2018, https://qz.com/1193912/love-and-producer-chinas-female-gamers-are-spending-millions-of-dollars-on-virtual-boyfriends. Accessed 1 Dec. 2022.

11 Duffy, Clare. "Microsoft Patented a Chatbot That Would Let You Talk to Dead People. It Was Too Disturbing for Production." *CNN Business,* 27 Jan. 2021, https://edition.cnn.com/2021/01/27/tech/microsoft-chat-bot-patent/index.html. Accessed 1 Dec. 2022.

12 Wanqing, Zhang. "The AI Girlfriend Seducing China's Lonely Men." *Sixth Tone*, 7 Dec. 2020, https://www.sixthtone.com/news/1006531/the-ai-girlfriend-seducing-chinas-lonely-men. Accessed 1 Dec. 2022.

13 Brown, Karen. "Something Bothering You? Tell It to Woebot." *New York Times*, 1 June 2021, https://www.nytimes.com/2021/06/01/health/artificial-intelligence-therapy-woebot.html. Accessed 1 Dec. 2022.

14 Czeisler M., Lane R., Petrosky E., et al. "Mental Health, Substance Use, and Suicidal Ideation During the COVID-19 Pandemic—United States, June 24–30, 2020." *MMWR Morb Mortal Wkly Rep*, vol. 69, no. 32, pp. 1049–1057, https://www.cdc.gov/mmwr/volumes/69/wr/mm6932a1.htm. Accessed 1 Dec. 2022.

15 Caron, Christina. "'Nobody Has Openings': Mental Health Providers Struggle to Meet Demand." *New York Times*, 14 Sep. 2021, https://www.nytimes.com/2021/02/17/well/mind/therapy-appointments-shortages-pandemic.html. Accessed 1 Dec. 2022.

16 At the time of writing (November 2022), its postpartum depression services had been granted Breakthrough Device Designation from the FDA, which is an intermediary investigative stage before full approval. Woebot Health. "Woebot Health Receives FDA Breakthrough Device Designation for Postpartum Depression Treatment." *Woebot Health,* 25 May 2021, https://woebothealth.com/woebot-health-receives-fda-breakthrough-device-designation/. Accessed 1 Dec. 2022.

17 Woebot Health. "About Us." *Woebot Health,* 2022, https://woebothealth.com/about-us/. Accessed 1 Dec. 2022.
18 Simonite, Tom. "The Therapist Is In—and It's a Chatbot App." *Wired,* 17 June 2020, https://www.wired.com/story/therapist-in-chatbot-app/. Accessed 1 Dec. 2022.
19 Brodwin, Erin. "I Spent 2 Weeks Texting a Bot about My Anxiety—and Found It to Be Surprisingly Helpful." *Business Insider,* 30 Jan. 2018, https://www.businessinsider.com/therapy-chatbot-depression-app-what-its-like-woebot-2018-1?r=US&IR=T. Accessed 1 Dec. 2022.
20 Brown, Karen. "Something Bothering You? Tell It to Woebot." *New York Times,* 1 June 2021, https://www.nytimes.com/2021/06/01/health/artificial-intelligence-therapy-woebot.html. Accessed 1 Dec. 2022.
21 Darcy, A., Daniels, J., Salinger, D., Wicks, P., Robinson, A. "Evidence of Human-Level Bonds Established with a Digital Conversational Agent: Cross-sectional, Retrospective Observational Study." *JMIR Formative Research*, vol. 5, no. 5, 2021. JMIR Publications, https://formative.jmir.org/2021/5/e27868/. Accessed 1 Dec. 2022.
22 Bram, Barclay. "My Therapist, the Robot." *New York Times,* 27 Sep. 2022, https://www.nytimes.com/2022/09/27/opinion/chatbot-therapy-mental-health.html. Accessed 1 Dec. 2022.
23 Oracle News Connect. "Global Study: 82% of People Believe Robots Can Support Their Mental Health Better Than Humans." *Oracle,* 2022, https://www.oracle.com/news/announcement/ai-at-work-100720/. Accessed 1 Dec. 2022.
24 Embodied. "Moxie." *Embodied Moxie,* 2022, https://embodied.com/products/buy-moxie-robot. Accessed 1 Dec. 2022.
25 ElliQ. "Introducing ElliQ." *Intuition Robotics,* 2022, https://elliq.com/. Accessed 1 Dec. 2022.
26 Dementia Australia. "Dementia Australia Takes Top Tech iAwards Honours for Ted the AI Avatar." *Dementia Australia,* 13 Oct. 2020, https://www.dementia.org.au/about-us/media-centre/media-releases/dementia-australia-takes-top-tech-iawards-honours-ted-ai. Accessed 1 Dec. 2022.

CHAPTER 7: PSYCHEDELIC WELLNESS

1 "Psilocybin." *How to Change Your Mind,* produced by Alison Ellewood, performance by Michael Pollan, season 1, episode 2, Netflix, 2022.
2 Miller, Laura. "The Trip of a Lifetime." *Slate,* 14 May 2018, https://slate.com/culture/2018/05/lsd-research-michael-pollans-how-to-change-your-mind-reviewed.html. Accessed 15 Dec. 2022.
3 Beckley Foundation. "Psychedelic Research Timeline." *Beckley Foundation,* 2016, https://www.beckleyfoundation.org/psychedelic-research-timeline-2/. Accessed 14 Dec. 2022.
4 Baer, Drake. "How Steve Jobs' Acid-Fueled Quest for Enlightenment Made Him the Greatest Product Visionary in History." *Business Insider,* 29 Jan. 2015, https://www.businessinsider.com/steve-jobs-lsd-meditation-zen-quest-2015-1?r=US&IR=T. Accessed 15 Dec. 2022.
5 Richert, Lucas. "The Psychedelic Renaissance." *Psychology Today,* 14 Aug. 2019, https://www.psychologytoday.com/gb/blog/hygieias-workshop/201908/the-psychedelic-renaissance. Accessed 14 Dec. 2022.
6 Tullis, Paul. "How Ecstasy and Psilocybin Are Shaking Up Psychiatry." *Nature,* 27 Jan. 2021, https://www.nature.com/articles/d41586-021-00187-9. Accessed 15 Dec. 2022.

7 Kelland, Kate. "Mental Health Crisis Could Cost the World $16 Trillion by 2030." *Reuters,* 9 Oct. 2018, https://www.reuters.com/article/us-health-mental-global-idUSKCN1MJ2QN. Accessed 15 Dec. 2022.
8 The Economist. "How to Make Better Use of Antidepressants." *The Economist,* 19 Oct. 2022, https://www.economist.com/science-and-technology/2022/10/19/how-to-make-better-use-of-antidepressants. Accessed 15 Dec. 2022.
9 Agrawal, Manish. "Psychedelics May Erase Cancer Patients' Depression, Anxiety." *Washington Post,* 2 April 2022, https://www.washingtonpost.com/health/2022/04/02/cancer-psychedelics-psilocybin-anxiety-depression/. Accessed 15 Dec. 2022.
10 Ibid.
11 Johns Hopkins Medicine Newsroom. "Psilocybin Treatment for Major Depression Effective for Up to a Year for Most Patients, Study Shows." *Johns Hopkins Medicine,* 15 Feb. 2022, https://www.hopkinsmedicine.org/news/newsroom/news-releases/psilocybin-treatment-for-major-depression-effective-for-up-to-a-year-for-most-patients-study-shows. Accessed 15 Dec. 2022.
12 Ge Huang, Vicky. "How to Invest in Psychedelics." *Business Insider,* 15 Sep. 2021, https://www.businessinsider.com/investing-psychedelics-biotech-billionaire-crypto-spacs-longevity-space-christian-angermayer-2021-9. Accessed 15 Dec. 2022.
13 Ibid.
14 COMPASS Pathways. "COMP360 Psilocybin Therapy Shows Potential in Open-Label Study in Type II Bipolar Disorder Presented at ACNP." *GlobeNewswire,* 8 Dec. 2022, https://www.globenewswire.com/news-release/2022/12/08/2569941/0/en/COMP360-psilocybin-therapy-shows-potential-in-open-label-study-in-type-II-bipolar-disorder-presented-at-ACNP.html. Accessed 15 Dec. 2022.
15 Ge Huang, Vicky. "How to Invest in Psychedelics." *Business Insider,* 15 Sep. 2021, https://www.businessinsider.com/investing-psychedelics-biotech-billionaire-crypto-spacs-longevity-space-christian-angermayer-2021-9. Accessed 15 Dec. 2022.
16 Bryant, Chris. "Magic Mushrooms Are Giving Investors a Bad Trip." *Bloomberg,* 14 April 2022, https://www.bloomberg.com/opinion/articles/2022-04-14/psychedelics-stocks-like-atai-life-sciences-are-having-a-bad-psilocybin-trip?leadSource=uverify%20wall. Accessed 15 Dec. 2022.
17 Angermayer, Christian. "Psychedelics, Quo Vadis—Recreational or Medical Use?" *Christian's World,* 18 July 2022. *LinkedIn,* https://www.linkedin.com/pulse/psychedelics-quo-vadis-recreational-medical-use-angermayer/. Accessed 15 Dec. 2022.
18 Tripp. "Home Page." *Tripp,* 2022, https://www.tripp.com/. Accessed 15 Dec. 2022.
19 Illing, Sean. "The Extraordinary Therapeutic Potential of Psychedelic Drugs, Explained." *Vox,* 8 Mar. 2019, https://www.vox.com/science-and-health/2019/1/10/18007558/denver-psilocybin-psychedelic-mushrooms-ayahuasca-depression-mental-health. Accessed 15 Dec. 2022.
20 Burkeman, Oliver. "How to Change Your Mind: The New Science of Psychedelics by Michael Pollan—Review." *The Guardian,* 22 May 2018, https://www.theguardian.com/books/2018/may/22/how-to-change-mind-new-science-psychedelics-michael-pollan-review. Accessed 15 Dec. 2022.

CHAPTER 8: AMBIENT HEALTH

1 ecoLogicStudio. “Air Bubble: Air-Purifying Eco-Machine.” *ecoLogicStudio,* ND, https://www.ecologicstudio.com/projects/air-bubble-air-purifying-eco-machine. Accessed 4 Dec. 2022.

2 Ibid.

3 United States Environment Protection Agency. “Indoor Air Quality.” *Report on the Environment,* 7 Sep. 2021, https://www.epa.gov/report-environment/indoor-air-quality. Accessed 1 Dec. 2022.

4 World Health Organization. “Air Pollution.” *World Health Organization,* 2022, https://www.who.int/health-topics/air-pollution#tab=tab_1. Accessed 1 Dec. 2022.

5 Ibid.

6 Global Times. “Nippon Paint’s Antivirus Kids Paint Passes American Laboratory Tests and Also Complies with Chinese Antiviral Group Standards.” *Global Times,* 21 Dec. 2020, https://www.globaltimes.cn/content/1210524.shtml. Accessed 4 Dec. 2022.

7 Wisma Atria. “Welcoming You Back Safely!” *Wisma Atria,* 2022, https://www.wismaonline.com/happenings/whats-on/welcoming-you-back-safely/. Accessed 1 Dec. 2022.

8 CDC. “Percent of U.S. Adults 55 and Over with Chronic Conditions.” *Centers for Disease Control and Prevention,* 6 Nov. 2015, https://www.cdc.gov/nchs/health_policy/adult_chronic_conditions.htm. Accessed 29 Dec. 2022.

9 Ford, ES., Bergmann, MM., Kroger, J., et al. “Healthy Living Is the Best Revenge: Findings from the European Prospective Investigation into Cancer and Nutrition-Potsdam Study.” *Archives of Internal Medicine,* 1 Aug. 2009, vol. 169, no. 15, pp. 1355–62, https://europepmc.org/article/med/19667296. Accessed 29 Dec. 2022.

10 Gulati, Gautam. Personal Interview. 17 Oct. 2022.

11 Three Garden Road. “First-in-HK WELL Building Platinum Standard.” *Three Garden Road,* 2016, https://www.threegardenroad.com/en/wellness-hub.html. Accessed 1 Dec. 2022.

12 Champion REIT. “Three Garden Road Becomes First Existing Building Awarded with WELL Certification at Platinum Level in Hong Kong.” *Asia Corporate New Network,* 10 Feb. 2020, https://www.acnnewswire.com/press-release/english/57192/three-garden-road-becomes-first-existing-building-awarded-with-well-certification-at-platinum-level-in-hong-kong. Accessed 4 Dec. 2022.

13 WELL. “WELL Hits New Milestone, Tops 4 Billion Square Feet of Space.” *International WELL Building Institute,* 3 Aug. 2022, https://resources.wellcertified.com/press-releases/well-hits-new-milestone-tops-4-billion-square-feet-of-space/. Accessed 1 Dec. 2022.

14 Mangia, Karen. “Working Well: Rachel Hodgdon of International WELL Building Institute on How Companies Are Creating Cultures That Support & Sustain Mental, Emotional, Social, Physical & Financial Wellness.” *Authority Magazine,* 20 July 2022. *Medium,* https://medium.com/authority-magazine/working-well-rachel-hodgdon-of-international-well-building-institute-on-how-companies-are-creating-f4385bcd2ea9. Accessed 1 Dec. 2022.

15 Petter, Olivia. “Equinox Hotel Review: Wellness Meets Glam in New York’s Hudson Yards.” *Independent,* 17 Mar. 2022, https://www.independent.co.uk/travel/hotels/equinox-hotel-review-new-york-b2031850.html?r=17449. Accessed 1 Dec. 2022.

16 Stieg, Cory. "Forget 'Smart' Houses: This $24.5 Million 'Wellness Mansion' in Beverly Hills Has Ergonomic Floors and Lights That Mimic Sunrise." *CNBC Make It*, 20 Sep. 2019, https://www.cnbc.com/2019/09/20/beverly-hills-mansion-includes-delos-wellness-features.html. Accessed 1 Dec. 2022.
17 Amieva, H., Benois-Pineau, J., Pech, M., et al. "Falls Detection and Prevention Systems in Home Care for Older Adults: Myth or Reality?" *JMIR Aging*, vol. 4, no. 4, 2021. JMIR Publications, https://aging.jmir.org/2021/4/e29744. Accessed 1 Dec. 2022.

CHAPTER 9: GREEN PRESCRIPTIONS

1 Williams, Florence. "This Is Your Brain on Nature." *National Geographic*, ND, https://www.nationalgeographic.com/magazine/article/call-to-wild. Accessed 29 Dec. 2022.
2 Kagawa, T., Kasetani, T., Miyazaki, Y., Park, B., Tsunetsugu, Y. "The Physiological Effects of Shinrin-Yoku (Taking in the Forest Atmosphere or Forest Bathing): Evidence from Field Experiments in 24 Forests across Japan." *Environ Health Preventive Medicine*, vol. 15, no. 1, 2010, pp. 18–26. *National Library of Medicine*, https://pubmed.ncbi.nlm.nih.gov/19568835/. Accessed 1 Dec. 2022.
3 Annerstedt, M. and Währborg, P. "Nature-Assisted Therapy: Systematic Review of Controlled and Observational Studies." *Scandinavian Journal of Public Health*, vol. 39, no. 4, 2011, pp. 371–88. *National Library of Medicine*, https://pubmed.ncbi.nlm.nih.gov/21273226/. Accessed 1 Dec. 2022.
4 Ibid.
5 White, M.P., Alcock, I., Grellier, J. et al. "Spending at Least 120 Minutes a Week in Nature Is Associated with Good Health and Wellbeing." *Scientific Reports*, vol. 9, no. 7730, 2019, https://doi.org/10.1038/s41598-019-44097-3. Accessed 1 Dec. 2022.
6 Savage, Maddy. "Friluftsliv: The Nordic Concept of Getting Outdoors." Worklife, 10 Dec. 2017. *BBC.com*, https://www.bbc.com/worklife/article/20171211-friluftsliv-the-nordic-concept-of-getting-outdoors. Accessed 1 Dec. 2022.
7 United States Environment Protection Agency. "Indoor Air Quality." *Report on the Environment*, 7 Sep. 2021, https://www.epa.gov/report-environment/indoor-air-quality. Accessed 1 Dec. 2022.
8 Nielsen. "The Nielsen Total Audience Report: April 2020." *Nielsen*, April 2020, https://www.nielsen.com/insights/2020/the-nielsen-total-audience-report-april-2020/. Accessed 1 Dec. 2022.
9 Livni, Ephrat. "This Is How Distance from Nature Is Affecting Our Health." *World Economic Forum*, 1 Mar. 2019, https://www.weforum.org/agenda/2019/03/psychoterratica-is-the-trauma-caused-by-distance-from-nature. Accessed 1 Dec. 2022.
10 Department for Environment, Food & Rural Affairs, Department of Health and Social Care, Natural England, Rebecca Pow MP. "New Sites to Test How Connecting People with Nature Can Improve Mental Health." *GOV.UK*, 19 Dec. 2020, https://www.gov.uk/government/news/new-sites-to-test-how-connecting-people-with-nature-can-improve-mental-health. Accessed 1 Dec. 2022.
11 GOV.UK. "Green Social Prescribing: Call for Expressions of Interest." *GOV.UK*, 3 Mar. 2021, https://www.gov.uk/government/publications/green-social-

prescribing-call-for-expressions-of-interest/green-social-prescribing-call-for-expressions-of-interest. Accessed 1 Dec. 2022.

12 Cook, Rachel. "Social Prescribing: The Power of Nature as Treatment." *Natural England*, 12 April 2022. GOV.UK, https://naturalengland.blog.gov.uk/2022/04/12/social-prescribing-the-power-of-nature-as-treatment/. Accessed 1 Dec. 2022.

13 Bligh, A., Squire, H., Ware, G. "From 3D Printing Drugs to Social Prescribing—Medicine Made for You Part 3." *The Conversation*, 3 Mar. 2020, https://theconversation.com/from-3d-printing-drugs-to-social-prescribing-medicine-made-for-you-part-3-132817. Accessed 1 Dec. 2022.

14 The Wildlife Trusts. "New Report Reveals That Prescribing Nature Is Excellent Value for Money." *The Wildlife Trusts*, 10 Oct. 2019, https://www.wildlifetrusts.org/news/new-report-reveals-prescribing-nature. Accessed 1 Dec. 2022.

15 Department for Environment, Food & Rural Affairs, The Rt Hon George Eustice MP. "George Eustice Speech on Environmental Recovery: 20 July 2020." *GOV.UK*, 20 July 2020, https://www.gov.uk/government/speeches/george-eustice-speech-on-environmental-recovery-20-july-2020. Accessed 1 Dec. 2022.

16 Merchant, Nilofer. "Got a Meeting? Take a Walk." *TED*, 2013, https://www.ted.com/talks/nilofer_merchant_got_a_meeting_take_a_walk#t-38870. Accessed 1 Dec. 2022.

17 The Spheres. "Learn about the Building." *The Spheres*, 2022, https://www.seattlespheres.com/. Accessed 1 Dec. 2022.

CHAPTER 10: METABOLIC MONITORING

1 Hammond, Claudia. "Do We Need to Walk 10,000 Steps a Day?" *BBC.com*, 28 July 2019, https://www.bbc.com/future/article/20190723-10000-steps-a-day-the-right-amount. Accessed 15 Dec. 2022.

2 Reynolds, Gretchen. "Do We Really Need to Take 10,000 Steps a Day for Our Health?" *New York Times*, 6 July 2021, https://www.nytimes.com/2021/07/06/well/move/10000-steps-health.html. Accessed 15 Dec. 2022.

3 Kelland, Kate. "One in Five Deaths Worldwide Linked to Unhealthy Diet." *World Economic Forum*, 4 April 2019, https://www.weforum.org/agenda/2019/04/one-in-five-deaths-worldwide-linked-to-unhealthy-diet/. Accessed 15 Dec. 2022.

4 Marshall-Koons, Pamela Denise. "Food Suicide." *The Gainesville Sun*, 2022, https://eu.gainesville.com/story/opinion/2021/11/02/food-suicide/8553164002/. Accessed 15 Dec. 2022.

5 Harvard T.H. Chan School of Public Health. "Close to Half of US Population Projected to Have Obesity by 2030." *Harvard T.H. Chan School of Public Health*, 18 Dec. 2019, https://www.hsph.harvard.edu/news/press-releases/half-of-us-to-have-obesity-by-2030/. Accessed 15 Dec. 2022.

6 CDC Newsroom. "New CDC report: More Than 100 million Americans Have Diabetes or Prediabetes." *Centers for Disease Control and Prevention*, 18 July 2017, https://www.cdc.gov/media/releases/2017/p0718-diabetes-report.html. Accessed 15 Dec. 2022.

7 Araújo, J., Cai, J., Stevens, J. "Prevalence of Optimal Metabolic Health in American Adults: National Health and Nutrition Examination Survey 2009–2016." *Mary Ann Liebert, Inc. Publishers*, 8 Feb. 2019, https://www.liebertpub.com/doi/10.1089/met.2018.0105#:~:text=Conclusions%3A%20Prevalence%20of%20metabolic%20health,serious%20implications%20for%20public%20health. Accessed 15 Dec. 2022.

8 Team Type 1 Foundation. "Phil Southerland." *Team Type 1 Foundation*, ND, https://www.teamtype1.org/bio/phil-southerland/. Accessed 15 Dec. 2022.

9 Ehlinger, Maija. "Fueled by $13.5 Million Investment, an Atlanta Pro Cyclist Is Rethinking Glucose Monitoring for Athletes." *Hypepotamus*, 12 May 2021, https://hypepotamus.com/feature/supersapiens-funding/. Accessed 15 Dec. 2022.
10 Supersapiens. "Home Page." *Supersapiens*, 2022, https://www.supersapiens.com/en-EN/?us=yes. Accessed 15 Dec. 2022.
11 Strategic Market Research LLP. "Continuous Glucose Monitoring (CGM) Market to Reach $16.33 Billion by 2030, Growing at a CAGR of 11.5%." *GlobeNewswire*, 13 Sep. 2022, https://www.globenewswire.com/en/news-release/2022/09/13/2515227/0/en/Continuous-Glucose-Monitoring-CGM-Market-to-Reach-16-33-Billion-by-2030-Growing-at-a-CAGR-of-11-5.html. Accessed 15 Dec. 2022.
12 Samsung Newsroom. "Samsung Researchers' Non-Invasive Blood Glucose Monitoring Method Featured in 'Science Advances.'" *Samsung Newsroom*, 29 Jan. 2020, https://news.samsung.com/global/samsung-researchers-non-invasive-blood-glucose-monitoring-method-featured-in-science-advances. Accessed 15 Dec. 2022.
13 Titcomb, James. "Apple Watch Could Add Blood Sugar and Alcohol Readings after Deal with UK Tech Company." *The Telegraph*, 1 May 2021, https://www.telegraph.co.uk/technology/2021/05/01/apple-watch-could-add-blood-sugar-alcohol-readings-deal-uk-tech/. Accessed 15 Dec. 2022.
14 Edwards, Phil. "When Running for Exercise Was for Weirdos." *Vox*, 9 Aug. 2015, https://www.vox.com/2015/8/9/9115981/running-jogging-history. Accessed 15 Dec. 2022.
15 Gregoire, Carolyn. "How Yoga Became a $27 Billion Industry—and Reinvented American Spirituality." *Huffpost*, 16 Dec. 2013, https://www.huffingtonpost.co.uk/entry/how-the-yoga-industry-los_n_4441767. Accessed 15 Dec. 2022.

CHAPTER 11: AUGMENTED CREATIVITY

1 Roose, Kevin. "An A.I.-Generated Picture Won an Art Prize. Artists Aren't Happy." *New York Times*, 2 Sep. 2022, https://www.nytimes.com/2022/09/02/technology/ai-artificial-intelligence-artists.html. Accessed 17 Dec. 2022.
2 Palmer, RJ. [@arvalis] "A new AI image generator appears to be capable of making art that looks 100% human made. As an artist I am extremely concerned." *Twitter*, 13 Aug. 2022, https://twitter.com/arvalis/status/1558623545374023680. Accessed 17 Dec. 2022.
3 Harwell, Drew. "He Used AI to Win a Fine-Arts Competition. Was It Cheating?" *Washington Post*, 2 Sep. 2022, https://www.washingtonpost.com/technology/2022/09/02/midjourney-artificial-intelligence-state-fair-colorado/. Accessed 17 Dec. 2022.
4 Young, James and Staaf, Martin. "Stable Diffusion—Harnessing the Creative Power of Generative AI." *BBDO*, ND, https://bbdo.com/thinking/638e1133f1e61dcd71ce2f7a. Accessed 17 Dec. 2022.
5 Reeps100. "Creating an A.I. Second Self." *Reeps100*, 2022, https://reeps100.com/project/second-self. Accessed 17 Dec. 2022.
6 Smith, John. "IBM Research Takes Watson to Hollywood with the First 'Cognitive Movie Trailer.'" *IBM*, 31 Aug. 2016, https://www.ibm.com/blogs/think/2016/08/cognitive-movie-trailer/. Accessed 17 Dec. 2022.
7 Roose, Kevin. "A Coming-Out Party for Generative A.I., Silicon Valley's New Craze." *New York Times*, 21 Oct. 2022, https://www.nytimes.com/2022/10/21/technology/generative-ai.html. Accessed 17 Dec. 2022.

8 Torres, Roberto. "GitHub Copilot Adds 400K Subscribers in First Month." *CIODive*, 1 Aug. 2022. *Industry Dive*, https://www.ciodive.com/news/github-copilot-microsoft-software-developer/628587/. Accessed 17 Dec. 2022.

9 Ibid.

10 Kalliamvakou, Eirini. "Research: Quantifying Github Copilot's Impact on Developer Productivity and Happiness." *GitHub*, 7 Sep. 2022, https://github.blog/2022-09-07-research-quantifying-github-copilots-impact-on-developer-productivity-and-happiness/. Accessed 17 Dec. 2022.

11 The Generalist. "Endless Media." *The Generalist*, 4 Dec. 2022, https://www.generalist.com/briefing/endless-media. Accessed 17 Dec. 2022.

12 Haverkamp, Hendrik. "A Teacher Allows AI Tools in Exams—Here's What He Learned." *The Decoder*, 30 Oct. 2022, https://the-decoder.com/a-teacher-allows-ai-tools-in-exams-heres-what-he-learned/. Accessed 17 Dec. 2022.

13 Vincent, James. "AI-Generated Answers Temporarily Banned on Coding Q&A Site Stack Overflow." *The Verge*, 5 Dec. 2022, https://www.theverge.com/2022/12/5/23493932/chatgpt-ai-generated-answers-temporarily-banned-stack-overflow-llms-dangers. Accessed 17 Dec. 2022.

14 Thompson, Clive. "On Bullshit, and AI-Generated Prose." *Medium*, 6 Dec. 2022, https://clivethompson.medium.com/on-bullshit-and-ai-generated-prose-611a0f899c5. Accessed 17 Dec. 2022.

15 The Economist. "Huge 'Foundation Models' Are Turbo-Charging AI Progress." *The Economist*, 11 June 2022, https://www.economist.com/interactive/briefing/2022/06/11/huge-foundation-models-are-turbo-charging-ai-progress. Accessed 17 Dec. 2022.

16 Vincent, James. "The Lawsuit That Could Rewrite the Rules of AI Copyright." *The Verge*, 8 Nov. 2022, https://www.theverge.com/2022/11/8/23446821/microsoft-openai-github-copilot-class-action-lawsuit-ai-copyright-violation-training-data. Accessed 17 Dec. 2022.

17 Clarke, Arthur C. *Profiles of the Future: An Inquiry into the Limits of the Possible.* Henry Holt & Company, 1984.

CHAPTER 12: REMOTE WORK FOR ALL

1 T-Mobile Nederland. "The Impossible Tattoo—Powered by 5G." *YouTube*, 7 Sep. 2020, https://www.youtube.com/watch?v=GSbaqCe747Q. Accessed 2 Dec. 2022.

2 Lo Scalzo, Flavio. "Tommy the Robot Nurse Helps Keep Italy Doctors Safe from Coronavirus." *Reuters*, 1 April 2020, https://www.reuters.com/article/us-health-coronavirus-italy-robots-idUSKBN21J67Y. Accessed 2 Dec. 2022.

3 Leithead, Alastair. "Inside America's Drone HQ." *BBC.com*, 5 April 2012, https://www.bbc.com/news/world-us-canada-17516156. Accessed 2 Dec. 2022.

4 Anderson, Brad. "Einride Pod Is the First Autonomous Electric Freight Truck to Hit Top Gear's Track." *Carscoops*, 22 Oct. 2020, https://www.carscoops.com/2020/10/einride-pod-is-the-first-autonomous-electric-freight-truck-to-hit-top-gears-track/. Accessed 2 Dec. 2022.

5 Einride. "Remote Pod Operator." *Einride*, ND, https://jobs.lever.co/einride/3823060f-3093-46fc-8a16-1f7cee88da29. Accessed 2 Dec. 2022.

6 McKinsey & Company. "Disrupting Transport: An Interview with Robert Falck of Einride." *McKinsey & Company*, 2 Aug. 2022, https://www.mckinsey.com/capabilities/operations/our-insights/global-infrastructure-initiative/voices/disrupting-transport-an-interview-with-robert-falck-of-einride. Accessed 2 Dec. 2022.

7 Einride. "Einride Will Hire Its First Remote Operator in 2020." *Einride,* 9 Mar. 2020, https://www.einride.tech/insights/einride-will-hire-its-first-remote-autonomous-truck-operator-in-2020. Accessed 2 Dec. 2022.

8 McKinsey & Company. "Disrupting Transport: An Interview with Robert Falck of Einride." *McKinsey & Company*, 2 Aug. 2022, https://www.mckinsey.com/capabilities/operations/our-insights/global-infrastructure-initiative/voices/disrupting-transport-an-interview-with-robert-falck-of-einride. Accessed 2 Dec. 2022.

9 Einride. "Remote Operation and the Future of Trucking." *Einride*, 7 Dec. 2021, https://www.einride.tech/insights/remote-operation-and-the-future-of-trucking. Accessed 2 Dec. 2022.

10 Gardner, Greg. "Want to Drive Your Truck by Remote Control? Einride Is Hiring." *Forbes*, 27 Feb. 2020, https://www.forbes.com/sites/greggardner/2020/02/27/want-to-drive-your-truck-by-remote-control-einride-is-hiring/?sh=6f8a22937fd6. Accessed 2 Dec. 2022.

11 Einride. "Tiffany and the Future of Shipping." *Einride*, 21 Mar. 2022, https://www.einride.tech/insights/tiffany-and-the-future-of-shipping. Accessed 2 Dec. 2022.

12 Lay, Belmont. "Miners in China Work from Home Using 5G-Enabled Machinery to Do Heavy Lifting." *Mothership*, 26 Aug. 2020, https://mothership.sg/2020/08/china-miners-5g-machinery/. Accessed 2 Dec. 2022.

13 Devanesan, Joe. "Japan's FamilyMart Hedges Bets on In-Store Robots." *Techwire Asia*, 22 July 2020, https://techwireasia.com/2020/07/japans-familymart-hedges-bets-on-in-store-robots/. Accessed 2 Dec. 2022.

14 Master Blaster. "Cafe Opens in Tokyo Staffed by Robots Controlled by Paralyzed People." *Sora News24*, 29 Nov. 2018, https://soranews24.com/2018/11/29/cafe-opens-in-tokyo-staffed-by-robots-controlled-by-paralyzed-people/. Accessed 2 Dec. 2022.

CHAPTER 13: WORK DECONSTRUCTED

1 Darbyshire, Madison. "The Lawyer Duo Who Job-Share at Partnership Level." *Financial Times*, 16 Oct. 2019, https://www.ft.com/content/f650bb6a-ca46-11e9-af46-b09e8bfe60c0. Accessed 2 Dec. 2022.

2 Davies, Nigel. "New Data Reveals How Remote Workers Are Getting Short Changed." *Forbes*, 19 April 2021, https://www.forbes.com/sites/nigeldavies/2021/04/19/new-data-reveals-how-remote-workers-are-getting-short-changed/?sh=c6b191b5de09. Accessed 2 Dec. 2022.

3 Priestley, Angela. "'Overlooked for Promotion, Perceived to Lack Commitment': The Perils of Part Time Work." *Women's Agenda*, 7 Feb. 2019, https://womensagenda.com.au/latest/overlooked-for-promotion-perceived-to-lack-commitment-the-perils-of-part-time-work/. Accessed 2 Dec. 2022.

4 Lorch, Danna. "Is Job Sharing the Solution to Our Flexible Work Problems?" *Fast Company*, 29 July 2021, https://www.fastcompany.com/90658962/is-job-sharing-the-solution-to-our-flexible-work-problems. Accessed 2 Dec. 2022.

5 S.N. "Why So Many Dutch People Work Part Time." *The Economist*, 12 May 2015, https://www.economist.com/the-economist-explains/2015/05/11/why-so-many-dutch-people-work-part-time. Accessed 2 Dec. 2022.

6 Barker, E., Day, B., Stanislas, B. "Happy Job Sharing & Caring Father's Day!" Civil Service Blog, 14 July 2019. *GOV.UK*, https://civilservice.blog.gov.uk/2019/06/14/happy-job-sharing-caring-fathers-day/. Accessed 2 Dec. 2022.

7 Roleshare. "Why Two Senior Directors at Aviva Think Rolesharing Is Great for Men." *Talk Roleshare Podcast*, season 1, episode 7, 15 Nov. 2019, https://www.roleshare.com/toolkit/podcasts/men-can-flex-aviva-group-sustainability-public-policy-director-sam-white-will-mcdonald. Accessed 2 Dec. 2022.
8 Roleshare. "FAQ." *Roleshare*, 2022, https://www.roleshare.com/faq. Accessed 2 Dec. 2022.
9 ADP Newsroom. "One Year into the Pandemic: ADP Research Institute® Uncovers How Working Conditions and Attitudes Have Changed in Global Study." *ADP Newsroom*, 28 April 2021, https://mediacenter.adp.com/2021-04-28-One-Year-into-the-Pandemic-ADP-Research-Institute-R-Uncovers-How-Working-Conditions-and-Attitudes-Have-Changed-in-Global-Study. Accessed 2 Dec. 2022.
10 Government Equalities Office, Behavioural Insights Team. "A Field Trial with Zurich Insurance to Advertise All Jobs as Part-Time." *GOV.UK*, 17 Nov. 2020, https://www.gov.uk/government/publications/a-field-trial-with-zurich-insurance-to-advertise-all-jobs-as-part-time. Accessed 2 Dec. 2022.
11 Zurich. "Zurich Sees Leap in Women Applying for Senior Roles after Offering All Jobs as Flexible." *Zurich*, 17 Nov. 2020, https://www.zurich.co.uk/media-centre/zurich-sees-leap-in-women-applying-for-senior-roles-after-offering-all-jobs-as-flexible. Accessed 2 Dec. 2022.
12 Webber, Ashleigh. "Flexible Working 'Nudges' Result in 30% Uplift in Job Applications." *Personnel Today*, 29 May 2020, https://www.personneltoday.com/hr/indeed-flexible-working-nudges-study/. Accessed 2 Dec. 2022.
13 Marchant, Natalie. "Zurich Added These 6 Words to Job Adverts and More Women Applied." *World Economic Forum*, 8 Dec. 2020, https://www.weforum.org/agenda/2020/12/zurich-flexible-working-women-diversity/. Accessed 2 Dec. 2022.
14 Cohen, Patricia. "This Plan Pays to Avoid Layoffs. Why Don't More Employers Use It?" *New York Times*, 20 Aug. 2020, https://www.nytimes.com/2020/08/20/business/economy/jobs-work-sharing-unemployment.html. Accessed 2 Dec. 2022.
15 Ang, Prisca. "DBS Bank to Roll Out Voluntary Job-Sharing Scheme Where 2 Employees Share One Full-Time Role." *Straits Times*, 18 Nov. 2020, https://www.straitstimes.com/business/banking/dbs-bank-to-roll-out-job-sharing-scheme-where-2-employees-share-one-full-time-role. Accessed 2 Dec. 2022.

CHAPTER 14: REFLECTIVE CULTURES

1 Television Academy. "Savage X Fenty Show." *Television Academy*, 2020, https://www.emmys.com/shows/savage-x-fenty-show. Accessed 2 Dec. 2022.
2 Ibid.
3 McKinnon, Tricia. "How Rihanna's Fenty Brand Is Leading in Diversity & Inclusion." *Indigo9 Digital*, 3 May 2022, https://www.indigo9digital.com/blog/fentydiversityinclusion. Accessed 2 Dec. 2022.
4 Robehmed, Natalie. "How Rihanna Created A $600 Million Fortune—and Became the World's Richest Female Musician." *Forbes*, 4 June 2019, https://www.forbes.com/sites/natalierobehmed/2019/06/04/rihanna-worth-fenty-beauty/?sh=59aabe9713de. Accessed 2 Dec. 2022.
5 Flanagan, Hanna. "Rihanna Says Her Quarantine Uniform Is Not 'All Leather and Sexy': 'I'm in a Robe Every Day'." *People*, 2 Oct. 2020, https://people.com/style/rihanna-on-body-confidence-quarantine-uniform/. Accessed 2 Dec. 2022.

6 Deloitte. "Missing Pieces Report: The Board Diversity Census." *Deloitte,* 2021, https://www2.deloitte.com/us/en/pages/center-for-board-effectiveness/articles/missing-pieces-report-board-diversity.html. Accessed 2 Dec. 2022.
7 Frey, William. "Less Than Half of US Children under 15 Are White, Census Shows." *Brookings,* 24 June 2019, https://www.brookings.edu/research/less-than-half-of-us-children-under-15-are-white-census-shows/. Accessed 2 Dec. 2022.
8 Dahlgreen, Will and Shakespeare, Anna-Elizabeth. "1 in 2 Young People Say They Are Not 100% Heterosexual." *YouGov,* 16 Aug. 2015, https://yougov.co.uk/topics/society/articles-reports/2015/08/16/half-young-not-heterosexual. Accessed 2 Dec. 2022.
9 Kishan, Saijel. "Economist Found $16 Trillion When She Tallied Cost of Racial Bias." *Bloomberg,* 20 Oct. 2020, https://www.bloomberg.com/news/articles/2020-10-20/racism-and-inequity-have-cost-the-u-s-16-trillion-wall-street-economist-says?leadSource=uverify%20wall. Accessed 2 Dec. 2022.
10 Devillard, S., Dobbs, R., Ellingrud, K., et al. "How Advancing Women's Equality Can Add $12 Trillion to Global Growth." *McKinsey Global Institute,* 1 Sep. 2015, https://www.mckinsey.com/featured-insights/employment-and-growth/how-advancing-womens-equality-can-add-12-trillion-to-global-growth. Accessed 2 Dec. 2022.
11 Dixon-Fyle, S., Dolan, K., Hunt, V., et al. "Diversity Wins: How Inclusion Matters." *McKinsey & Company,* 19 May 2020, https://www.mckinsey.com/featured-insights/diversity-and-inclusion/diversity-wins-how-inclusion-matters. Accessed 2 Dec. 2022.
12 Black in Fashion Council. "Welcome to the Black in Fashion Council." *Black in Fashion Council,* 2020, https://www.blackinfashioncouncil.com/. Accessed 2 Dec. 2022.
13 Ibid.
14 Evans, Morgan. "The Black in Fashion Council Founders on Creating an 'Accountability Culture' in the Industry." *People,* 26 June 2020, https://people.com/style/black-in-fashion-council-founders-lindsay-peoples-wagner-sandrine-charles-interview/. Accessed 2 Dec. 2022.
15 Fields, Aryn. "The Human Rights Campaign & Black in Fashion Council Release First-Ever 'Black in Fashion' Index." *Human Rights Campaign,* 29 Sep. 2021, https://www.hrc.org/press-releases/the-human-rights-campaign-black-in-fashion-council-release-first-ever-black-in-fashion-index. Accessed 2 Dec. 2022.
16 Alliance for Global Inclusion. "2022 Global Inclusion Index Survey." *Alliance for Global Inclusion,* 2022, https://www.allianceforglobalinclusion.com/index-results/2022. Accessed 2 Dec. 2022.
17 FairHQ. "Grow a Diverse and Inclusive Company." *FairHQ,* 2022, https://fairhq.co/. Accessed 4 Dec. 2022.

CHAPTER 15: BIG BRAND REDEMPTION

1 Gelles, David. *The Man Who Broke Capitalism.* Simon & Schuster, 31 May 2022.
2 Andersen, Kurt. "How Jack Welch Revolutionized the American Economy." *New York Times,* 2 June 2022, https://www.nytimes.com/2022/06/02/books/review/the-man-who-broke-capitalism-david-gelles.html. Accessed 2 Dec. 2022.
3 Philanthropy News Digest. "Microsoft Leads Ranking of 'Just' Companies for Third Straight Year." *Candid,* 19 Oct. 2020, https://philanthropynewsdigest.org/news/microsoft-leads-ranking-of-just-companies-for-third-straight-year. Accessed 3 Jan. 2023.

4 Foley, Kevin. "The Certified B Corporation: A Definition and Brief History of How It All Started?" *Valley to Summit,* 27 May 2019, https://www.valleytosummit.net/the-certified-b-corporation-a-definition-and-brief-history-of-how-it-all-started. Accessed 2 Dec. 2022.
5 Ibid.
6 Feloni, Richard. "More Than 2,600 Companies, Like Danone and Patagonia, Are on Board with an Entrepreneur Who Says the Way We Do Business Runs Counter to Human Nature and There's Only One Way Forward." *Business Insider,* 8 Dec. 2018, https://www.businessinsider.com/b-corporation-b-lab-movement-and1-cofounder-2018-11?op=1&r=US&IR=T. Accessed 4 Dec. 2022.
7 B Lab. "About B Corp Certification: Measuring a Company's Entire Social and Environmental Impact." *B Lab,* 2022, https://www.bcorporation.net/en-us/certification. Accessed 4 Dec. 2022.
8 B Lab Global. "How Can Business Act with Purpose?" *B Lab Forces for Good* podcast, episode 1, 12 Oct. 2022, https://www.bcorporation.net/en-us/news/blog/forces-for-good-podcast-episode-1-purpose. Accessed 4 Dec. 2022.
9 B Lab. "Frequently Asked Questions: Everything You Need to Know about B Lab and the B Corp Movement." *B Lab,* 2022, https://www.bcorporation.net/en-us/faqs. Accessed 4 Dec. 2022.
10 Danone. "B Corp." *Danone,* ND, https://www.danone.com/about-danone/sustainable-value-creation/BCorpAmbition.html. Accessed 26 Dec. 2022.
11 B Lab Europe. "Behind the B Movement Builders: The Key Role of Multinationals in the B Corp Movement to Achieve Systemic Change." *Medium,* 2 May 2022, https://bcorpeurope.medium.com/behind-the-b-movement-builders-the-key-role-of-multinationals-in-the-b-corp-movement-to-achieve-732c74e01e56. Accessed 2 Dec. 2022.
12 Toussaint, Kristen. "The backlash against B Lab." *Fast Company,* 19 Oct. 2022, https://www.fastcompany.com/90794381/how-b-lab-is-responding-to-b-corp-backlash. Accessed 2 Dec. 2022.
13 Kassoy, A., Houlahan, B., Gilbert, J. "Passing the Torch: A Note from B Lab's Co-Founders." *B Lab,* 7 July 2022, https://www.bcorporation.net/en-us/news/blog/passing-the-torch-note-b-lab-co-founders. Accessed 5 Dec. 2022.

CHAPTER 16: IMPACT HUBS

1 Bogost, Ian. "The Wildly Appealing, Totally Doomed Future of Work." *The Atlantic,* 26 Sep. 2019, https://www.theatlantic.com/technology/archive/2019/09/why-wework-was-destined-fail/598891/. Accessed 1 Dec. 2022.
2 Ibid.
3 Ibid.
4 Hern, Alex. "Covid-19 Could Cause Permanent Shift Towards Home Working." *The Guardian,* 13 Mar. 2020, https://www.theguardian.com/technology/2020/mar/13/covid-19-could-cause-permanent-shift-towards-home-working. Accessed 1 Dec. 2022.
5 PwC. "PwC's US Remote Work Survey." *PwC,* 12 Jan. 2021, https://www.pwc.com/us/en/services/consulting/business-transformation/library/covid-19-us-remote-work-survey.html. Accessed 1 Dec. 2022.
6 Haag, Matthew. "Facebook Bets Big on Future of NYC, and Offices, With New Lease." *New York Times,* 3 Aug. 2020, https://www.nytimes.com/2020/08/03/nyregion/facebook-nyc-office-farley-building.html. Accessed 1 Dec. 2022.
7 Living Wage Foundation. "The UK's First Living Wage Building Launches in South London." *Living Wage Foundation,* 26 April 2019, https://www.livingwage.

org.uk/news/uk%E2%80%99s-first-living-wage-building-launches-south-london. Accessed 5 Dec. 2022.
8 3Space International House. "BuyGiveWork." *3Space International House,* ND, https://www.3spaceinternational.co.uk/buygivework. Accessed 1 Dec. 2022.
9 3Space. "Impact." 3Space *International House*, ND, https://www.3spaceinternational.co.uk/impact. Accessed 3 Jan. 2023.
10 Urban Land Institute. "Health and Social Equity in Real Estate: State of the Market." *Urban Land Institute,* 10 Nov. 2020, https://knowledge.uli.org/reports/research-reports/2020/health-and-social-equity-in-real-estate. Accessed 1 Dec. 2022.
11 Urban Land Institute. "Health and Social Equity in Real Estate: Examples from the Field." *Urban Land Institute,* 2020, https://knowledge.uli.org/-/media/files/research-reports/2020/uli-healthandsocialequityinrealestate_fieldex_finalv5.pdf?rev=e5f4573a51274296937bb6888f2f3dcf&hash=F731A7C7E05B75FE4F00B0D53313C821. Accessed 1 Dec. 2022.

CHAPTER 17: UNNATURALLY BETTER

1 Eschner, Kat. "Winston Churchill Imagined the Lab-Grown Hamburger." *Smithsonian Magazine,* 1 Dec. 2017, https://www.smithsonianmag.com/smart-news/winston-churchill-imagined-lab-grown-hamburger-180967349/. Accessed 16 Dec. 2022.
2 Joe, Tanuvi. "Eat Just Serves Cultured Meat to Diners at 1880 Restaurant Singapore in a World First." *Green Queen*, 23 Dec. 2020, https://www.greenqueen.com.hk/eat-just-serves-cultured-meat-to-diners-at-1880-restaurant-singapore-in-a-world-first/. Accessed 16 Dec. 2022.
3 Research and Markets. "2022 Worldwide Market for Cultured Meat Report—Featuring 3D Bio-Tissues, Agulos Biotech and Aleph Farms Among Others." *GlobeNewswire*, 2 Feb. 2022, https://www.globenewswire.com/en/news-release/2022/02/02/2377373/28124/en/2022-Worldwide-Market-for-Cultured-Meat-Report-Featuring-3D-Bio-Tissues-Agulos-Biotech-and-Aleph-Farms-Among-Others.html. Accessed 16 Dec. 2022.
4 The Future Market. "Exploring and Building the Future of Food." *The Alpha Food Labs Future Market*, 2022, https://thefuturemarket.com/. Accessed 16 Dec. 2022.
5 Zewe, Adam. "Toward Customizable Timber, Grown in a Lab." *MIT New Office*, 25 May 2022, https://news.mit.edu/2022/lab-timber-wood-0525. Accessed 26 Dec. 2022.
6 Califf, Robert and Mayne, Susan. "FDA Spurs Innovation for Human Food from Animal Cell Culture Technology." *US Food and Drug Administration*, 16 Nov. 2022, https://www.fda.gov/news-events/press-announcements/fda-spurs-innovation-human-food-animal-cell-culture-technology. Accessed 16 Dec. 2022.
7 Crippa, M., Solazzo, E., Guizzardi, D. et al. "Food Systems Are Responsible for a Third of Global Anthropogenic GHG Emissions." *Nature Food*, no. 2, pp. 198–209, 8 Mar. 2021, https://www.nature.com/articles/s43016-021-00225-9#cite-as. Accessed 16 Dec. 2022.
8 Clean Water Action. "The Meat Industry—Environmental Issues & Solutions." *Clean Water Action*, 2022, https://cleanwater.org/meat-industry-environmental-issues-solutions. Accessed 16 Dec. 2022.
9 Sanchez, Maricel. "'We're Reimagining Meat to Spare Land and Resources, but Never Flavour': Interview with Nicolas Morin-Forest, CEO and Co-founder of Gourmey." *EU-Startups*, 23 Feb. 2022, https://www.eu-startups.com/2022/02/

were-reimagining-meat-to-spare-land-and-resources-but-never-flavour-interview-with-nicolas-morin-forest-ceo-and-co-founder-of-gourmey/. Accessed 16 Dec. 2022.

10 The Good Food Institute. "2021 State of the Industry Report: Cultivated Meat and Seafood." *The Good Food Institute*, 2021, https://gfi.org/wp-content/uploads/2022/04/2021-Cultivated-Meat-State-of-the-Industry-Report-1.pdf. Accessed 16 Dec. 2022.

11 VitroLabs Inc. "Home Page." *VitroLabs Inc*, 2022, https://www.vitrolabsinc.com/. Accessed 16 Dec. 2022.

12 KLM. "World First in the Netherlands by KLM, Shell and Dutch Ministry for Infrastructure and Water Management: First Passenger Flight Performed with Sustainable Synthetic Kerosene." *KLM Royal Dutch Airlines*, 8 Feb. 2021, https://news.klm.com/world-first-in-the-netherlands-by-klm-shell-and-dutch-ministry-for-infrastructure-and-water-management-first-passenger-flight-performed-with-sustainable-synthetic-kerosene/. Accessed 16 Dec. 2022.

13 Instinctif Partners. "Touchlight Receives Grant to Advance Rapid, Scalable and Thermostable Doggybone DNA Vaccine Platform." *Touchlight*, 29 Nov. 2022, https://www.touchlight.com/news/touchlight-receives-grant-to-advance-doggybone-dna-vaccine-platform/. Accessed 16 Dec. 2022.

CHAPTER 18: CALCULATED CONSUMPTION

1 Kaufman, Mark. "The Carbon Footprint Sham." *Mashable*, 2022, https://mashable.com/feature/carbon-footprint-pr-campaign-sham. Accessed 1 Dec. 2022.

2 Edie Newsroom. "Quorn Rolls Out Carbon Footprint Labelling." *Edie*, 10 Jan. 2020, https://www.edie.net/quorn-rolls-out-carbon-footprint-labelling/. Accessed 1 Dec. 2022.

3 Smithers, Rebecca. "Quorn to Be First Major Brand to Introduce Carbon Labelling." *The Guardian*, 9 Jan. 2020, https://www.theguardian.com/environment/2020/jan/09/quorn-to-be-first-major-brand-to-introduce-carbon-labelling. Accessed 1 Dec. 2022.

4 London, Lela. "Allbirds Is the First Fashion Brand to Label Its Carbon Footprint Like Calories." *Forbes*, 15 April 2020, https://www.forbes.com/sites/lelalondon/2020/04/15/allbirds-is-the-first-fashion-brand-to-label-its-carbon-footprint-like-calories/?sh=7aaff41270db. Accessed 1 Dec. 2022.

5 Ibid.

6 Martinko, Katherine. "Allbirds Wants Fashion Industry to Embrace Carbon Footprint Labels." *Treehugger*, 20 April 2021, https://www.treehugger.com/allbirds-fashion-industry-embrace-carbon-footprint-labels-5179644. Accessed 1 Dec. 2022.

7 Ho, Sally. "Allbirds Launches Carbon Footprint Count for Every Sneaker in Its Collection." *Green Queen*, 21 Oct. 2020, https://www.greenqueen.com.hk/allbirds-launches-carbon-footprint-count-for-every-sneaker-in-its-collection-carbon-labels/. Accessed 1 Dec. 2022.

8 Oatly. "Oat Drink with Carbon Dioxide Equivalents." *Oatly*, ND, https://www.oatly.com/en-gb/stuff-we-make/climate-footprint. Accessed 1 Dec. 2022.

9 Vestre. "The Growing Importance of Epds. Why It Matters and How You Use Them." *Vestre News*, 1 Feb. 2021, https://vestre.com/fr/actualites/de-limportance-croissante-des-dep-comment-les-utiliser?_geom=%E2%9C%AA. Accessed 1 Dec. 2022.

10 Much Better Adventures. "We've Added Carbon Labels to All Our Trips ... and Call on the Rest of the Travel Industry to Do the Same." *Much Better Adventures*,

2 Feb. 2021, https://www.muchbetteradventures.com/magazine/carbon-label-to-all-trips-and-calls-on-the-travel-industry-to-follow-suit/. Accessed 1 Dec. 2022.
11 Yu, Ivy. "Alibaba's Tmall Pilots Carbon Labeling to Drive Sustainable Consumption." *Alizila: News from Alibaba,* 7 April 2022, https://www.alizila.com/alibabas-tmall-pilots-carbon-labeling-to-drive-sustainable-consumption/. Accessed 1 Dec. 2022.
12 Vaughan, Adam. "Tesco Drops Carbon-Label Pledge." *The Guardian,* 30 Jan. 2012, https://www.theguardian.com/environment/2012/jan/30/tesco-drops-carbon-labelling. Accessed 1 Dec. 2022.
13 Rosenbloom, Stephanie. "At Wal-Mart, Labeling to Reflect Green Intent." *New York Times,* 15 July 2009, https://www.nytimes.com/2009/07/16/business/energy-environment/16walmart.html. Accessed 1 Dec. 2022.
14 MacDonagh, John. "Carbon Pledges Continue to Create New Opportunities for Startups." *PitchBook,* 10 Sep. 2022, https://pitchbook.com/newsletter/carbon-pledges-continue-to-create-new-opportunities-for-startups. Accessed 1 Dec. 2022.
15 Allbirds. "Don't Hide Your Pollution. Label It." *Allbirds,* 2022, https://www.allbirds.com/pages/carbon-footprint-calculator. Accessed 1 Dec. 2022.
16 Buxton, Amy. "Norwegian Consumers Ditch Red Meat after Carbon Footprint Is Printed on Oda Grocery Receipts." *Green Queen,* 11 Jan. 2022, https://www.greenqueen.com.hk/red-meat-carbon-footprint-oda-norway/. Accessed 1 Dec. 2022.

CHAPTER 19: GUILT-FREE INDULGENCE

1 Peters, Adele. "The Newest Plant-Based Meat Brand Comes from a 19-Year-Old Founder." *Fast Company,* 9 July 2019, https://www.fastcompany.com/90373837/the-newest-plant-based-meat-brand-comes-from-a-19-year-old-founder. Accessed 5 Dec. 2022.
2 Martinez, Jocelyn. "Bella Hadid Is 'Freaking the F Out' about Spicy Vegan Chicken Nuggets." *VegNews,* 25 Aug. 2020, https://vegnews.com/2020/8/bella-hadid-is-freaking-the-f-out-about-spicy-vegan-chicken-nuggets. Accessed 2 Dec. 2022.
3 Agence France-Presse. "Welcome to Tokyo's Gome Pit: A Pop-Up Bar in a Rubbish Dump Designed to Make Drinkers Think about Sustainability." *South China Morning Post,* 29 Jan. 2019, https://www.scmp.com/news/asia/east-asia/article/2184075/welcome-tokyos-gome-pit-pop-bar-rubbish-dump-designed-make. Accessed 2 Dec. 2022.
4 Habib, R., Hardisty, D., White, K. "The Elusive Green Consumer." *Harvard Business Review,* July-Aug. 2019, https://hbr.org/2019/07/the-elusive-green-consumer. Accessed 2 Dec. 2022.
5 Better Future. "The *New York Times* Announces the Mylo™ Consortium." *Bolt Threads,* 19 Nov. 2020, https://boltthreads.com/blog/the-new-york-times-announces-the-mylo-consortium/. Accessed 2 Dec. 2022.
6 Skydiamond. "About Us." *Skydiamond,* ND, https://skydiamond.com/about-us. Accessed 2 Dec. 2022.
7 Ecotricity. "Our Story: 27 Years of Ecotricity." *Ecotricity,* ND, https://www.ecotricity.co.uk/our-story/27-years-of-ecotricity. Accessed 2 Dec. 2022.
8 Gillespie, Tom. "Eco-Friendly Diamonds Developed Using Carbon Sucked from the Air—'Bling without the Sting'." *Sky News,* 30 Oct. 2020, https://news.sky.com/story/eco-friendly-diamonds-developed-using-carbon-sucked-from-the-air-bling-without-the-sting-12118523. Accessed 2 Dec. 2022.

9 Skydiamond. "About Us." *Skydiamond,* ND, https://skydiamond.com/about-us. Accessed 2 Dec. 2022.

CHAPTER 20: SECONDHAND STATUS

1 Grobe, Max. "Take a Look Inside This Fake Supreme Store in China." *Highsnobiety,* 2018, https://www.highsnobiety.com/p/supreme-store-fake-china/. Accessed 19 Dec. 2022.
2 Sherwood, Alice. "Spot the Difference: The Invincible Business of Counterfeit Goods." *The Guardian,* 10 May 2022, https://www.theguardian.com/fashion/2022/may/10/spot-the-difference-the-invincible-business-of-counterfeit-goods. Accessed 19 Dec. 2022.
3 Castaño, R., Perez, M., Quintanilla, C. "Constructing Identity through the Consumption of Counterfeit Luxury Goods." *Qualitative Market Research: An International Journal,* vol. 13, no. 3, p. 17, 15 June 2010. DeepDyve, https://www.deepdyve.com/lp/emerald-publishing/constructing-identitythrough-the-consumption-of-counterfeit-luxury-JfO4pjvSJL. Accessed 19 Dec. 2022.
4 The Economist. "Fashion as an Asset Class." *The Economist,* 18 Dec. 2021, https://www.economist.com/christmas-specials/2021/12/18/fashion-as-an-asset-class. Accessed 21 Dec. 2022.
5 SR2020. "StockX: The Stock Market for Things." *HBS Digital Initiative,* 24 Mar. 2020, https://d3.harvard.edu/platform-digit/submission/stockx-the-stock-market-for-things/. Accessed 19 Dec. 2022.
6 ThredUP. "2022 Resale Report." *ThredUP,* May 2022, https://www.thredup.com/resale/#decade-in-resale. Accessed 19 Dec. 2022.
7 Andjelic, Ana. "Veblen Is Wrong: Towards the New Aspiration Economy." *DataDrivenInvestor,* 23 Jan. 2020. *Medium,* https://medium.datadriveninvestor.com/veblen-is-wrong-the-new-aspiration-economy-765c3d5456d. Accessed 19 Dec. 2022.
8 McKinsey & Company. "Is Luxury Resale the Future of Fashion?" *McKinsey & Company,* 14 Dec. 2020, https://www.mckinsey.com/industries/retail/our-insights/is-luxury-resale-the-future-of-fashion. Accessed 19 Dec. 2022.
9 Segran, Elizabeth. "This 24-Year-Old Designer Just Made $1 Million Selling Used Clothes Online." *Fast Company,* 22 June 2020, https://www.fastcompany.com/90512591/meet-the-24-year-old-designer-who-made-1-million-on-depop. Accessed 19 Dec. 2022.
10 Ibid.
11 Reflaunt. "Concierge Retail Service." *Reflaunt,* 2022, https://www.reflaunt.com/services/concierge-resale-service. Accessed 19 Dec. 2022.
12 IKEA. "Inter IKEA Sustainability Summary Report FY17." *IKEA,* 2017, https://preview.thenewsmarket.com/Previews/IKEA/DocumentAssets/502623.pdf. Accessed 19 Dec. 2022.

CHAPTER 21: NEW COLLECTIVISM

1 Head, Nathan. [@NathanHeadPhoto]. "My BAYC + BAKC airdrop amount rn, I honestly don't know what to do this is a lot of money." *Twitter,* 17 Mar. 2022, https://twitter.com/NathanHeadPhoto/status/1504441134499700739. Accessed 3 Dec. 2022.
2 Lutz, Sander. "ApeCoin Gains 22% after Debut of Bored Ape-Themed Video with Eminem and Snoop Dogg." *Decrypt,* 26 June 2022, https://decrypt.co/103880/

apecoin-gains-22-after-debut-of-bored-ape-themed-video-with-eminem-and-snoop-dogg. Accessed 3 Dec. 2022.
3 ApeCoin DAO. [0xfcbb...5439]. "AIP-91: Ape&Talent—Platform to Connect Talent within the Ape Community—Ecosystem Fund Allocation." *Snapshot, ND,* https://snapshot.org/#/apecoin.eth/proposal/0xbaf724416aa6e56c5458e498fb044dbfe-41fa63f59eb05ac829cdfa6ea4787c8. Accessed 3 Dec. 2022.
4 Newton, Casey. "There's Something Off about Apecoin." *The Verge,* 23 Mar. 2022, https://www.theverge.com/22992086/bored-ape-yacht-club-apecoin-venture-capital-yuga-labs-money. Accessed 3 Dec. 2022.
5 Pahwa, Nitish. "The Feds Think Bored Ape Yacht Club Was Up to Some Monkey Business." *Slate,* 12 Oct. 2022, https://slate.com/technology/2022/10/bored-ape-yacht-club-yuga-labs-sec-crypto-nfts-apecoin.html. Accessed 3 Dec. 2022.
6 World Cooperative Monitor. "World Cooperative Monitor: New Ranking of the Largest Cooperatives Is Now Available." *World Cooperative Monitor,* 23 Jan. 2020, https://monitor.coop/sites/default/files/basic-page-attachments/wcm-2019pressrelease-226234832.pdf. Accessed 3 Dec. 2022.
7 Green Bay Packers. "2022 Green Bay Packers Annual Meeting of Shareholders." *Green Bay Packers,* 2022, https://www.packers.com/community/shareholders. Accessed 3 Dec. 2022.
8 Goal. "Are Barcelona Fan-Owned? Catalan Club's Model & Elections Explained." *Goal,* 20 July 2020, https://www.goal.com/en-gb/news/are-barcelona-fan-owned-catalan-clubs-model-elections-explained/1ggsvoyel0lzv1a2xvn5pdt5v5. Accessed 3 Dec. 2022.
9 Alleyne, M., Canon, C., Evans, A., et al. "Exit to Community: A Community Primer." *Media Enterprise Design Lab, College of Media, Communication and Information,* 31 Aug. 2020. *University of Colorado Boulder,* https://www.colorado.edu/lab/medlab/2020/08/31/exit-community-community-primer. Accessed 3 Dec. 2022.
10 Ibid.
11 Ibid.
12 Ibid.
13 Alleyne, M., Canon, C., Evans, A., et al. "Exit to Community: A Community Primer." *Media Enterprise Design Lab, College of Media, Communication and Information,* 31 Aug. 2020. *University of Colorado Boulder,* https://www.colorado.edu/lab/medlab/sites/default/files/attached-files/exittocommunityprimer-web.pdf. Accessed 3 Dec. 2022.
14 Gelles, David. "Give Gig Economy Workers Equity? The S.E.C. Is Considering It." *New York Times,* 6 Nov. 2018, https://www.nytimes.com/2018/11/06/business/dealbook/gig-economy-equity-sec-rule-701-uber-airbnb.html. Accessed 3 Dec. 2022.
15 Sabia, L., Bell, R., Bozward, D. "Using Equity Crowdfunding to Build a Loyal Brand Community: The Case of Brewdog." *The International Journal of Entrepreneurship and Innovation,* 14 Mar. 2022. Sage Journals, https://journals.sagepub.com/doi/full/10.1177/14657503221086101. Accessed 3 Dec. 2022.
16 Alleyne, M., Canon, C., Evans, A., et al. "Exit to Community: A Community Primer." *Media Enterprise Design Lab, College of Media, Communication and Information,* 31 Aug. 2020. *University of Colorado Boulder,* https://www.colorado.edu/lab/medlab/sites/default/files/attached-files/exittocommunityprimer-web.pdf. Accessed 3 Dec. 2022.

CHAPTER 22: GOOD GOVERNMENT

1 Acemoglu, D., Johnson, S., Robinson, J. *An African Success Story: Botswana. Massachusetts Institute of Technology Department of Economics Working Paper Series,* July 2001, https://dspace.mit.edu/bitstream/handle/1721.1/63256/africansuccessst00acem.pdf. Accessed 18 Dec. 2022.

2 Transparency International. "Corruption Perceptions Index 2021." *Transparency International,* 2021, https://www.transparency.org/en/cpi/2021. Accessed 18 Dec. 2022.

3 Harvey, Ross. "Botswana's Backsliding: A Story of Governance Demise." *Good Government Africa,* 13 April 2022, https://gga.org/botswanas-backsliding-a-story-of-governance-demise/. Accessed 26 Dec. 2022.

4 Edelman. "2022 Edelman Trust Barometer." *Edelman,* 2022, https://www.edelman.com/trust/2022-trust-barometer. Accessed 26 Dec. 2022.

5 Futures Centre. "Surabaya, Indonesia Introduces a Plastic Waste Bus Fare Scheme." *Futures Centre,* 11 Dec. 2022, https://www.thefuturescentre.org/signal/surabaya-indonesia-introduces-a-plastic-waste-bus-fare-scheme/. Accessed 18 Dec. 2022.

6 World Government Summit. "Edge of Government 2019: Powered by You." *World Government Summit,* 2019, https://edge.worldgovernmentsummit.org/. Accessed 18 Dec. 2022.

7 IBM Center for the Business of Government. "About the Center for the Business of Government: Connecting Research to Practice." *IBM Center for the Business of Government,* 2021, https://www.businessofgovernment.org/about. Accessed 18 Dec. 2022.

8 "A Conversation with Berks County Commissioner Christian Leinbach." *The Good Government Show,* season 2, episode 14, 24 Nov. 2022, https://goodgovernmentshow.com/. Accessed 18 Dec. 2022.

9 The World Bank. "Home Page." *The World Bank,* 2022, https://www.worldbank.org/en/programs/futureofgovernment. Accessed 18 Dec. 2022.

10 McNulty, Jennifer. "Youth Activism Is on the Rise Around the Globe, and Adults Should Pay Attention, Says Author." *UC Santa Cruz Newscenter,* 17 Sep. 2019, https://news.ucsc.edu/2019/09/taft-youth.html. Accessed 18 Dec. 2022.

CHAPTER 23: THE 15-MINUTE CITY

1 Willsher, Kim. "Paris Mayor Unveils '15-Minute City' Plan in Re-Election Campaign." *The Guardian,* 7 Feb. 2020, https://www.theguardian.com/world/2020/feb/07/paris-mayor-unveils-15-minute-city-plan-in-re-election-campaign. Accessed 2 Dec. 2022.

2 Moreno, Carlos. "The 15-Minute City." *TED,* ND, https://www.ted.com/talks/carlos_moreno_the_15_minute_city?language=en. Accessed 2 Dec. 2022.

3 Willsher, Kim. "Paris Mayor Unveils '15-Minute City' Plan in Re-Election Campaign." *The Guardian,* 7 Feb. 2020, https://www.theguardian.com/world/2020/feb/07/paris-mayor-unveils-15-minute-city-plan-in-re-election-campaign. Accessed 2 Dec. 2022.

4 Paris 2024. "The Olympic and Paralympic Village." *Paris 2024,* ND, https://www.paris2024.org/en/olympic-and-paralympic-village-0/. Accessed 5 Dec. 2022.

5 Dillet, Romain and Lomas, Natasha. "How Four European Cities Are Embracing Micromobility to Drive Out Cars." *TechCrunch+,* 20 Nov. 2020, https://techcrunch.com/2020/11/20/how-four-european-cities-are-embracing-micromobility-to-drive-out-cars/. Accessed 2 Dec. 2022.

6 Portland Plan. "5b. 20-Minute Neighborhoods." *Portland Plan*, 2022, https://www.portlandonline.com/portlandplan/index.cfm?a=288098&c=52256. Accessed 2 Dec. 2022.
7 Warner, Kelsey. "Neom's The Line Will Be a Futuristic Lab for the '15-Minute City.'" *The National*, 25 Jan. 2021, https://www.thenationalnews.com/business/property/neom-s-the-line-will-be-a-futuristic-lab-for-the-15-minute-city-1.1144977. Accessed 2 Dec. 2022.
8 VanMoof. "Time to Ride the Future." *VanMoof*, 6 June 2020, https://www.youtube.com/watch?v=kMpqVfnuyII. Accessed 2 Dec. 2022.
9 Gigg, Peter. "The Truth Hurts: How Vanmoof Got Banned from French TV." *VanMoof Blog*, 30 June 2020, https://www.vanmoof.com/blog/en/the-truth-hurts-how-vanmoof-got-banned-from-french-tv. Accessed 2 Dec. 2022.
10 Ibid.
11 National Association of City Transportation Officials. "136 Million Trips Taken on Shared Bikes and Scooters across the U.S. in 2019." *National Association of City Transportation Officials*, 27 Aug. 2020, https://nacto.org/2020/08/27/136-million-trips-taken-on-shared-bikes-and-scooters-across-the-u-s-in-2019/. Accessed 2 Dec. 2022.
12 CB Insights. "The Micromobility Revolution: How Bikes and Scooters Are Shaking Up Urban Transport Worldwide." *CB Insights*, 13 Oct. 2021, https://www.cbinsights.com/research/report/micromobility-revolution/. Accessed 2 Dec. 2022.
13 Citroën International. "AMI, 100% Electric Mobility Accessible to All." *Citroën International*, ND, https://www.citroen.com/en/Highlight/131/ami-100-electric-mobility-accessible-to-all. Accessed 2 Dec. 2022.
14 Bennett, Paige. "Paris Plans to Be Completely Cyclable by 2026." *World Economic Forum*, 28 Oct. 2021, https://www.weforum.org/agenda/2021/10/paris-plans-completely-cyclable-by-2026/. Accessed 2 Dec. 2022.
15 Heineke, K., Kloss, B., Scurtu, D. "The Future of Micromobility: Ridership and Revenue after a Crisis." *McKinsey & Company*, 16 June 2020, https://www.mckinsey.com/industries/automotive-and-assembly/our-insights/the-future-of-micromobility-ridership-and-revenue-after-a-crisis. Accessed 2 Dec. 2022.
16 Block, India. "Giant Net City Car-Free Neighbourhood in Shenzhen Will Cover Two Million Square Metres." *Dezeen*, 11 June 2020, https://www.dezeen.com/2020/06/11/wechat-car-free-city-tencent-net-city-shenzhen-nbbj/. Accessed 2 Dec. 2022.
17 Wray, Sarah. "Green Jobs, Public Transport and '15-Minute Cities' Top C40 Mayors' Agenda." *Cities Today*, 16 July 2020, https://cities-today.com/green-jobs-public-transport-and-15-minute-cities-top-mayors-agenda-for-covid-19-recovery/. Accessed 2 Dec. 2022.
18 Ricker, Thomas. "VanMoof Founders on S3 E-Bike Issues, Delays, and New At-Home Support." *The Verge*, 16 Sep. 2020, https://www.theverge.com/2020/9/16/21437704/vanmoof-interview-s3-electric-bike-issues-delays-mobile-service-network. Accessed 2 Dec. 2022.
19 Reuters. "Dutch E-Bike Maker VanMoof Raises $128 Million to Expand." *Reuters*, 1 Sep. 2021, https://www.reuters.com/business/autos-transportation/dutch-e-bike-maker-van-moof-raises-128-million-expand-2021-09-01/. Accessed 3 Dec. 2022.

CHAPTER 24: INHUMAN DELIVERY

1 Heater, Brian. "Alphabet's Wing Drones Hit 200,000 Deliveries as It Announces Supermarket Partnership." *TechCrunch*, 1 Mar. 2022, https://techcrunch.com/2022/03/01/alphabets-wing-drones-hit-200000-delivers-as-it-announces-supermarket-partnership/. Accessed 16 Dec. 2022.

2 Edwards, Sarah. "Alphabet-Owned Drone Marks 200,000 Deliveries Milestone." *Thomas Insights*, 1 Aug. 2022, https://www.thomasnet.com/insights/alphabet-owned-drone-marks-200-000-deliveries-milestone/. Accessed 16 Dec. 2022.

3 Crumley, Bruce. "Zipline Discusses Its Newly Awarded Global Drone Delivery Innovation." *DroneDJ*, 4 Nov. 2022, https://dronedj.com/2022/11/04/zipline-discusses-its-newly-awarded-global-drone-delivery-innovation/. Accessed 16 Dec. 2022.

4 Hamilton, Isobel. "A Tiny Irish Drone Startup Is Delivering Emergency Cake, Pizza, and Medical Supplies to Moneygall, the Ancestral Home of Barack Obama." *Business Insider*, 3 June 2020, https://www.businessinsider.com/drone-delivery-startup-manna-adapted-to-coronavirus-pandemic-2020-5?r=US&IR=T. Accessed 16 Dec. 2022.

5 Koetsier, John. "Drone Delivery Is Live Today, and It's 90% Cheaper Than Car-Based Services." *Forbes*, 18 Aug. 2021, https://www.forbes.com/sites/johnkoetsier/2021/08/18/drone-delivery-is-live-today-and-its-90-cheaper-than-car-based-services/?sh=76f7bf924d02. Accessed 16 Dec. 2022.

6 Koetsier, John. "Drone Delivery Is Here. Right Now. Live. For Real. And It's Awesome." *John Koetsier*, 17 June 2021, https://johnkoetsier.com/drone-delivery-is-here-right-now-live-for-real-and-its-awesome/. Accessed 16 Dec. 2022.

7 Ibid.

8 Daleo, Jack. "Irish Drone Delivery Firm Manna to Launch in US This Year." *FreightWaves*, 10 Aug. 2022, https://www.freightwaves.com/news/irish-drone-delivery-firm-manna-to-launch-in-us-this-year. Accessed 16 Dec. 2022.

9 UPS Newsroom. "UPS Flight Forward Adds Innovative New Aircraft, Enhancing Capabilities and Network Sustainability." *United Parcel Service of America*, 8 April 2021, https://about.ups.com/ae/en/newsroom/press-releases/innovation-driven/ups-flight-forward-adds-new-aircraft.html. Accessed 16 Dec. 2022.

10 Levin, Alan. "First Aerial Delivery Drone Granted Design Approval by FAA." *Bloomberg*, 7 Sep. 2022, https://www.bloomberg.com/news/articles/2022-09-07/first-delivery-drone-granted-design-approval-by-us-regulators?leadSource=uverify%20wall. Accessed 16 Dec. 2022.

11 Supporting European Aviation. "Europe Is Now in the Fast Lane to Implementing UAS Traffic Management Systems." *Supporting European Aviation*, 23 June 2021, https://www.eurocontrol.int/article/europe-now-fast-lane-implementing-uas-traffic-management-systems. Accessed 16 Dec. 2022.

12 Federal Aviation Administration. "Package Delivery by Drone (Part 135)." *US Department of Transportation*, 21 June 2021, https://www.faa.gov/uas/advanced_operations/package_delivery_drone. Accessed 16 Dec. 2022.

13 Koetsier, John. "Drone Delivery Is Here. Right Now. Live. For Real. And It's Awesome." *John Koetsier*, 17 June 2021, https://johnkoetsier.com/drone-delivery-is-here-right-now-live-for-real-and-its-awesome/. Accessed 16 Dec. 2022.

14 Vincent, James. "Alphabet's Drone Delivery Service Wing Hits 100,000 Deliveries Milestone." *The Verge*, 25 Aug. 2021, https://www.theverge.com/2021/8/25/22640833/drone-delivery-google-alphabet-wing-milestone. Accessed 16 Dec. 2022.

CHAPTER 25: URBAN FORESTS

1 Baker, Aryn. "What It's Like Living in One of the Hottest Cities on Earth—Where It May Soon Be Uninhabitable." *Time,* 12 Sep. 2019, https://time.com/longform/jacobabad-extreme-heat/. Accessed 2 Dec. 2022.

2 McKinsey Sustainability. "Protecting People from a Changing Climate: The Case for Resilience." *McKinsey & Company,* 8 Nov. 2021, https://www.mckinsey.com/capabilities/sustainability/our-insights/protecting-people-from-a-changing-climate-the-case-for-resilience. Accessed 2 Dec. 2022.

3 Sekkappan, Cheryl. "The Most Stunning Green Architecture in Singapore." *TimeOut,* 23 Dec. 2021, https://www.timeout.com/singapore/things-to-do/the-most-stunning-green-architecture-in-singapore. Accessed 2 Dec. 2022.

4 C40 Cities Climate Leadership Group, Nordic Sustainability. "Cities100: Medellín's Interconnected Green Corridors." *C40 Knowledge,* Oct. 2019, https://www.c40knowledgehub.org/s/article/Cities100-Medellin-s-interconnected-green-corridors?language=en_US. Accessed 2 Dec. 2022.

5 Ausloos, Manuel. "Heatwave in Paris Exposes City's Lack of Trees." *Reuters,* 5 Aug. 2022, https://www.reuters.com/world/europe/heatwave-paris-exposes-citys-lack-trees-2022-08-04/. Accessed 2 Dec. 2022.

6 Seoul Metropolitan Government. "Promoting the Creation of 'Urban Wind Path Forests' That Send Clean and Cool Air from the Forest to the City." *Seoul Metropolitan Government,* 21 Oct. 2020, http://english.seoul.go.kr/promoting-the-creation-of-urban-wind-path-forests-that-send-clean-and-cool-air-from-the-forest-to-the-city/. Accessed 2 Dec. 2022.

7 Stefano Boeri Architetti. "Vertical Forest." *Stefano Boeri Architetti,* ND, https://www.stefanoboeriarchitetti.net/en/project/vertical-forest/. Accessed 2 Dec. 2022.

8 Thought Leaders Interviews. "Stefano Boeri and the Archipelago City, to Save the Environment." *Webuild Value Digital magazine,* 22 Dec. 2021, https://www.webuildvalue.com/en/thought-leaders-interviews/interview-stefano-boeri-archipelago-city.html. Accessed 2 Dec. 2022.

9 Stefano Boeri Architetti. "Projects." *Stefano Boeri Architetti,* ND, https://www.stefanoboeriarchitetti.net/en/projects/. Accessed 2 Dec. 2022.

10 Arch Daily. "Trudo Vertical Forest / Stefano Boeri Architetti." *Arch Daily,* 2021, https://www.archdaily.com/976910/trudo-vertical-forest-stefano-boeri-architetti. Accessed 2 Dec. 2022.

11 Stefano Boeri Architetti. "Liuzhou Forest City." *Stefano Boeri Architetti,* ND, https://www.stefanoboeriarchitetti.net/en/project/liuzhou-forest-city/. Accessed 2 Dec. 2022.

12 Stefano Boeri Architetti. "Smart Forest City Cancun." *Stefano Boeri Architetti,* ND, https://www.stefanoboeriarchitetti.net/en/project/smart-forest-city-cancun/. Accessed 2 Dec. 2022.

13 ArchifyNow. "Ronald Lu & Partners Wins Worldwide Competition with New "Treehouse" Concept." *Archify.com,* 17 Feb. 2022, https://www.archify.com/hk/archifynow/ronald-lu-partners-wins-worldwide-competition-with-new-treehouse-concept. Accessed 2 Dec. 2022.

14 Carlo Ratti Associati. "Jian Mu Tower." *Carlo Ratti Associati,* ND, https://carloratti.com/project/jian-mu-tower/. Accessed 2 Dec. 2022.

CHAPTER 26: NU-AGRICULTURE

1 Harari, Yunval Noah. *Sapiens: A Brief History of Humankind.* Harper, 10 Feb. 2015.

2 Roser, Max. "Employment in Agriculture." *Our World in Data*, 2013, https://ourworldindata.org/employment-in-agriculture. Accessed 2 Dec. 2022.

3 United Nations. "Growing at a Slower Pace, World Population Is Expected to Reach 9.7 Billion in 2050 and Could Peak at Nearly 11 Billion around 2100." *United Nations*, 17 June 2019, https://www.un.org/development/desa/en/news/population/world-population-prospects-2019.html. Accessed 2 Dec. 2022.

4 World Health Organization, Food and Agriculture Organization of the United Nations. "Global and Regional Food Consumption Patterns and Trends." *Diet, Nutrition and the Prevention of Chronic Diseases*, 2003, https://www.fao.org/3/ac911e/ac911e05.htm. Accessed 2 Dec. 2022.

5 Ritchie, Hannah and Roser, Max. "Land Use." *Our World in Data*, Sep. 2019, https://ourworldindata.org/land-use. Accessed 2 Dec. 2022.

6 McKinsey Sustainability. "Feeding the World Sustainably." *McKinsey Quarterly*, 2 June 2020, https://www.mckinsey.com/capabilities/sustainability/our-insights/feeding-the-world-sustainably. Accessed 2 Dec. 2022.

7 Viviano, Frank. "This Tiny Country Feeds the World." *National Geographic magazine*, Sep. 2017, https://www.nationalgeographic.com/magazine/article/holland-agriculture-sustainable-farming. Accessed 2 Dec. 2022.

8 Ÿnsect. "Agtech Startup Ÿnsect Extends Its Series C to $372 Million to Improve Global Food Security and Sustainability with the First Carbon Negative and Largest Vertical Farm in the World." *Ÿnsect*, 6 Oct. 2020, http://www.ynsect.com/en/agtech-startup-ynsect-extends-its-series-c-to-372-million-to-improve-global-food-security-and-sustainability-with-the-first-carbon-negative-and-l-argest-vertical-farm-in-the-world-2/. Accessed 2 Dec. 2022.

9 World Bank Live. "Featured Speaker: Talash Huijbers." *World Bank Live*, 19 Jan. 2022, https://live.worldbank.org/experts/talash-huijbers. Accessed 2 Dec. 2022.

10 Baldock, Kyle. "Agrourbana's Plan to Grow the Best Greens in Santiago." *Association for Vertical Farming*, 27 Mar. 2019, https://vertical-farming.net/blog/2019/03/27/agrourbana-vertical-farm-solar-power/. Accessed 2 Dec. 2022.

11 Berman, Robby. "NASA's Idea for Making Food from Thin Air Just Became a Reality—It Could Feed Billions." *Big Think*, 19 July 2019, https://bigthink.com/health/protein-from-air/. Accessed 2 Dec. 2022.

12 The Index Project. "Designs for Life: The Inventions That Build a Better World." *New York Times* [paid post], ND, https://www.nytimes.com/paidpost/the-index-project/the-inventions-that-build-a-better-world.html. Accessed 2 Dec. 2022.

13 Morin, Roc. "The Man Who Would Make Food Obsolete." *The Atlantic*, 28 April 2014, https://www.theatlantic.com/health/archive/2014/04/the-man-who-would-make-eating-obsolete/361058/. Accessed 2 Dec. 2022.

14 Solar Foods. "Impact." *Solar Foods*, 2022, https://solarfoods.com/impact/. Accessed 2 Dec. 2022.

15 Solar Foods. "Solein Submitted to the European Commission for Novel Food Approval." *Solar Foods*, 2 Nov. 2021, https://solarfoods.com/solein-submitted-to-the-european-commission-for-novel-food-approval/. Accessed 2 Dec. 2022.

16 Solar Foods. "Solar Foods Receives Novel Food Regulatory Approval for a Protein Grown with CO2 and Electricity." *Solar Foods*, 26 Oct. 2022, https://solarfoods.com/solar-foods-receives-novel-food-regulatory-approval/. Accessed 2 Dec. 2022.

17 Lascelles, Alice. "Can Making Food from CO2 Help Our Overburdened Planet?" *Financial Times*, 29 May 2020, https://www.ft.com/content/ad5ad0f4-e2bf-4c8a-b890-de3f5df920ba. Accessed 2 Dec. 2022.
18 Ibid.

CHAPTER 27: WASTE-FREE PRODUCTS

1 Phillips, Dom. "Brazil Carnival Revellers Warned That All That Glitters Is Not Good for the Planet." *The Guardian*, 11 Feb. 2018, https://www.theguardian.com/world/2018/feb/11/brazil-carnival-rio-glitter-microplastics-environment. Accessed 2 Dec. 2022.
2 Fairs, Marcus. "The Circular Economy 'Will Never Work with the Materials We Have' Says Cyrill Gutsch of Parley for the Oceans." *Dezeen*, 16 June 2020, https://www.dezeen.com/2020/06/16/circular-economy-plastic-biofabricated-materials-cyrill-gutsch-interview/. Accessed 2 Dec. 2022.
3 Clark, Murray. "The Mad Miracle Science of a Lab-Grown Hoodie." *GQ*, 21 Oct. 2022, https://www.gq-magazine.co.uk/fashion/article/the-north-face-eye-junya-watanabe-earth-hoodie. Accessed 2 Dec. 2022.
4 Notpla. "We Make Packaging Disappear." *Notpla*, 2022, https://www.notpla.com/. Accessed 5 Dec. 2022.
5 Vollebak. "Clothes from the Future." *Vollebak*, 2022, https://vollebak.com/. Accessed 5 Dec. 2022.
6 Weiss, Sabrina. "This T-Shirt Is 100% Plant and Algae. It Biodegrades in 12 Weeks." *Wired*, 24 Aug. 2019, https://www.wired.co.uk/article/vollebak-algae-plant-shirt. Accessed 5 Dec. 2022.
7 Ibid.
8 H&M Group. "Creating H&M's Most Sustainable Collection Ever." *H&M Group*, 15 May 2020, https://hmgroup.com/our-stories/creating-hms-most-sustainable-collection-ever/. Accessed 2 Dec. 2022.

CHAPTER 28: MILLIONS OF MICROGRIDS

1 Day, Lewin. "Rivian R1T Powers Patient's Vasectomy after Clinic Power Outage." *The Drive*, 1 Sep. 2022, https://www.thedrive.com/news/doctor-performs-vasectomy-running-surgery-on-a-rivian-r1t. Accessed 30 Nov. 2022.
2 Brody, S., Rogers, M., and Siccardo, G. "Why, and How, Utilities Should Start to Manage Climate-Change Risk." McKinsey & Company, 24 April 2019, https://www.mckinsey.com/industries/electric-power-and-natural-gas/our-insights/why-and-how-utilities-should-start-to-manage-climate-change-risk. Accessed 30 Nov. 2022.
3 Armstrong, Martin. "The Price of Solar Power Has Fallen by Over 80% Since 2010. Here's Why." *World Economic Forum*, 4 Nov. 2021, https://www.weforum.org/agenda/2021/11/renewable-energy-cost-fallen/. Accessed 30 Nov. 2022.
4 Ellerbeck, Stefan. "These Regions Produce a Lot of Carbon Emissions—Here's What They Plan to Do about It." *World Economic Forum*, 26 Aug. 2022, https://www.weforum.org/agenda/2022/08/electricity-capacity-power-renewable-energy/. Accessed 30 Nov. 2022.
5 Katz, Cheryl. "The Batteries That Could Make Fossil Fuels Obsolete." *Future Planet*, 17 Dec. 2020. *BBC.com*, https://www.bbc.com/future/article/20201217-renewable-power-the-worlds-largest-battery. Accessed 30 Nov. 2022.
6 Helman, Christopher. "Why Tesla's Powerwall Is Just Another Toy for Rich Green People." *Forbes*, 1 May 2015, https://www.forbes.com/sites/

christopherhelman/2015/05/01/why-teslas-powerwall-is-just-another-toy-for-rich-green-people/?sh=2a4d7d5046e4. Accessed 30 Nov. 2022.
7 Alamalhodaei, Aria. "Tesla Has Installed 200,000 Powerwalls around the World So Far." *TechCrunch*, 26 May 2021, https://techcrunch.com/2021/05/26/tesla-has-installed-200000-powerwalls-around-the-world-so-far/. Accessed 5 Dec. 2022.
8 Lambert, Fred. "Tesla's Virtual Power Plant Had Its First Event Helping the Grid—Looks Like the Future." *Electrek*, 18 Aug. 2022, https://electrek.co/2022/08/18/teslas-virtual-power-plant-first-event-helping-grid-future/. Accessed 30 Nov. 2022.
9 Alvarez, Simon. "Tesla Solar + Powerwall More Than Covers Monthly Payment after a Week of VPP Events." *Teslarati*, 10 Sep. 2022, https://www.teslarati.com/tesla-powerwall-covers-monthly-payment-after-vpp-events/. Accessed 5 Dec. 2022.
10 Musk, Elon. [@elonmusk]. "With the new lower Tesla pricing, it's like having a money printer on your roof if you live a state with high electricity costs. Still better to buy, but the rental option makes the economics obvious." *Twitter*, 18 Aug. 2019, https://twitter.com/elonmusk/status/1163025594180726784?lang=en. Accessed 30 Nov. 2022.
11 Woody, Todd. "How Ford's Electric Pickup Can Power Your House for 10 Days." *Bloomberg*, 31 May 2022, https://www.bloomberg.com/news/articles/2022-05-31/how-the-ford-f-150-can-be-a-backup-home-generator?leadSource=uverify%20wall. Accessed 30 Nov. 2022.
12 Husk Powering Systems. "Husk Power Systems—First Minigrid Company to Power 100 Communities & 5,000 Small Business Customers." *Husk Powering Systems*, 10 Dec. 2020, https://huskpowersystems.com/husk-power-systems-first-minigrid-company-to-power-100-communities-5000-small-business-customers/. Accessed 30 Nov. 2022.
13 EcoEnergy. "Our History." *EcoEnergy*, 2016, https://ecoenergyfinance.org/history/. Accessed 5 Dec. 2022.
14 Seaborg. "Rethinking Nuclear." *Seaborg Technologies*, 2022, https://www.seaborg.com/. Accessed 5 Dec. 2022.

CHAPTER 29: MAKING WEATHER

1 NASA Langley Research Center Aerosol Research Branch. "Global Effects of Mount Pinatubo." *NASA Earth Observatory*, 15 June 2001, https://earthobservatory.nasa.gov/images/1510/global-effects-of-mount-pinatubo. Accessed 15 Dec. 2022.
2 Novak, Matt. "Weather Control as a Cold War Weapon." *Smithsonian Magazine*, 5 Dec. 2011, https://www.smithsonianmag.com/history/weather-control-as-a-cold-war-weapon-1777409/. Accessed 15 Dec. 2022.
3 Fowler, Tara. "For $100,000, This Company Will Guarantee You a Rain-Free Wedding." *People*, 28 Jan. 2015, https://people.com/celebrity/for-100000-this-company-will-guarantee-you-a-rain-free-wedding/. Accessed 15 Dec. 2022.
4 Lampitt, R., Achterberg, E., Anderson, T., et al. "Ocean Fertilization: A Potential Means of Geoengineering?" *Philosophical Transactions of the Royal Society*, vol. 366, no. 1882, pp. 3919–3945. The Royal Society Publishing, 29 Aug. 2008, https://royalsocietypublishing.org/doi/10.1098/rsta.2008.0139. Accessed 15 Dec. 2022.
5 McKibben, Bill. "Dimming the Sun to Cool the Planet Is a Desperate Idea, Yet We're Inching Toward It." *New Yorker*, 22 Nov. 2022, https://www.newyorker.com/news/annals-of-a-warming-planet/dimming-the-sun-to-cool-the-planet-

is-a-desperate-idea-yet-were-inching-toward-it?utm_source=NYR_REG_GATE. Accessed 15 Dec. 2022.
6 Ibid.
7 The Association of Siamese Architects under Royal Patronage. "ASA Experimental Design Competition 2022: Design Brief." *The Association of Siamese Architects under Royal Patronage*, 2022, https://www.asacompetition.com/brief-en. Accessed 15 Dec. 2022.
8 The Association of Siamese Architects under Royal Patronage. "Re-Freeze the Artic." *The Association of Siamese Architects under Royal Patronage*, 2019, https://www.asacompetition.com/post/re-freeze-the-arctic. Accessed 15 Dec. 2022.
9 Ibid.
10 Holland, Oscar. "Scientists and Designers Are Proposing Radical Ways to 'Refreeze' the Arctic." *CNN.com*, 1 Sep. 2019, https://edition.cnn.com/style/article/refreeze-arctic-design-scn/index.html. Accessed 15 Dec. 2022.
11 Sherwin, Cian. "Real Ice." *For Tomorrow*, 2022, https://fortomorrow.org/explore-solutions/real-ice. Accessed 15 Dec. 2022.
12 Ibid.

CHAPTER 30: BEYOND NET ZERO

1 Global Footprint Network. "Earth Overshoot Day." *Global Footprint Network*, 2022, https://www.footprintnetwork.org/our-work/earth-overshoot-day/. Accessed 17 Dec. 2022.
2 Vivobarefoot. "Unfinished Business 2022." *Vivobarefoot*, 2022, https://www.vivobarefoot.com/uk/unfinished-business. Accessed 17 Dec. 2022.
3 Bloom. "The Bloom Story." *Bloom*, ND, https://www.bloommaterials.com/the-bloom-story/. Accessed 16 Dec. 2022.
4 Gelles, David. "Billionaire No More: Patagonia Founder Gives Away the Company." *New York Times*, 21 Sep. 2022, https://www.nytimes.com/2022/09/14/climate/patagonia-climate-philanthropy-chouinard.html. Accessed 16 Dec. 2022.
5 Interface. "Carbon Negative." *Interface*, 2022, https://www.interface.com/US/en-US/sustainability/carbon-negative.html. Accessed 16 Dec. 2022.
6 Milman, Oliver. "'World's Most Sustainable Spirit': The Vodka Made with CO2 Captured From Air." *The Guardian*, 20 Oct. 2021, https://www.theguardian.com/food/2021/oct/20/vodka-made-with-co2-captured-from-air-sustainable-spirit. Accessed 16 Dec. 2022.
7 Sheep Inc. "Home Page." *Sheep Inc*, 2022, https://eu.sheepinc.com/. Accessed 16 Dec. 2022.
8 Kellogg, Carolyn. "Ikea Is Changing Its Long-Lived Billy Bookshelf. Is Print Dead?" *Los Angeles Times*, 12 Sep. 2011, https://www.latimes.com/archives/blogs/jacket-copy/story/2011-09-12/ikea-is-changing-its-long-lived-billy-bookshelf-is-print-dead. Accessed 16 Dec. 2022.
9 "IKEA: Making a $40 Billion Company Climate Positive." *Azeem Azhar's Exponential View*, season 5, episode 10. *Harvard Business Review*, 2022, https://hbr.org/podcast/2020/12/ikea-making-a-40-billion-company-climate-positive. Accessed 17 Dec. 2022.
10 Ibid.
11 PepsiCo. "PepsiCo Unveils Ambitious New Agriculture Goals." *PepsiCo*, 20 April 2020, https://www.pepsico.com/our-stories/story/pepsico-unveils-ambitious-new-agriculture-goals. Accessed 16 Dec. 2022.
12 Ibid.

13 Ralph Lauren Newsroom. "Ralph Lauren Corporate Foundation and Soil Health Institute Unveil New US Regenerative Cotton Program." *Ralph Lauren Corporation*, 26 Oct. 2021, https://corporate.ralphlauren.com/pr_211026_Regenerative-Cotton.html. Accessed 16 Dec. 2022.
14 Kering. "Kering and Conservation International Announce First Grantees for Regenerative Fund for Nature." *Kering*, 3 Sep. 2021, https://www.kering.com/en/news/kering-and-conservation-international-announce-first-grantees-for-regenerative-fund-for-nature. Accessed 17 Dec. 2022.
15 SMI. "Fashion Task Force Unveils Its Manifesto for Regenerative Fashion." *SMI*, 20 April 2022, https://www.sustainable-markets.org/news/fashion-task-force-unveils-its-manifesto-for-regenerative-fashion-/. Accessed 17 Dec. 2022.
16 Quote Catalog. "The Greatest Danger for Most of Us Is Not That Our Aim Is Too High and We Miss It, but That It Is Too Low and We Reach It." *Quote Catalog*, 2022, https://quotecatalog.com/quote/michelangelo-buonarroti-the-greatest-da-b7KRRA1. Accessed 16 Dec. 2022.

CONCLUSION

1 Hawaii Research Center for Futures Studies. "Publications." *University of Hawaii at Mānoa*, 2022, https://manoa.hawaii.edu/futures-center/publications/. Accessed 29 Dec. 2022.
2 Haden, Jeff. "20 Years Ago, Jeff Bezos Said This 1 Thing Separates People Who Achieve Lasting Success from Those Who Don't." *Inc.com*, 6 Nov. 2017, https://www.inc.com/jeff-haden/20-years-ago-jeff-bezos-said-this-1-thing-separates-people-who-achieve-lasting-success-from-those-who-dont.html. Accessed 18 Dec. 2022.

INDEX

**Italics* indicate illustrations

Milton Keynes UK
Ingram Content Group UK Ltd.
UKHW020721140824
446906UK00008B/20

9 781646 871469